Sociology of the Arts

Series Editors
Katherine Appleford
Kingston University London, UK

Anna Goulding
University of Newcastle, UK

Dave O'Brien
University of Edinburgh, UK

Mark Taylor
University of Sheffield, UK

This series brings together academic work which considers the production and consumption of the arts, the social value of the arts, and analyses and critiques the impact and role of cultural policy and arts management. By exploring the ways in which the arts are produced and consumed, the series offers further understandings of social inequalities, power relationships and opportunities for social resistance and agency. It highlights the important relationship between individual, social and political attitudes, and offers significant insights into the ways in which the arts are developing and changing. Moreover, in a globalised society, the nature of arts production, consumption and policy making is increasingly cosmopolitan, and arts are an important means for building social networks, challenging political regimes, and reaffirming and subverting social values across the globe.

More information about this series at
http://www.palgrave.com/gp/series/15469

Peter Campbell

Persistent Creativity

Making the Case for Art, Culture and the Creative Industries

Peter Campbell
University of Liverpool
Liverpool, UK

ISSN 2569-1414   ISSN 2569-1406   (electronic)
Sociology of the Arts
ISBN 978-3-030-03118-3   ISBN 978-3-030-03119-0   (eBook)
https://doi.org/10.1007/978-3-030-03119-0

Library of Congress Control Number: 2018960252

This Palgrave Macmillan imprint is published by the registered company Springer Nature Switzerland AG
The registered company address is: Gewerbestrasse 11, 6330 Cham, Switzerland

The thing that hath been, it is that *which shall be; and that which is done* is *that which shall be done: and* there is *no new* thing *under the sun. Is there* any *thing whereof it may be said, See, this* is *new? it hath been already of old time, which was before us.* There is *no remembrance of former* things; *neither shall there be* any *remembrance of* things *that are to come with* those *that shall come after.*

(Ecclesiastes 1:9–11)[1]

To my first reader

Preface

This book mirrors my academic career thus far. I first encountered the recently established UK government 'Department for Culture, Media and Sport', and its stated concern of developing 'creative industries', whilst studying a module on 'Leisure in Modern Britain' as an undergraduate in the late 1990s. A decade later as a PhD student, I found myself researching cultural policy and the development of these creative industries in more detail. Another decade on, as a full-time academic continuing to research this field, I now lead an undergraduate module of my own on 'Culture, Economy and Cities', attempting to explain such matters to students mostly unborn when I began my own studies. This book considers how over the course of this twenty year period the concept of 'creativity', and attempts to leverage its apparent power, became increasingly prominent. Whilst a range of critiques have been made of this concept, and whilst at points it seemed vulnerable to crisis, creativity has shown a remarkable persistence.

This book therefore attempts to understand and explain this persistence. It considers the development of an 'agenda' around creativity and looks into how this agenda is validated and applied. It demonstrates that although this 'Creativity Agenda' became particularly prominent during the 1990s, it is not an entirely new phenomenon, but rather represents the intensification of a range of historical precursors. Once established, this agenda deploys the idea of creativity in myriad ways, which are examined here in terms of their mutual coherence. Given that this era also saw an increased concern with the notion of 'evidence-based policy', this book considers how the case is made for art, culture and the creative industries, the challenges this evidence-making task presents, and the role of specific actors in establishing forms of evidence which substantiate and shape the Creativity Agenda, enabling its persistence.

In addition to considering the persistence of certain conceptions of creativity, and the role of evidence in this, the book also considers the application of the Creativity Agenda in the specific site of Liverpool, England, demonstrating how the city draws on this agenda, and in so doing has helped to further its development. Despite a dominant 'success story' around creativity, however, it is argued that there is a need to consider this story more precisely, and to continue to question the nature of policies and methods in this field, lest the more problematic aspects of the Creativity Agenda also persist, as they have to date.

—

The completion of this book has relied on a range of support. Firstly, the support of the UK Research Councils has been vital. My doctoral research, during which I first explored some of these issues, was funded as part of an AHRC/ESRC Impact Fellowship in Cultural Policy and Regeneration, and I was able to develop these ideas—particularly those considered in Chapter 4 on the nature of the methods used to make the case for arts and culture—due to funding from the AHRC Cultural Value Project. Some material in this chapter has previously been published as:

Campbell, P. Cox, T. & O'Brien, D. (2017) The social life of measurement: how methods have shaped the idea of culture in urban regeneration. *Journal of Cultural Economy, 10(1)*, 49–62.

The material from this article has been revised and is reused here under the terms of the Creative Commons 4.0 License. This book would also not exist without a period of research leave generously provided by my academic home, the Department of Sociology, Social Policy and Criminology at the University of Liverpool. I would not wish to set myself the mammoth task of listing all my colleagues, both within the University and elsewhere, who have been of support in the completion of this book, so I will restrict myself to singling out for special acknowledgement those with whom I have been fortunate enough to collaborate with directly in publishing work on these subjects so far: Tamsin Cox, Stephen Crone, Dave O'Brien, Mark Taylor and Stuart Wilks-Heeg. I cannot fling enough appreciative adjectives in your direction, but these names represent simply the tip of an iceberg of academic support: if you are reading this, you know who you are. Finally, my parents indicated that they deserved some acknowledgement for helping me to cart my belongings into the house in which this book was mostly written, but I owe them thanks for much more than that, as they surely know.

Liverpool, UK   Peter Campbell

Contents

List of Figures

1

Introduction: 'Persistent Creativity'?

In the early twenty-first century, the potential of the creative economy, made up of creative workers fulfilling creative occupations, or working in creative industries, is increasingly celebrated and encouraged. These creative workers—or, more simply, 'creatives'—might be seen to constitute a creative class, or to live in a creative city. This creative city may not only house these creative workers, but also have creative leaders, exercising creative entrepreneurial energies, forging ahead in unchartered political waters, just as their counterparts in industry creatively innovate with new businesses and products. Or, rather, these have at least come to be popular notions.

This book aims to establish how such conceptions of creativity have come to prominence, how they are substantiated, how they are taken up in practice and how they persist. As the mentions above of creative *industries* and creative *occupations* hint at, the *economic* role played by creativity is seen as increasingly important in these processes. Creativity thus becomes central to what we may term an 'economic imaginary' (Campbell 2014). Oakley and O'Connor provide a useful summary of Sum and Jessop's work regarding this term explaining how 'any course

© The Author(s) 2019
P. Campbell, *Persistent Creativity*, Sociology of the Arts,
https://doi.org/10.1007/978-3-030-03119-0_1

of collective action necessarily demands that we select from a range of possibilities and develop these within a particular, simplifying narrative in order to become generally accepted' (2015, p. 13). The idea of creativity has increasingly played a role in such simplifying narratives from the 1990s onwards. It is important to note, however, that the 'economic imaginary' is not merely a way of understanding or framing events, but that it also helps to privilege certain activities, to construct them and their broader contexts (Jessop 2004). The economic imaginary is thus not 'imaginary' in the sense of 'fictional'. Rather, it enables a coherent account of a complex reality, and in so doing plays a role in shaping that reality. In this, we can usefully reflect on the 'Thomas theorem' of sociology set out in the early twentieth century: if we *define* situations as real, they *are* real in their consequences (Thomas and Thomas 1928, p. 572) or, as Becker notes in an intensification of this theorem, 'to a sociologist, nothing is more real than what people have agreed on' (2014, p. 185). The chapters that follow will discuss how particular notions of, and roles for, creativity are agreed upon, and how these notions come to be taken up and promoted. In addition to considering what the real consequences of these positions are, the issue of *how* this creativity is defined as real will also be considered. Indeed, the time and resources expended in generating evidence to substantiate the role and nature of creativity can be seen as one of the 'real consequences' of this imaginary. The challenges and patterns which are found when such evidence is sought, though, are of particular concern here. The aim, therefore, is to establish where this dominant position regarding creativity comes from, what it consists of, how it is substantiated, and how it frames and shapes tangible action.

As the focus here is on the ways in which particular ideas around creativity are not only shaped but promoted and enacted, this book uses the shorthand label of the 'Creativity Agenda' to refer to the set of ideas which came to prominence and which have been increasingly endorsed, promoted, and enacted from the late 1990s on. To give a sense of the nature, scope, and scale of the application of this agenda, we can consider Mould's recent summary of events:

Since the turn of the new millennium, many urban and regional governments from all over the world, from Sydney to Sheffield, from Manila to Madison, have been enabling strategies of development purporting to stimulate creativity among its inhabitants and, perhaps more predominantly, to bring in talented, educated and creative people from elsewhere in the hope of benefiting from their economic growth potential. Moreover gargantuan financial sums have been spent on these endeavours. (2017, p. 1)

In concert with this assessment, this book argues that although the agenda which drives such spending started to make its mark in earnest relatively recently, once established, it has proven in many ways to be remarkably durable. It is this durability and persistence that the book seeks to investigate, and to which the 'persistent creativity' of the title refers.

The title also refers to the process of 'making the case for art, culture and the creative industries'. As noted, the role of evidence in supporting the Creativity Agenda is one that will be considered in detail, and one which raises the important issue of the definition of terms. Even in the brief sketch at the outset of this chapter, we can see the idea of creativity being used in many different senses. Does this common terminology indicate commonality in the activities referred to and, if so, what is the nature of this common creativity? Questions such as this persist alongside the development of the Creativity Agenda, and this book argues that a need for a more precise consideration of how such questions may be answered also persists. One issue which will recur throughout is the challenge of *defining* creativity in a meaningful way, but no matter how this is done, one fundamental aspect to the rise of the Creativity Agenda is a sustained emphasis on the importance of artistic, expressive activity; whenever creativity is discussed, 'culture' is seldom far behind.

In essence, then, the questions that will be considered here are about how and why creativity is conceived in certain forms, and the persistence of these conceptions. Given that the Creativity Agenda has become a global phenomenon, it is not possible to interrogate its every manifestation, and so discussion here will largely focus on a particularly influential site for the agenda, the UK. In the UK, we can see clear manifestations of the Creativity Agenda which are mirrored internationally, and which demonstrate the durability referred to above. Here it is useful to consider statements from policymakers in the UK over a twenty year period which provide a picture of 'Persistent Creativity' in miniature:

- In 1998, following the recent establishment of the 'Department for Culture, Media and Sport' (DCMS) within UK government, the book 'Creative Britain' was published in which Baron Smith of Finsbury, the first Secretary of State for DCMS, outlined the importance of 'creative industries' to government policy, to the future of the economy, and to society more broadly. Smith positioned creative industries as "where the wealth and the jobs of the future are going to be generated from" (1998, p. 31), and his government's goal as being to "put these industries properly on the political map for the first time ever" (p. 142). In addition, creativity was identified as bringing many wider benefits, such as fostering "social inclusion through shared emotions" (p. 24).

Ten years later, the picture looked remarkably similar:

- In 2008, DCMS, in partnership with the Department for Business, Enterprise and Regulatory Reform, and the Department for Innovation, Universities and Skills, published a report also entitled 'Creative Britain' in which the importance of 'creative industries' to the government, to the future of the economy, and to society more broadly were outlined once more. In this report creative industries were positioned as being important "in the coming years" (DCMS et al. 2008, p. 1), as important to the government in their aim of creating "the jobs of the future" (p. 4) and as "increasingly vital" to the UK economy (p. 6). The report outlined a vision of a Britain "in ten years' time where the local economies in our biggest cities are driven by creativity" (p. 6). In addition to this economic role, however, it was noted that such industries "also bring wider social and cultural benefits" (p. 58).

Another ten years on, this picture persists:

- In 2018, Nesta—a body originally established by New Labour in 1998, but operating as a charity since 2012 (see Oakley et al. 2014)—published the report 'Creative Nation' (Mateos Garcia et al. 2018). In this report, the UK's Minister for Digital and the Creative Industries emphasised the value of these creative industries—"British creative industries [...] are an engine of growth"—and noted that supporting them will ensure that the country is "fit for the future" (p. 4).

The following chapters will consider how this constancy is achieved, and some of the challenges raised by the conception of creativity that persists throughout this period. Chapter 2 will examine how, although it has come to prominence comparatively recently, this persistent position rests on deeper foundations. It considers the emergence of culture and the arts as an object of political intervention, and the idea of the arts as central to wider social benefits. It also traces the emergence of a particular concern with quantification across society that gradually encroaches on the field of culture, and an increasing focus on economic valuation in the context of neoliberal ideology, alongside theorising regarding the rise of a 'new' economy, the emergence of which is deemed in some ways to have the potential to 'regenerate' urban areas.

Chapter 3 considers the forms of 'creativity' which the Creativity Agenda seeks to promote. The terms 'creative industries', 'creative economy', 'creative class' and 'creative city' are discussed and defined, and it is argued that despite the common terminology, these terms can be understood and deployed in mutually contradictory forms. This poses questions for the coherence of the Creativity Agenda. Nevertheless, however utilised, the term always seems to privilege the arts and culture in one form or another, but the fact that it can be deployed in such a flexible fashion helps to account in part for its continual rise.

Chapter 4 is based on research into the ways in which the case is made for the benefits of arts and culture. It outlines the prominence of an economic case for culture in recent years, and a continuing emphasis on the need for evidence in this area to be clearer and more robust.

Given the persistence of such an emphasis over many years, the challenges that are presented when attempts are made to develop this evidence base are considered. Chapter 5 is also based on research into the methods used to establish the case for creativity, and specifically examines the statistical evidence base in relation to the 'creative industries' referred to above. The issue of definition raised in Chapter 3 continues to be pertinent here, and this chapter explains how the creative industries come to be defined and measured, and how the statistics which these measurements produce are understood. The patterns shown in these statistics as the Creativity Agenda rises are discussed, and the changing definition of creativity underlying these statistics is traced. It is argued that here, as in many domains, methods serve not simply to measure, but to actively constitute creativity in certain forms (e.g. Rose 1991, p. 676).

Chapter 6 discusses the deployment of the Creativity Agenda in the specific location of Liverpool, England. Liverpool is positioned as an early adopter of the Creativity Agenda, and the role of Liverpool's tenure as European Capital of Culture in 2008 is considered. As well as tracing how bodies in the city drew on the Creativity Agenda prior to 2008, and how the European Capital of Culture competition has become aligned to this agenda, this chapter considers how evidence relating to Liverpool's tenure serves to bolster this agenda up to the present day. Nevertheless, it is also argued that this case, like others, raises serious questions regarding the limitations of any deployment of this agenda in light of persistent structural inequalities. Chapter 7 thus argues for the need to clarify the Creativity Agenda, to consider what activities are represented as creative, and to ask in what way their creativity is understood. Without asking such questions, a vague, unified sense of creativity risks obscuring the realities of the economic performance that has become central to the agenda, allowing myths to prevail, and also of increasingly operating in a way which is, paradoxically, ever less creative. Whilst this chapter points to signs that those who push this agenda are attempting to consider some of these issues, it also points to interventions that suggest resistance to change. Chapter 8 follows this in drawing conclusions regarding the state of play after twenty years. It indicates that the Creativity Agenda seems to have become unquestionable in certain quarters, but that as it continues to demonstrate the contradictions raised in previous chapters, there is a risk that the imaginary around creativity, always somewhat problematic, is becoming increasingly detached from reality.

References

Becker, H. S. (2014). *What about Mozart? What about murder? Reasoning from cases*. Chicago: University of Chicago Press.

Campbell, P. (2014). Imaginary success?—The contentious ascendance of creativity. *European Planning Studies, 22*(5), 995–1009.

DCMS, BERR, & DIUS. (2008). *Creative Britain: New talents for the new economy*. London: DCMS.

Jessop, B. (2004). Critical semiotic analysis and cultural political economy. *Critical Discourse Studies, 1*(2), 159–174.

Mateos Garcia, J., Klinger, J., & Stathoulopoulos, K. (2018). *Creative nation: How the creative industries are powering the UK's nations and regions*. London: Nesta.

Mould, O. (2017). *Urban subversion and the creative city*. London: Routledge.

Oakley, K., & O'Connor, J. (2015). The cultural industries: An introduction. In K. Oakley & J. O'Connor (Eds.), *The Routledge companion to the cultural industries* (pp. 1–32). London: Routledge.

Oakley, K., Hesmondhalgh, D., Bell, D., & Nisbett, M. (2014). The national trust for talent? NESTA and New Labour's cultural policy. *British Politics, 9*(3), 297–317.

Rose, N. (1991). Governing by numbers: Figuring out democracy. *Accounting, Organizations and Society, 16*(7), 673–692.

Smith, C. (1998). *Creative Britain*. London: Faber and Faber.

Thomas, W. I., & Thomas, D. S. (1928). *The child in America: Behavior problems and programs*. New York: Alfred A. Knopf.

2

Presages of Persistent Creativity

Whilst this book concentrates on the persistence of a set of ideas regarding creativity in the early twenty-first century, in earlier periods there are indications of what is to come. Understanding these helps explain the role which creativity comes to hold in the present day. This chapter thus examines how the ground is cleared for the 'Creativity Agenda' introduced in Chapter 1. As such, it considers periods in which the language of creativity which becomes so prominent is yet to be regularly deployed, but in which a range of factors which foreshadow what is to come are in play. These factors, long extant, become more prominently and intensively intertwined in the era of the Creativity Agenda. This chapter therefore places the relatively recent arrival of the Creativity Agenda in the context of this longer history of factors that will become key to its development. These are the emergence of culture as an object of political concern; a drive to understand the world through 'objective' evidence gathering; the increasing dominance of the economic over other forms of value, in tandem with emerging ideas around a 'new' economy; and the idea that art and culture may be used to achieve 'regeneration'. These strands are not entirely separate, nor are they the only important factors in understanding the Creativity Agenda, but as they are interwoven, they form the foundations on which later endeavours rest.

© The Author(s) 2019
P. Campbell, *Persistent Creativity*, Sociology of the Arts,
https://doi.org/10.1007/978-3-030-03119-0_2

Before Creativity

In Chapter 1, a persistent, and consistent, position regarding the role of creativity from the 1990s to the 2010s was briefly traced. Immediately prior to this period, however, the idea of culturally creative practices being of increasing economic importance could be viewed with scepticism, suspicion or even be barely considered at all. Moss (2002), for instance, discusses the development by local government in Sheffield, England of a 'Cultural Industries Quarter' in the 1980s. This is characterised as a 'very daring use of taxpayers' money' (p. 214) which was regarded at the time of its establishment as an 'extraordinary, either brave or foolish, use of public money' (p. 211). Although there are similar efforts to promote what would later be referred to as 'creative' industries at this time, it is worth considering O'Connor's assessment of the position of local government more broadly in this period, as made in the early 1990s:

> Our investigations found that the current level of awareness of the potential of the arts and cultural industries was generally low, and that some local authorities were organisationally ill-equipped to develop and implement an arts and cultural industries strategy. (1992, p. 56)

At this point, not only is organisational capacity low, but so even is *awareness* of the potential for cultural industries. Speaking of a specific research location in the UK, O'Connor adds:

> No local authority in Greater Manchester has yet developed a strategy for the arts and cultural industries. Awareness of the potential of the arts and cultural industries is extremely patchy. Often the term Cultural Industry is poorly understood, and the contribution of the Arts to any economic regeneration strategy is seen as entirely marginal. (1992, p. 66)

In this location, as in others, intervention in this field remained under-developed by the later 1990s. Speaking of a research project carried out in this period, Banks and O'Connor note that, in Manchester, as in other UK cities, the idea that activities such as music, arts and media were economically regenerative and productive (rather than simply a drain on the public purse) and that cultural production could provide 'real' jobs and careers (and not just hobbies or distractions) seemed a new and irreverent claim. (2017, p. 638)

On the surface, this therefore seems like a remarkably rapid transformation. In the early 1990s, we have reports that the economic contribution of culture and the arts is given low, or no, priority, yet by the late 1990s, although still seen as a 'new' area for activity, national policymakers are asserting that the creative industries which encompass these activities are central to future economic success (Smith 1998, p. 31), with this position persisting in subsequent decades, as sketched in Chapter 1. Whilst it may seem to arrive relatively quickly, however, it is not the case that at this point in time, a range of actors including government suddenly 'get' creativity, and then maintain this position. Rather, this now persistent discourse around creativity can be seen not as fundamentally novel, but as the intensification and intertwining of a range of extant positions.

Creativity: Persistent Forever?

Although the aim here is to outline the historic factors that presage the operation of a subsequently persistent Creativity Agenda, it would be problematic to agree with the UK Business Secretary Greg Clark that 'Britain's creative industries have been at the heart of our economy for centuries' (BEIS 2018), or the even stronger assertion from chairman of 'Creative England' (a not-for-profit organisation seeking to promote creative industries), and ex-Special Advisor to the Secretary of State for Culture, Media and Sport in the UK, John Newbigin OBE, that 'the creative industries are as old as human society itself' (2007). As previously noted, the potential for misunderstanding and imprecision when the language of 'creativity' is utilised will be a common theme throughout this book; Chapter 5 will consider the definition of 'creative industries' in detail, but it is sufficient here to point out that it is problematic to argue that these creative industries are thousands, or even hundreds, of years old. Indeed, the term itself has only been in common usage since the 1990s, and many of the activities this term covers have only operated in a manner resembling their current form for a matter of decades. Whilst creativity in some form characterises human existence, and thus is indeed 'as old as human society itself', the creativity which characterises the Creativity Agenda taken up by policymakers, and the conditions which provide the circumstances for its development can be specified more concretely than this. The specific conditions that shape this recent usage are thus considered below.

Cultural Policy and Its Justifications

The brief outline in Chapter 1 showed a persistent case for creativity being made by government ministers, and so one factor enabling the rise of the Creativity Agenda is for the field of culture and creativity to be seen as a suitable one for political intervention. Whilst any attempt to define 'cultural policy' is fraught with difficulty, perhaps inherently so (see Gray 2010), if we consider intervention by the state in the field of the arts, we can see intervention in some form occurring over a long period, and becoming more prominent over time. Hesmondhalgh et al. note that public funding for national cultural institutions in the UK began in the mid-eighteenth century (2015a, p. 5), although Minihan (1977) demonstrates that by the early nineteenth-century culture retained a very low priority in government, which held that culture and the arts 'should be fostered primarily by those who enjoyed them' (p. 17), with the state playing a minimal role. She also, however, outlines a direction of travel away from this position over the course of the nineteenth century. In terms of what this emergent cultural policy seeks to achieve, Hesmondhalgh et al. (2015a, p. 7) rightly argue that summarising the goals of cultural policy is challenging, especially in comparison with other policy fields, but that it can often be seen to operate in areas such as seeking to narrate the 'national story', protecting heritage, regulating and censoring cultural forms and a concern with cultural production and consumption.

Cultural policy in the nineteenth century could not be concerned with the production or consumption of, for instance, the commodities of the music industry as we know them today, as neither these commodities nor this industry yet existed. Nevertheless, whilst meaningful cultural policy was minimal at this stage, and whilst the language of 'creativity' was not as pervasive as it would later become, it is instructive to note that some of the arguments made even in the earliest stages of cultural policy as to why government intervention in this field is required, and how it could be beneficial, foreshadow the justifications for the Creativity Agenda of the twenty-first century. At this point, for instance, we can identify incipient versions of the idea that artistic objects and practices are 'core' to wider economic and social benefits that later come to greater prominence. Minihan identifies debates over the role of government in the purchase of the Parthenon marbles removed by Thomas Bruce, 7th Earl of Elgin, in the early 1800s as key to the establishment of early substantial cultural policy in the UK, and notes that the Select Committee appointed to consider the purchase of the marbles put forth the supporting argument that the fine arts are '[intimately] connected with the advancement of everything valuable in Science, Literature, and Philosophy' and notably adds that, even at this point in time, 'the observation was not new' (1977, p. 14). This broad-ranging role can perhaps be linked to the developments in the use of the terminology of 'culture' as the eighteenth century gave way to the nineteenth traced by Williams (1958), in which the 'culture of the arts' is linked to a general refined state of being 'cultured', analogous to earlier uses of the term related to development of the land (rather than of human capacities) that persist in terms such as 'agriculture' and 'horticulture'. The developing uses of the term Williams outlines, including 'the general state of intellectual development in society as a whole' and 'the general body of the arts' (p. xvi) can be seen to intermingle and overlap, a process aided by the use of a common term. As later chapters will emphasise, this idea that cultural activity is connected with and core to many wider benefits is a key aspect of the Creativity Agenda, and the deployment of common terminology similarly helps to bolster this case in later periods.

The points made in debate in favour of the purchase of the Parthenon marbles by the Irish MP John Croker in the early nineteenth century would thus not be out of place in the early twenty-first century. He argued that the acquisition of this ancient statuary by the state would be,

> for the use of the people, for the encouragement of arts, the increase of manufactures, the prosperity of trades, and the encouragement of industry; not merely to please the eye of the man of taste, but to create, to stimulate, to guide the exertions of the artist, the mechanic and even the labourer. (cited in Minihan 1977, p. 17)

The idea that artistic practice may stimulate creativity and economic output, and at the same time bring together people from many different social strata is therefore not a novel, or recent, position. Indeed, Minihan cites arguments such as these from throughout the nineteenth century. For example, a Select Committee report twenty years after the discussion of the purchase of the Parthenon marbles in 1836 on 'Arts and their Connexion with Manufactures' emphasises the *economic* role the arts may play, and the need for further intervention to promote this:

> The arts have received little encouragement in this country [...yet] the connexion between art and manufactures is most important: and for this merely economical reason (were there no higher motive) it equally imports us to encourage art in its loftier attributes. (cited in Minihan 1977, p. 43)

Encourage the 'lofty' arts, and we may reap the benefits of increased economic output. Crudely put, perhaps, but such ideas would not be alien to a Culture Secretary in the 1990s or the early 2000s. In addition to being connected with *wider* 'manufactures', we will also see such arguments become increasingly dominant in the context of artistic practice in and of itself. Despite an increasing prominence throughout the nineteenth century, however, the marginality of cultural policy in this period must be emphasised. Even if a Culture Secretary in the 1990s would be sympathetic to some of these historic positions, it must be noted that in the UK at least, there was no such Secretary *until* the 1990s (Hesmondhalgh et al. 2015a, p. 60). Indeed, only two 'White Paper' policy documents on the arts and culture have ever been published in the UK, and the first, from 1965—'A Policy For The Arts: The First Steps'—argues that government support for the arts up to this point had been 'on a relatively modest scale' and, in fact, 'on no more than a poor law relief basis' (Lee 1965, pp. 16, 19). Whilst this 1965 White Paper paved the way for some transformation of this situation (the paper's author was the first to occupy the role of 'Minister of State for the Arts', and Hesmondhalgh et al. argue, for instance, that 'serious' support for the arts in the UK can be dated to the 1960s (2015b, p. 108)), it is important to note that it does not seek to make an exclusively economic case. The arts are positioned as central to 'civilised communities' and their contribution to the gaiety of the nation is presented as cause enough for increased support. Also, whilst this first White Paper came from the Labour Party, who play a large role in the story of creativity under consideration here, Hesmondhalgh et al. point out that up until the 1990s, Labour 'like most social democratic parties, generally treated culture and the arts as utterly marginal' (2015a, p. 23).

In briefly considering the political precursors of the Creativity Agenda, then, we see elements of paradox which will persist. On the one hand, government support of cultural practice is deemed important for the wider benefits it may have, and often for the specifically economic benefits that will 'ripple out' from artistic activity, with bold claims such as 'every thing valuable' ultimately being linked to the arts. On the other hand, despite such claims, tangible cultural policy or supporting resources may remain thin on the ground.

Evidence, Numbers and Culture

Whilst certain ideas around the benefits of culture and creativity can thus be located in historical periods, a substantial policy focus on these areas only develops in the late twentieth century. This is also true of the increasing focus on generating evidence to substantiate the nature of these benefits. Chapters 4 and 5 consider the increasing trend for political support of culture or creativity to be based on, or to seek to generate, justifying 'evidence' of some form. In this era of 'evidence-based policy', there is a particular emphasis on the gathering and utilisation of numerical data. In this, we also see an intensification of practices with long-standing roots. Porter's work on the conquering march of statistical measures refers to a 'great explosion of numbers' in a range of fields in the 1820s and 1830s (1986, p. 11) and gives contemporaneous accounts of the increasing importance of numerical data to policymakers (p. 37). In the early stages of cultural policy discussed above, however, the case for the importance of culture is generally not made using statistical evidence. The nineteenth-century Select Committees referred to, for instance, draw largely on expert testimony to demonstrate the economic role of culture. It is pertinent to note, however, that contemporary commentators find the use of this form of evidence to be questionable at best (e.g. Mechanics' Magazine 1837, pp. 323–329). Such questioning of the evidence base around culture and creativity also persists in later periods, as will be seen in later chapters.

It is likely that one reason for the absence of significant bodies of numerical evidence in the field of culture and cultural policy until well after the general 'explosion of numbers' in the early nineteenth century is the marginality of cultural policy referred to above. If the wider importance of cultural activity is argued for, but afforded no significant political resources, then it is of no great consequence if arguments about its effects stay at the level of anecdote or statements of faith. As well as its political marginality, the comparative absence of the application of statistical measures in the cultural field is likely due to activity in this field being particularly resistant to the use of such measures. Even where there is some historical evidence of attempts to *measure* aspects of artistic achievement, such as in de Piles' 'painter's scale' of the early eighteenth century ([1708] 1766), it is clear that these are not intended to be 'objective' measures. De Piles, the 'leading and official theorist' of the Royal Academy of Painting and Sculpture established by Louis XIV (Puttfarken 1985, p. xii) is quite explicit that his numerical rankings of artists were created '*plutôt pour me divertit que pour attirer les autres dans mon sentiment*' (de Piles [1708] 1766, p. 387), and Puttfarken concludes that, 'although highly acclaimed in the eighteenth century [the scale] is now considered his most notorious contribution to criticism' (1985, p. 42).

Whilst after the eighteenth century an attempt to score and rank artistic output may be considered 'notorious', we can also see glimpses of scientism applied to the cultural realm in the late nineteenth century. In a consideration of Solvay's work beginning in this period on 'energetic' theories of value, Max Weber pours scorn on attempts to 'scientifically' measure various phenomena centred on meaning, including the arts, using quantitative methods and mathematical formulae, characterising Solvay's viewpoint thus:

> Music, for instance, gives rise to cerebral states that cause modifications to occur in the process of oxidization; and these in turn serve the purpose of an improved utilization of the released organic energy [...] Therefore, the energetical significance [of music] has been proved; consequently it is, like all similar phenomena, "in principle" measurable. ([1909] 2012, p. 255)

For Weber, any such measurements are not appropriate for the task of ascertaining value:

> It is a ridiculous pastime to invent mathematical symbols for this value judgement: if [performing] such puny tricks had any sense at all, the coefficients corresponding to those symbols would have to be completely different for *every single valuating subject* [...] the height of absurdity is of course reached when those who emit these puffs of hot air attitudinize as if they were offering something of a "scientific" nature. ([1909] 2012, p. 255, original emphasis)

Whilst Weber would not see fit to address such activities were they not being attempted to some degree, at this point in time such attempts to quantitatively measure cultural value remain comparatively rare. Once again, however, here we can see incipient developments that will intensify in later periods, albeit in somewhat different forms. What characterises the period of 'persistent creativity' that is to come, is not so much attempts to quantify artistic practice itself, but rather to establish a secure evidence base regarding the wider 'instrumental' effects of culture and creativity—that is to say that whilst they may have value in and of themselves, they can usefully be put to work supporting other outcomes. The available literature suggests that, in concert with its marginal political position, substantial research data regarding such instrumental outcomes remains notable by its absence up until the final quarter of the twentieth century, despite a long history of assertions regarding the range of beneficial outcomes, and the leveraging of these assertions in making the case for political intervention (as seen above). As Chapter 4 will consider in more detail, whilst the broader social benefits of artistic activity have been strongly argued for, particularly since the 1960s, the 'significant body of evidence' produced since this date 'was anecdotal and there were significant gaps in the documentation of work' (Reeves 2002, p. 7).

Given the importance to the Creativity Agenda of the specifically *economic* role attributed to creativity, it is also instructive to note that, despite a similar hinterland to the other phenomena considered in this chapter, the specific study of the arts within the field of economics also does not flourish until the 1960s (Frey 2003, p. 3). Relatedly, Velthuis and Coslor note that, although having been used as a deliberate source of economic investment since at least the seventeenth century, the use of art in such a manner intensifies dramatically in the twentieth century. It is particularly instructive in this consideration of the development of numerical evidence to note their point that it was also in the 1960s that, '*The Times* of London was the first to make art explicitly comparable to stocks by publishing a graph representing the price development of art, akin to a stock index' (2012, p. 475).

Economic Value and Neoliberal Ideology

Following this period, we see an increasing emphasis on the need to produce evidence to make the case for culture and creativity, often focussed on economic outcomes. In considering the role played by evidence-making in the persistence of the Creativity Agenda, though, there is a further paradox. The value of creativity is continually asserted, but continually uncertain; continually demonstrated but never fully established. This pattern starts to become more prominent in the 1980s in concert with the intensification at this time of claims around the economic role of culture. As we saw above, in this period a local government intervention to develop cultural businesses could still be seen as 'brave or foolish', but in the broader policy arena, Matarasso notes that prominent statements around the economic outcomes of cultural activity are made in a much clearer and more strident manner in this period than in earlier stages of cultural policymaking,

> for instance in the Arts Council Chairman's 1985 lecture on 'The Political Economy of the Arts' in which Lord Rees-Mogg claimed that 'The Arts Council gives the best value for money in job creation of any part of the state system'. (2009, p. 7)

Similarly, in 1986 the Arts Council produced a report, 'Partnership: Making Arts Money Work Harder', which argued for a more multivalent role for the arts in developing industry and building communities, but one clearly focussed on economic factors. This period has thus been characterised as one in which researchers 'adopted arguments according to the prevailing business mood of the decade', attempting to make the economic case for the arts to argue against cuts in government spending (Lorente 1996, p. 6). The major reference point for later work which aims to provide more robust evidence on the specifically *economic* role that artistic practice may play is Myerscough's 'The Economic Importance of the Arts in Britain' (1988). Such economic outcomes are important to the Creativity Agenda with its emphasis on creative *industries*, the 'wealth of the future' and so forth, and in many ways Myerscough's work lays clear foundations for much that follows. Indeed, the successful international exporting of Myerscough's model (Comedia 2004, p. 8; Hesmondhalgh et al. 2015a, p. 62) presages the international proliferation of UK models of measurement of the creative industries examined further in Chapter 5. In considering the historical development of 'evidence' for the role of culture, Hughes emphasises the fact that Myerscough's work demonstrates an inflection point in research in this field, and in 1989 is able to convincingly refer to an 'almost scandalous lack of empirical research into the operation of the arts sector' (p. 34) before this time, praising Myerscough's efforts to rectify this situation, although also raising some points of critique. Hughes points to methodological questions regarding Myerscough's work, arguing that in places it seems to inappropriately inflate the role of the arts, veering away from an attempt to simply present the position of arts practice with clarity, and closer to advocacy for the cultural sector. As later chapters will argue, though, this is yet another way in which Myerscough's work lays the foundations for subsequent practice.

Again, it should be noted here that whilst concern with measuring the outcomes of cultural practice intensifies in this period, this concern is not new. To return to consideration of 'instrumentalist' arguments around supporting the arts more broadly, Belfiore (2006) argues that rather than being a modern invention, such instrumentality can be traced back to Classical Greece. In addition to this longer history regarding the uses to which art can be put, the Creativity Agenda thrives due to an intensification of a historical trend towards the domination of all other forms of value by economic value. On the development of this trend, it is instructive to consider the position of Taylor:

> The philosophers and political economists of the eighteenth century sensed that theirs was an age of profound changes and that such changes were especially manifest in the distinctions and relationships between economic, ethical and aesthetic life. That the emergent nineteenth century theoretical orthodoxy attempted to reduce these three to one – utility – in the face of a romantic rearguard action to at least maintain two – the economic and the aesthetic – only serves to illustrate the importance of what was at stake. (2015, p. 9)

This 'reduction' to utilitarian positions on value is argued to continue in recent times, however the dominance of economic logics in the 1980s is assigned by Taylor not only to these broader historical trends but to the specific dominance in this more recent period of neoliberal ideology (2015, p. 28).

Whilst the term 'neoliberal' has become unhelpfully unmoored in recent years, and can be used by some as little more than an ambiguous term of disapproval, Taylor is undoubtedly correct that in understanding the conditions in which the Creativity Agenda comes to prominence neoliberalism is a useful concept. As with 'creativity', to define the term succinctly is difficult, but Davies' perceptive account of neoliberalism includes many useful guides. Firstly, given this chapter's concern with historical precursors and time frames, Davies argues that neoliberalism forms 'a roughly coherent paradigm' that traverses the globe from the late 1970s onwards (2014, p. 2), with the common thread in this paradigm being 'an attempt to replace political judgement with economic evaluation, including, but not exclusively, the evaluations offered by markets' (2014, p. 3). We can thus see how the developing contextual conditions for the rise of the Creativity Agenda traced above intertwine and intensify in this era. Davies considers the role of quantitative data in this paradigm, and its apparent ability to reduce uncertainty and the need for political judgement, emphasising how,

> from a neoliberal perspective, price provides a logical and phenomenological ideal of how human relations can be mediated without the need for rhetorical, ritualized or deliberately performative modes of communication. [...] The reduction of complex and uncertain situations to a single number, as achieved by a market, appears as a route out of the hermeneutic pluralism and associated dangers of politics. (2014, p. 4)

This reduction of all forms of value to a single signifier in order to, at least 'ideally', avoid the complexity of politics echoes the impulse explicitly stated by the early statistical societies who played a key role in the expansion of numerical measures in the nineteenth century, noted above. Porter, for instance, refers in the establishment of the London Statistical Society in the 1830s to their 'first and most essential rule' which was 'to exclude all opinions' (1986, p. 36). Again we see a paradox in operation here, as Rose outlines:

> Paradoxically, in the same process in which numbers achieve a privileged status in political decisions, they simultaneously promise a

"de-politicization" of politics, redrawing the boundaries between politics and objectivity by purporting to act as automatic technical mechanisms for making judgments, prioritizing problems and allocating scarce resources. (1991, p. 674)

As will be discussed further in the consideration of the evidence base around creative industries in Chapter 5, apparently 'objective' measures, rather than exiting the field of judgement, may merely obscure important assumptions and ideological stances, and this is particularly the case when dealing with quantitative information, often presented as though the result of a purely technical measurement process. Whilst we can understand the focus on *economic* measures in making the case for culture and creativity in a neoliberal era, therefore, we should also be ready to question the means by which such forms of 'evidence' operate. Nevertheless, as discussed in Chapter 4, from the 1990s onwards, in line with the emergence of the Department for Culture, Media and Sport in the UK, we see an increased concentration on the need for the cultural sector to make its case in ways which at least gesture towards clear, demonstrable outcomes. What work such as Myerscough's aligns with is a sense towards the end of the twentieth century that we increasingly enter a period in which, by focussing specifically on economic outcomes, the arts can attempt to make their case clearly and uncontestably, in a manner which is (supposedly) beyond political argumentation. If 'creativity', however conceived, results in increased tax revenue, increased spending by tourists, higher value goods and other 'objectively' measurable outcomes then, from certain perspectives, it is only 'rational' to continue to push the Creativity Agenda.

We should, however, exercise caution before assuming that as the twentieth-century ends, the cultural realm has been abandoned to the operations of economic markets. Davies argues that it is rather the case that the state comes increasingly to justify decisions in terms that are 'commensurable with the logic of markets' (2014, p. 6) utilising related techniques of evaluation to give at least the impression that clean, rational measures are taking precedent over the messy subjectivity of judgement. To return to the question of policymaking, these techniques of evaluation are embedded in the 'new public management' which is characteristic of government from the late twentieth century, with its 'focus on management, not policy, and on performance appraisal and efficiency' (Bevir and Rhodes 2003, p. 82). Such ideas present particular problems for the cultural realm where judgement and subjectivity seem particularly important. It should also be noted that the ideology of neoliberalism also works to emphasise competition, with measurement enabling ranking, evaluation and scoring (Davies 2014, p. 30). This increasing emphasis on competition is intensified by the sense that 'winning' the creativity game is particularly important to future success in light of broader economic trends.

A 'New' Economy

In tandem with this increasing concern with economic forms of valuation, there is a developing sense that the economy *itself* is undergoing significant transformation in the late twentieth century. Prior to the 1990s, there is essentially no substantial policy which uses the language of the 'creative industries', and no policy statements as clear as Smith's to the effect that these will be central to the 'wealth of the future' (1998, p. 31). Yet one clear thread in the Creativity Agenda is the sense that a fundamental transformation is emergent and persistently emergent; creativity may be of some importance now, but it will be even *more* important in future, and so those who do not take preparatory action will, in an era of global competition, be left behind. This sense of the need to prepare for the arrival, or intensification, of a transformational economic state of affairs also has a longer history which aligns with, and prepares the way for, the Creativity Agenda.

Theorising regarding an emergent 'new' economy develops in the final half of the twentieth century and intensifies in its final quarter. The specific character of these 'new' economic circumstances is conceived of in various ways, but a growing emphasis is placed on the economic importance of intangible goods such as meaningful symbols and knowledge. In a broader consideration of the specifics of creative work, for instance, Banks argues that it is in the 1950s in the UK that jobs in 'cultural industries began to attain a greater popularity and currency' (2017,

p. 91). Banks also argues that at the start of the 1950s, C. Wright Mills' study *White Collar* ([(1951)] 2002) is prescient in identifying 'a new set of workplaces and occupations in the post-war United States, based on knowledge and information, services and symbol production' (Banks 2017, p. 91). Prominent management theorists such as Drucker emphasise similar points in the 1950s, whilst also noting the fact that these ideas were yet to be widely adopted:

> The man who works exclusively or primarily with his hands is the one who is increasingly unproductive. Productive work in today's society and economy is work that applies vision, knowledge and concepts – work that is based on the mind rather than on the hand. [...] Educated people are the "capital" of a developed society [...] This may sound obvious. But it is so new that it is not yet recognized. (1959, p. 120)

This emphasis on the importance of 'knowledge' to current and future economic success in a 'knowledge economy' continues into the 1960s. Kerr, for instance, draws on Machlup's work on 'The Production and Distribution of Knowledge in the United States' (1962) to make the following claim in a tract expressing the importance of the university system:

> The production, distribution, and consumption of "knowledge" in all its forms is said to account for 29 percent of gross national product, according to Fritz Machlup's calculations; and "knowledge production" is growing at about twice the rate of the rest of the economy. Knowledge has certainly never in history been so central to the conduct of an entire society. (Kerr [1963] 2001, p. 66)

Considering the specifics of the increased importance of *cultural* work, Banks (2017, p. 92) also points to the work of Berger at this time on 'youthfulness' as a human characteristic (not necessarily dependent on age). Berger questions which adult occupations tolerate or reward such 'youthfulness', and his 'youthful careers' include 'bohemian businessmen' (1963, p. 332) whose motivating interests may be more 'expressive' than commercial, and 'show business' occupations including musician, actor and comedian (p. 335), in addition to 'satellite show business careers such as disc jockeying and modeling' (p. 337). Interestingly for the discussion here, Berger refers to these occupations explicitly as 'creative' ones, but unlike the celebratory narratives around creativity which are to come, concludes at this stage that 'opportunities for a successful career in bohemian business are probably not very good' (p. 334).

Such creative or cultural work could be said to be based on intangible 'knowledge' of some kind, but clearly there are many other fields in which intangible factors also play a key role. Nevertheless, even though it is yet to blossom, the roots of the Creativity Agenda start to grow much stronger in this context. Miller, for instance, argues that 'the creative industries as a discourse' begins in the 1960s with an increasing emphasis on the economic importance of 'post-industrial activities' (2009, p. 93). Similarly, Hesmondhalgh et al. trace elements of New Labour's cultural policy position to the eventual mainstream acceptance of the economic importance of 'information and knowledge', based on the work of theorists in the 1960s and 1970s such as Drucker, Bell and Porat (2015a, pp. 52–53).

Bell's work in the 1970s on the 'post-industrial society' is a key reference point in this area, and Bell offers this succinct description: 'the post-industrial society is an information society, as industrial society is a goods-producing society' (1974, p. 467). 'Information' is also central to Porat's work around this time, which acknowledges the prior work of Machlup on the measurement of the contribution of 'knowledge', and seeks to define the share of economic wealth which 'originates with the production, processing and distribution of information goods and services' (1977, p. 8). Garnham's work on how this 'information society' thinking underlies later positions on creativity is particularly informative, especially his emphasis on the fact that at this original stage, there is no especially prominent role for cultural work or creative industries in these theories (2001, p. 453). Nevertheless, the later rise of the Creativity Agenda can in part be explained by what Garnham argues is,

> an attempt by the cultural sector and the cultural policy community to share in its relations with the government, and in policy presentation in the media, the unquestioned prestige that now attaches to the

information society and to any policy that supposedly favours its development. (2005, p. 20)

For Garnham, Bell's version of 'information society' thinking has scientific work at its core, and the 'application of Weberian rationalization to the production of knowledge itself' (2000, p. 141). Garnham also emphasises how this vision of the information society that helps pave the way for the Creativity Agenda has a key role for the creative, innovative individual entrepreneur, aligning with the economic theories of Joseph Schumpeter. For Schumpeter, the economy is driven forward by the act of entrepreneurship which consists of enacting 'new combinations' of the means of production (1934, p. 68), with the application of such innovations rendering existing products and markets obsolete via a process of 'creative destruction' (Scott 2006). 'Creativity' is thus central, in certain senses, to economic transformation and success. As Garnham notes, key here are 'entrepreneurs and technologists' (2005, p. 22). Other strands to the development of this form of thinking include the increasing importance of business information systems, along with the 'information specialists' working around these systems, including 'lawyers, accountants, [and] management consultants' (p. 23), and the progressive shift away from work in manufacturing towards work in services in some locations.

Although each of these theorists has somewhat different interests and draws somewhat different conclusions, broadly speaking over this period we see an increasing sense that intangible factors such as knowledge and information, embodied in 'human capital', will be decisive to future economic growth and success in a competitive, globalised economy, and the creative entrepreneur is often positioned as increasingly important to these developments. On this issue of entrepreneurship, we see again how the roots of the Creativity Agenda can be productively entangled, as 'creative' entrepreneurship comes to be seen in an era of neoliberalism not simply as a positive attribute in the realm of business, but also comes to be valued over a number of domains, including government. Jessop (2002), for example, traces the development of the economy over the latter half of the twentieth century from a Fordist model within what he terms a 'Keynesian Welfare Nation State' which experiences crises in the 1970s and 1980s, leading to the emergence of a new model aligning with the ideological positions discussed thus far, which he terms the 'Schumpeterian Competition State'. This change entails a move from centralised, standardised production and state operation towards the promotion of entrepreneurship, inter-regional competition and a shift towards the exaltation of flexibility and free enterprise over a discourse more focussed on central planning.

This increased emphasis on the flexible creative entrepreneur also provides fertile ground for the later Creativity Agenda. Davies (2014) convincingly outlines the role assigned to market competition in neoliberal times, and the fact that 'creativity' is explicitly aligned in the work of influential thinkers such as Schumpeter as being a central factor in competitive entrepreneurship:

> One of the central messages that the competitiveness gurus sought to disseminate amongst policy elites over the 1980s and 1990s was that western economies could no longer compete internationally on price, but now needed to compete on quality, innovation and differentiation. Doing so involved identifying those elements of a population or locality that couldn't be easily mimicked by competitors, and then converting those into a source of competitive advantage. [...] The Schumpeterian idea of the disruptive, self-governing entrepreneur provides the philosophical anthropology underpinning this vision, and the race is to see which nation can best release this economic heroism. (2014, p. 113)

It is the economic crises referred to above which necessitate such 'new' competitive responses that also bring the Creativity Agenda another step closer. It is important to emphasise, therefore, that this discussion of 'new' economic times does not merely involve a discursive shift of emphasis by policymakers, or the emergence of a popular new theoretical trend, but is reflected in tangible circumstances. Although there are continuities that should not be overlooked, there is no doubt that the operations of the economy in many territories did indeed undergo significant changes in the final quarter of the twentieth century, and a brief examination of some macro patterns of employment helps to give a quick sense of the scale and speed of these changes. In the UK, for instance, in 1979 when a Conservative government embodying many of the neoliberal values discussed above first came to power, 6.7 million people were employed in manufacturing. In ten years, this figure fell by 25% to just over 5 million, and over the next twenty years, this figure would drop by another 50% to just over 2.5 million (ONS 2018a). By comparison, over the same period of 1979–2009, employment in 'administrative and support service activities' increased by over 100% from 1 million to 2.4 million (ONS 2018b).

As Pratt (2008, p. 109) points out, however, it is important to note that the 'old' industries under consideration are not in absolute decline when considered from a global perspective, but rather are located in sites where labour costs are lower. Britain, for instance, is no longer 'the workshop of the world' as it could claim to be in the nineteenth century, but this is not because there is no longer any need for such a workshop. Nevertheless, in locations such as Britain where 'old' industries are transformed, attacked, or abandoned, we see in response to this period of crisis the emergence of the idea that cultural and creative practices may help to fill the gap. Kong summarises the overall trend thus:

> The loss of jobs in traditional industrial sectors with the collapse of the industrial base in many cities, the need to adapt to the processes of economic restructuring of the 1970s and early 1980s, and growing competition in the new post-industrial service economy prompted governments to reexamine their cultural policies and mine the potential role of cultures for economic gain. (2000, p. 387)

Considering this period, it has been argued that regardless of whether discussion has used the terminology of an emergent 'post-industrial society', or a shift away from a Keynesian welfare state to a 'post-Fordist' society, or an era of 'postmodernism', or 'post-materialism', 'what united all these diagnoses was a sense that 'culture'—knowledge, creativity, the arts but also the sciences—were becoming more important in society and economy' (Bakhshi et al. 2009, p. 7). Certainly as we move towards the era of 'persistent creativity', there is an increasing emphasis on the economic role that activity which could be labelled as 'creative' may play. Given the focus here on culture and the arts, it should be noted that as we move into the 1990s, some argue that the 'newness' of this newly emergent economy can be especially characterised by phenomena that are cultural and symbolic in nature. Lash and Urry, for example, support the notion that the economic importance of tangible outputs and physical capital is declining and draw this distinction regarding the nature of the transformation that is occurring:

> What is increasingly produced are not material objects, but *signs*. These signs are of two types. Either they have a primarily cognitive content and are post-industrial or informational goods. Or they have primarily an aesthetic content and are what can be termed postmodern goods. (1994, p. 4)

What is clearly developing as the twentieth century closes, then, is a sense that heavy industry, manufacturing, physical labour and so on will not lead to competitive advantage in the future. Information, symbols, signs, aesthetics, culture—these are the way forward, and promoting creativity not just in the sense that aligns with the symbolic and the cultural, but also in the sense that involves creation of new competitive businesses will be key to securing competitive advantage. In this context, it is no surprise that an agenda around the power of creativity takes hold.

Art for Economic and Social 'Regeneration'

In considering the means by which the fallout from the economic transitions and crises discussed above can be resolved, the terminology of 'regeneration' is increasingly used from the 1980s onwards (Jones and Evans 2008, p. 2), and the notion of a specific role for culture in achieving this regeneration is one that we will see emerge as vital to the promotion of the Creativity Agenda. As such, this concept will be considered further in future chapters, but as its usage begins before the main period of 'persistent creativity' under consideration, this chapter ends by briefly considering some relevant precursors. Like many of the terms in use here, the notion of regeneration is not a simple one to pin down, but it is largely associated with attempts to restore or revive urban centres. Evans (2011, p. 7) states that the term is 'associated with extremes of social decline, multiple deprivation and disadvantage and in economic terms, below-average performance'. It is, therefore, the city or town that is struggling, whose socio-economic life has experienced a significant downturn or slump, and which without intervention will continue its decline that is in need of some form of regeneration (Jones and Evans 2008, p. 161). A role for culture, the arts and creativity in achieving such regeneration, however, has not always been prominent. Evans points out, for instance, that mainstream policy programmes aimed at achieving regeneration in such deprived zones,

> such as central government Single Regeneration Budget, New Deal for Communities and their predecessors originating in the 1970s – the European Structural Development Fund and European Social Funding – have traditionally lacked a cultural dimension and 'culture' is not one of the key domains that feature in how improvement is measured and regeneration investment is assessed. (Evans 2011, p. 7)

The 'discovery' of culture as a tool for urban regeneration, and its subsequent journey from the margins of regeneration policy and practice are difficult to date and map precisely, but certain patterns are relatively clear. In terms of time frame, Taylor argues for substantial growth in this agenda in the UK over the 1980s, with increased development in the 1990s (2006, p. 5). Vickery notes that until this point urban regeneration was largely led by property development (2007, p. 29), and that during the 1990s the role allocated to culture in urban regeneration schemes often remained linked to physical or spatial developments, being most visibly manifest through alteration of the design of the urban environment and the installation of public artworks (2007, pp. 18–19).

When culture is more closely attached to a 'regeneration' agenda, as we may expect from the discussion thus far, its beneficial effects are often posited as being ultimately economic, mirroring broader trends in cultural policy:

In the West, cultural policy had lost its prime modernising link to nation- and citizen- building by the 1960s (often before), and was increasingly linked to agendas of community, personal expression and self-development; to social issues (e.g., multiculturalism and neighborhood renewal); and – from the 1980s – to economic policy. (O'Connor 2005, p.47)

Nevertheless, its more socially 'regenerative' potential also forms part of the narrative regarding the role culture may play in regeneration, as Chapter 4 will discuss in more detail. Again, this is not an entirely novel development. Minihan argues that in the nineteenth century, 'among art's promoters, social concerns powerfully buttressed aesthetic interests' (1977, p. 27) and the range of positive outcomes attributed to the arts was broad-ranging; claims regarding the positive role the arts may play for improving health, for instance, date back at least a century (e.g. Leahy 2014, p. 12).

Discussions of 'regeneration' can be placed in this context, and in the context of the broader trends outlined above, which raise the issue of how cultural policy may increasingly be aligned to other policy agendas. Gray (2007) discusses the trend for cultural policy to become closely 'attached' to other policy agendas, noting a particular intensification of these tendencies from the late 1970s into the 1980s. Due to a comparative lack of political interest and power in the cultural sector at this point, Gray emphasises how justification for cultural funding became increasingly reliant on demonstrating the 'effectiveness' of the arts, primarily in the economic arena, but also in other ways. He refers to research considering the role of cultural resources in achieving economic growth, but also in countering social exclusion, and in achieving personal development and community empowerment (2007, p. 206). Others similarly note that over this period arts and culture are discussed in relation to their ability to 'reduce crime and deviance, and increase health and mental wellbeing' (Belfiore 2002, p. 97). These outcomes increasingly become a major focus of policy discussion and, as noted above, the need to not only *assert* but attempt to *demonstrate* these outcomes with numerical evidence becomes ever more prominent, as do actual interventions: by the late 1990s, Zukin could argue that in the context of 'an absence of traditional resources for competing for capital investment and jobs', cultural strategies for development,

> reflect[ed] the growing importance, in all mature urban centres, of a symbolic economy based on such abstract products as financial instruments, information and 'culture' – i.e. art, food, fashion, music and tourism. (1998, p. 826)

By this time, then, the expectations that culture and creativity can aid in 'regenerating' and sustaining urban centres are increasingly accepted, and so we are ready to enter the period of 'persistent creativity'.

Conclusion

The emergence in the 1990s of the Creativity Agenda traced in Chapter 1 was presaged by longer term trends. Over many decades, there has been a shift from a position in which state intervention in the field of the arts and cultural policy in any substantial form was seen as being essentially inappropriate, to one in which arguments that supporting artistic pursuits will lead to beneficial outcomes gain increasing traction. As ideological positions which place an increased emphasis on the primacy of economic value and the deployment of seemingly objective technical measures come to dominate, the 'need' to provide evidence of these beneficial outcomes intensifies, particularly in establishing measures of *economic* success. Aligned with this is a developing sense that intangible, symbolic work is particularly important in the transforming economic times of the late twentieth century and so those who create such symbols may also embody creativity in their ability to act as dynamic entrepreneurs, transforming the economy through the process of creative destruction. Given these wider transformations, it can be posited that it is only rational for policymakers to seek to prepare for an 'inevitable' creative future, especially given the primacy of narratives of inter-city and inter-country competition that come to the fore. This is especially so when economic transitions have left urban and industrial centres in a state of decline and so in need of some form of 'regeneration'.

To return to the period of early 'brave or foolish' interventions in the cultural economy where this chapter began, we can see how these interventions pick up on these themes. Wynne argues in the early 1990s that 'successful regeneration strategies' need to be based on a 'new economy' given the decline of 'traditional industries' (1992, pp. 1, 5), points echoed by Redhead's consideration of the Sheffield Cultural Industries Quarter considered at the outset. Redhead argues that this development, driven by local government,

> clearly filled a requirement in the Sheffield region, once the bottom fell out of traditional heavy industry there. Cultural industries tended to replace traditional ones. (1992, p. 49)

Although by this point we are yet to encounter the specific language of 'creativity' in any sustained form in the context of such developments, this term manages to draw together many of the ideas and practices discussed above and knot them together in a seemingly coherent fashion.

With these foundations laid, and with these positions overlapping in ways that provide fertile soil for its growth, we therefore enter an era in which we increasingly see value ascribed to 'creativity'. These trends are thus not new so much as increasingly intense. Many of the elements that come to characterise the discourse around creativity in the twenty-first century can be seen to be espoused much earlier, for instance the idea that creative practice can be at the 'core' of wider industrial outputs, or that culture can be beneficial in myriad ways. Despite the increasing emphasis on the generation of 'evidence' to sustain such positions, therefore, it is important to bear in mind that these positions have not originally emerged *from* such evidence, and predate a prevailing concern with evidence. Also, despite an increased focus on economic priorities, it is worth noting Bianchini's influential consideration of case studies from Western Europe in the early period of culture-led regeneration which argues that,

> the direct impact of 1980s cultural policies on the generation of employment and wealth was relatively modest, in comparison with the role of culture in constructing positive urban images, developing the tourism

industry, attracting inward investment, and strengthening the competitive position of cities. (1993, p. 2)

Given the concerns of the Creativity Agenda, we would expect this position to change as it rises to greater prominence. The specific nature of this agenda will therefore be examined in the next chapter. As the foundations traced above have many complementary characteristics, we will see that the narrative around creativity is in many ways a compelling one. We have also seen, however, that these trends contain elements of paradox and contradiction, and so must investigate whether the sense of creativity that comes to be prominently deployed is a coherent one.

References

Arts Council of Great Britain. (1986). *Partnership: Making arts money work harder*. London: Arts Council.

Bakhshi, H., Desai, R., & Freeman, A. (2009). *Not rocket science: A roadmap for arts and culture R&D*. Retrieved from https://mpra.ub.uni-muenchen.de/52710/1/MPRA_paper_52710.pdf.

Banks, M. (2017). *Creative justice: Cultural industries, work and inequality*. London: Rowman & Littlefield.

Banks, M., & O'Connor, J. (2017). Inside the whale (and how to get out of there): Moving on from two decades of creative industries research. *European Journal of Cultural Studies, 20*(6), 637–654.

BEIS. (2018, March 28). [Tweet]. Retrieved from https://twitter.com/beisgovuk/status/978874630030155776?s=11.

Belfiore, E. (2002). Art as a means of alleviating social exclusion: Does it really work? A critique of instrumental cultural policies and social impact studies in the UK. *International Journal of Cultural Policy, 8*(1), 91–106.

Belfiore, E. (2006). The unacknowledged legacy: Plato, the *Republic* and cultural policy. *International Journal of Cultural Policy, 12*(2), 229–244.

Bell, D. (1974). *The coming of post-industrial society*. London: Heinemann.

Berger, B. M. (1963). On the youthfulness of youth cultures. *Social Research, 30*(3), 319–342.

Bevir, M., & Rhodes, R. A. W. (2003). *Interpreting British governance*. London: Routledge.

Bianchini, F. (1993). Culture, conflict and cities: Issues and prospects for the 1990s. In F. Bianchini & M. Parkinson (Eds.), *Cultural policy and urban regeneration* (pp. 199–213). Manchester: Manchester University Press.

Comedia. (2004). *Culture and regeneration: An evaluation of the evidence.* Nottingham: Comedia.

Davies, W. (2014). *The limits of neoliberalism: Authority, sovereignty and the logic of competition.* London: Sage.

de Piles, R. ([1708] 1766). *Cours de peinture par principes.* Retrieved from http://gallica.bnf.fr/ark:/12148/bpt6k5814705x/f6.image.

Drucker, P. F. (1959). *Landmarks of tomorrow.* New York: Harper & Brothers.

Evans, G. (2011). Cities of culture and the regeneration game. *London Journal of Tourism, Sport and Creative Industries, 5*(6), 5–18.

Frey, B. S. (2003). *Arts & economics: Analysis & cultural policy* (2nd ed.). Berlin: Springer-Verlag.

Garnham, N. (2000). 'Information Society' as theory or ideology. *Information, Communication & Society, 3*(2), 139–152.

Garnham, N. (2001). Afterword: The cultural commodity and cultural policy. In S. Selwood (Ed.), *The UK cultural sector—Profile and policy issues* (pp. 445–458). London: Policy Studies Institute.

Garnham, N. (2005). From culture to creative industries. *International Journal of Cultural Policy, 11*(1), 15–29.

Gray, C. (2007). Commodification and instrumentality in cultural policy. *International Journal of Cultural Policy, 13*(2), 203–215.

Gray, C. (2010). Analysing cultural policy: incorrigibly plural or ontologically incompatible? *International Journal of Cultural Policy, 16*(2), 215–230.

Hesmondhalgh, D., Oakley, K., Lee, D., & Nisbett, M. (2015a). *Culture, economy and politics—The case of New Labour.* Basingstoke: Palgrave Macmillan.

Hesmondhalgh, D., Nisbett, M., Oakley, K., & Lee, D. (2015b). Were New Labour's cultural policies neo-liberal? *International Journal of Cultural Policy, 21*(1), 97–114.

Hughes, G. (1989). Measuring the economic value of the arts. *Policy Studies, 9*(3), 152–165.

Jessop, B. (2002). *The future of the capitalist state.* Cambridge: Polity.

Jones, P., & Evans, J. (2008). *Urban regeneration in the UK.* London: Sage.

Kerr, C. ([1963] 2001). *The uses of the university* (5th ed.). London: Harvard University Press.

Kong, L. (2000). Culture, economy, policy: Trends and developments. *Geoforum, 31*(4), 385–390.

Lash, S., & Urry, J. (1994). *Economies of signs and space*. London: Sage.

Leahy, H. R. (2014). The art of giving and receiving. In Contemporary Art Society & Whitechapel Gallery (Eds.), *The best is not too good for you: New approaches to public collections in England* (pp. 8–13). London: Whitechapel Gallery.

Lee, J. (1965). *A policy for the arts: The first steps*. London: Her Majesty's Stationery Office.

Lorente, P. (1996). *The role of museums and the arts in the urban regeneration of Liverpool*. Leicester: Centre for Urban History.

Machlup, F. (1962). *The production and distribution of knowledge in the United States*. Princeton: Princeton University Press.

Matarasso, F. (2009). *Playing as the world burns? Art and society today*. Retrieved from http://www.academia.edu/1713828/Playing_as_the_World_Burns_Art_and_society_today.

Mechanics' Magazine. (1837). *Further remarks on the report of the committee on the arts and principles of design*. London: Cunningham and Salmon.

Miller, T. (2009). From creative to cultural industries. *Cultural Studies, 23*(1), 88–99.

Mills, C.W. ([1951] 2002). *White collar*. Oxford: Oxford University Press.

Minihan, J. (1977). *The nationalization of culture*. London: Hamish Hamilton.

Moss, L. (2002). Sheffield's cultural industries quarter 20 years on: What can be learned from a pioneering example? *International Journal of Cultural Policy, 8*(2), 211–219.

Myerscough, J. (1988). *The economic importance of the arts in Britain*. London: Policy Studies Institute.

Newbigin, J. (2007). *Creative policy—What should the government do about creative industries?* Retrieved from https://web.archive.org/web/20130510012843/www.uel.ac.uk/risingeast/archive07/debate/newbigin.htm.

O'Connor, J. (1992). Local government and cultural policy. In D. Wynne (Ed.), *The culture industry: The arts in urban regeneration* (pp. 56–69). Aldershot: Avebury.

O'Connor, J. (2005). Creative exports: Taking cultural industries to St. Petersburg. *International Journal of Cultural Policy, 11*(1), 45–60.

ONS. (2018a). *UK workforce jobs SA: C Manufacturing (thousands)*. Retrieved from https://www.ons.gov.uk/employmentandlabourmarket/peopleinwork/employmentandemployeetypes/timeseries/jwr7/lms.

ONS. (2018b). *UK workforce jobs SA: N Administrative & support service activities (thousands)*. Retrieved from https://www.ons.gov.uk/employmentandlabourmarket/peopleinwork/employmentandemployeetypes/timeseries/jwt2/lms.

Porat, M. (1977). *The information economy: Definition and measurement*. Retrieved from https://files.eric.ed.gov/fulltext/ED142205.pdf.

Porter, T. M. (1986). *The rise of statistical thinking 1820–1900*. Princeton: Princeton University Press.

Pratt, A. C. (2008). Creative cities: The cultural industries and the creative class. *Geografiska Annaler: Series B, Human Geography, 90*(2), 107–117.

Puttfarken, T. (1985). *Roger De Piles' theory of art*. New Haven: Yale University Press.

Redhead, S. (1992). The popular music industry. In D. Wynne (Ed.), *The culture industry: The arts in urban regeneration* (pp. 42–55). Aldershot: Avebury.

Reeves, M. (2002). *Measuring the economic and social impact of the arts: A review*. London: Arts Council England.

Rose, N. (1991). Governing by numbers: Figuring out democracy. *Accounting, Organizations and Society, 16*(7), 673–692.

Schumpeter, J. A. (1934). *The theory of economic development*. Harvard: Harvard University Press.

Scott, A. J. (2006). Entrepreneurship, innovation and industrial development. *Small Business Economics, 26*(1), 1–24.

Smith, C. (1998). *Creative Britain*. London: Faber and Faber.

Taylor, C. (2006). Beyond advocacy: Developing an evidence base for regional creative industry strategies. *Cultural Trends, 15*(1), 3–18.

Taylor, C. (2015). *Cultural value: A perspective from cultural economy*. Retrieved from http://eprints.whiterose.ac.uk/91869/1/Taylor%20Cultural%20Value%20Final%20Nov%202015.pdf.

Velthuis, O., & Coslor, E. (2012). The financialization of art. In K. Knorr Cetina & A. Preda (Eds.), *The Oxford handbook of the sociology of finance* (pp. 471–487). Oxford: Oxford University Press.

Vickery, J. (2007). *The emergence of culture-led regeneration: A policy concept and its discontents*. Warwick: Centre for Cultural Policy Studies.

Weber, M. ([1909] 2012). "Energetical" theories of culture. In H. H. Bruun & S. Whimster (Eds.), *Max Weber: Collected methodological writings* (pp. 252–268). London: Routledge.

Williams, R. (1958). *Culture and society 1780–1950*. London: Chatto and Windus.

Wynne, D. (1992). Cultural industries. In D. Wynne (Ed.), *The culture industry: The arts in urban regeneration* (pp. 1–12). Aldershot: Avebury.

Zukin, S. (1998). Urban lifestyles: Diversity and standardisation in spaces of consumption. *Urban Studies, 35*(5–6), 825–839.

3

The Creativity Agenda(s)

Given persistent promotion of the potential of creativity, it is important to consider what form this creativity is understood to take. This chapter will thus examine specific conceptions of the nature of creativity which have flourished since the 1990s. Many have pointed to the near irresistibility of this agenda; who, after all, would want to stifle creative impulses? What negative outcomes could arise from an increase in creativity? To endorse creativity implies one is in favour of vitality, change, progress. The potential range of meanings for the term is broad, however, and so given that the language of creativity is notable by its comparative absence until this point in time, but quickly becomes dominant, it is thus necessary to consider the deployment of this terminology in some detail and ask whether the common labelling of phenomena as creative ones in this period emerges from some common core, or if instead it serves to draw together a range of disparate activities. This chapter thus begins by establishing the dominant position creativity achieves in the period from the late 1990s onwards, how this aligns with the precursors identified in Chapter 2, and also how this ascent is both rapid and wide-ranging by considering its global reach. Following this, it is argued that in this period we can locate a range of

© The Author(s) 2019
P. Campbell, *Persistent Creativity*, Sociology of the Arts,
https://doi.org/10.1007/978-3-030-03119-0_3

both overlapping and contradictory uses of the terminology of 'creativity'. This reinforces concerns about the meaning of this term, and raises the prospect that a common language obscures the reality of multiple subtly different Creativity *Agendas* (in the plural), which can conveniently be treated as though convergent and singular. By subsuming a range of different practices under the attractive banner of 'creativity', there is thus a risk that those pushing this agenda proceed as though they have a clear frame of reference in which to operate, when this may not be the case. It is thus necessary to ask in more detail what exactly *is* the creativity of the Creativity Agenda that persists in the early twenty-first century? In considering the multiple applications of the term, this chapter will conclude with a consideration of whether in the prominence and persistence of the Creativity Agenda we see something akin to the discursive trait of *catachresis*: 'application of a term to a thing which it does not properly denote' (Catachresis, n.d.). Although logically problematic, catachresis can play a role in amplifying the power and reach of discourse, serving, as Jäger and Maier have it, to 'bridge contradictions and increase plausibility' (2009, p. 48).

This chapter will consider these notions in light of key concepts which emerged in the late 1990s and early 2000s, and which have been the object of much analysis since this time: the 'creative industries' and the 'creative economy'; the 'creative class', aligned with ideas around creative innovation and entrepreneurship; and the notion of the 'creative city'. It will be argued that the often interchangeable usage of these terms is problematic as this is a field in which seemingly trivial terminological differences can obscure more important conceptual ones. Nevertheless, it will also be argued that in their deployment, an alignment of the notion of creativity with culture and the arts remains prominent, although not always logical.

The Rise and Rise of the Creativity Agenda

In considering how the value of creativity is promoted in this period, it can be noted that UK policy positions on the creative industries are particularly influential. Olma argues that the positions which emerge in the late 1990s align directly with the themes of global competition and economic transformation encountered in the previous chapter:

> The central idea behind the British initiative was that in order to stay on top of the global value chain, a national economy needs to specialise in creativity and innovation. (2016, p. 40)

Such ideas continue to be utilised in some form when the value of creativity is discussed, both within the UK and beyond, and across the political spectrum. To summarise an early and clear espousal of the Creativity Agenda, we can point to the New Statesman Arts Lecture delivered in 2001 by Labour peer Baron Evans of Temple Guiting (then Chair of the Council for Museums, Archives and Libraries). Building on the themes introduced in Chapter 2, this lecture covered the main elements of the emergent Creativity Agenda in short order, touching on the importance of a 'New Economy' based on 'culture and creativity'; the importance of Britain's 'creative industries' to its global position; the difficulties of 'measurement' for this economic activity, but the clear importance of creative industries to growth and GDP in spite of this; the role of culture in building 'social capital' and achieving 'social regeneration', with this social capital ultimately helping to 'create economic value'; the need for more 'entrepreneurship' to strengthen the creative industries, and also a note on the potential dangers in the rise of New Public Management-style audit techniques in enacting cultural policy (Evans, M. 2001, pp. 45–47). The Creativity Agenda had thus taken a coherent form, ready to be championed by prominent figures in a relatively short period of time.

The consolidation of this agenda was also comparatively rapid. By 2007, Schlesinger was able to persuasively argue that creativity had become established as a 'hegemonic term in an increasingly elaborated framework of policy ideas' (p. 377), pointing to the promotion of creativity and innovation as a means of delivering economic growth and success in the context of global competition. Focussing particularly on its role within policy circles, Schlesinger also argued that during its first decade of deployment the discourse of creativity had become so strong that it could be characterised as 'an object of unceasing advocacy by its proponents [...and] an obligatory starting point for those who wish to enter into dialogue with policymakers' (2007, p. 378). Schlesinger thus argues that during the 2000s, advocating the value of creativity, and particularly the 'creative economy', became a 'doctrine', and one bolstered not only by a range of 'evidence' (as considered further in the ensuing chapters), but also by a series of arguments regarding the risk that competitive advantage would be lost amongst the increasingly important and innovative creative industries unless action was taken, such as the development of 'creative hubs' (p. 385). Indeed, key policy documents commissioned by the UK's Department for Culture, Media and Sport (DCMS) at this point in time argued that creative industries were both a 'significant part of the knowledge economy' (The Work Foundation 2007, p. 30) and 'certain to become even more important in the future' (p. 188).

Having taken a fairly coherent form, and having become well established, these ideas continued their pattern of persistence into the 2010s. A report for a DCMS committee on 'supporting the creative economy' from 2013, for instance, characterised the role of creativity as follows:

Creativity is the key to both cultural and economic progress in an increasingly competitive world. In the United Kingdom, we rightly celebrate the successes and achievements of our artists and designers, our musicians and engineers, our writers and creative entrepreneurs. Our creative industries define us as a nation and provide a visible celebration of our diversity and ingenuity. If we are to sustain this success, and build on it, the Government must do all it reasonably can to help. (House of Commons 2013, p. 9)

By this point in time, Labour, the political party most strongly associated with the rapid rise of the Creativity Agenda in the UK, who governed from 1997 to 2010, were no longer in power, and so we can see how this agenda persists across party lines. Both the social and economic importance of creativity also continued to be emphasised by prominent figures in the field. Sir Peter Bazalgette, the former Chair of Arts Council England and former non-executive director of the DCMS board, for instance, argued that after the 2008 financial crash, in a search for industries that may counter economic problems, Britain's politicians 'all seem to have seized on the creative industries' (2009), and in his first speech as Chair of Arts Council England in 2013 argued that 'there is no city in Britain that does not understand the importance of the arts and culture, both as central to the life of the city and to the local economy' (Higgins 2013). More recently, the 2017 Conservative Party manifesto argued that arts and culture 'are at the heart of regeneration of much of modern Britain' (Conservative and Unionist Party 2017, p. 25), and following a Conservative electoral victory (and encouragement from the Confederation of British Industry [CBI 2014]), the wider discourse of creativity is echoed in the UK government's 'Industrial Strategy Sector Deal' for the creative industries of 2018, which leverages quantitative data in arguing that the creative industries are 'at the heart of the nation's competitive advantage', and that 'creative strengths' across the country can be further encouraged by government, promoting growth through entrepreneurship and innovation (HM Government 2018, p. 2).

A Global Agenda

Once established, then, the Creativity Agenda is a persistent one. Broadly, this agenda emphasises the importance of government policy in promoting creativity, positions artistic and cultural practice as a key aspect of this creativity, places an emphasis on 'evidence', has a dominant concern with economic value and a sense of an emerging 'new' economy which must be prepared for in order to reap economically and socially 'regenerative' outcomes, and allocates a special role to entrepreneurial innovation in driving this process forward. Whilst this agenda is particularly prominent in the UK, and whilst the UK plays a key role in its dissemination, we can see that this agenda also rises and persists globally. It is not the case that the impetus to adopt the Creativity Agenda is an irresistible force, and there are locations where the 'internationalization' of this agenda is resisted (see, for instance, O'Connor [2005] on experience in Russia), but it is fair to say that once it emerges, the Creativity Agenda establishes a remarkable reach.

In 2010, for instance, Bell and Jayne (p. 209) summarise how attempts to promote the 'creative city' and 'creative industries' have been taken up across the globe, and Brouillette emphasises the rapid speed with which these ideas have spread (2014, p. 1). Updating his work from 2007 referred to above, in 2017 Schlesinger writes on the 'global orthodoxy' established surrounding the creative economy, with the concept being,

> used supra-nationally, at nation-state or sub-state levels, and in the region or city. Consequently, creative nations, regions and cities, are now so much part of the competitive landscape that everyone takes them for granted. (2017, p. 77)

To give a sense of this global spread, we can point to some key developments from the research literature in the first decade in which this agenda was established. Ideas around creative cities, classes and industries were influential in Australia in the early 2000s (Gibson and Klocker 2005), and these same ideas are taken up in a wide range of locations, 'even in sparsely populated Scandinavia' (Lysgård 2013, p. 185). At the turn of the century, Wang notes that creative industries become 'the hottest buzzword' in Hong Kong (2004, p. 13), and Keane posits that 'the creative industries came to mainland China in late 2004' (2009, p. 431), with an emphasis on both economic and social outcomes (p. 439). In 2004, sites in South Korea were also officially designated as 'cities of culture' and 'creative cities' to promote tourism and creative industries (Lee 2007, p. 339), and 2004 also saw the establishment of the increasingly popular UNESCO 'Creative Cities Network', with designations of 'official Cities of Literature, Cities of Film, Cities of Music, and so on, reflect[ing] its desire to "help unlock the creative, social and economic potential of cultural industries"' (Brouillette 2014, p. 1). Bertacchini and Borrione note that the 'creative discourse' arrives in earnest in Italy with the 2007 'White Paper on Italian Creativity' (2013, p. 136), and Heinze and Hoose report on German policy around the same time presenting cultural industries as vital to economic growth, and a driver of innovation more broadly (2013, p. 517).

The Creativity Agenda thus took root in a number of countries over a comparatively quick period, and in the following decade this pattern persisted. A United Nations report in 2008 was described as the first to give the UN's view on 'this exciting new topic' (UN 2008, p. iii) based on 'the interface between creativity, culture and economics', which 'contributes to entrepreneurship [and] fosters innovation' (p. 3), but which, it is argued, requires further evidence for fully informed policymaking. By 2009, Evans identifies 'creative city – and "space" – promotion' as truly global phenomena (p. 1005), as are the promotion of the creative industries and the creative class (Chapain and Lee 2009). Regarding the global march of the Creativity Agenda, Schlesinger argues that,

> a clear turning point was reached inside the EU by 2010, by which time the creative economy had become part of the EC's *doxa* [...and] by 2012, the question of how to measure the [creative and cultural industries] was firmly on the EU agenda. (2017, pp. 79–80)

Claims around the relative economic importance of creativity in Europe and Asia continued into the mid-2010s (e.g. Vasiliu 2014; Chenyan 2014), as did related policymaking, evidence gathering and general promotion. As noted above, in 2018 the UK reasserted its commitment to the creative industries in its overall Industrial Strategy by publishing details of a 'sector deal' aiming to develop partnerships between government and industry, the creative industries being one of only six sectors to be the object of such a deal.

Given that this book concentrates on the UK case, it is worth emphasising the influence of UK policy positions on this global spread. Schlesinger refers to the UK as one of the 'key ideas factories' (2009, p. 17) in this field, and Olma argues that the main success of the British work on the creative industries is in its export to 'continental policy makers' (2016, p. 42), a point echoed, and expanded, by O'Connor's consideration of attempts to build an evidence base in this area:

> the [DCMS] Creative Industries Mapping Document itself became a lead export, as governments and cities in Europe (especially the new or aspirant EC member countries), in Latin America and particularly in the Far

East saw a new idea for the dynamic association of culture, economics and a new wave of modernisation. (2007, p. 41)

To point to just some specific locations, Singapore and Hong Kong are noted as being 'strongly influenced' by the UK model of creative industries (Flew and Cunningham 2010, p. 114), as well as Italy, Spain, China (De Propris et al. 2009, p. 11), Indonesia (Fahmi et al. 2016, p. 67) and Lithuania (Rindzevičiūtė et al. 2016, p. 598).

The Many Meanings of Creativity

Despite the apparent success of this narrative, however, at the same time as the proliferation of the Creativity Agenda, a slimmer set of literature gives rise to questions as to how meaningful this seemingly coherent agenda actually is. Positions range from those voicing caution over the need for clarity around the notion of creativity, to others suggesting the term is close to meaningless (and, indeed, that this lack of meaning, far from being a problem to be overcome, can actually help to *explain* the rapid take-up noted above). The remainder of this chapter therefore discusses the predominant usages of the term, seeking to explain the rise of the terminology of creativity, and to engage with these questions as to how appropriate its usage actually is.

Even at the outset of the period under consideration, we can see notes of caution being raised with regards to the concept of creativity and the manner in which it is deployed. As early as 2000, Chatterton argues that the 'most fundamental issue' in the discourse of the 'creative city', for instance, is the question of what is meant by the term, concluding that 'the term creativity is so ambiguous and overused that it is rendered meaningless' (p. 393), with others similarly arguing that in this period the language of creativity becomes so widely used that it loses any clear meaning (Bilton and Leary 2002, p. 49; Olma 2016, p. 39), or that in the process of achieving an increasing prominence, it becomes 'banal' (Schlesinger 2007, p. 377).

Even if the term is not seen as being so widely or ambiguously deployed as to become meaningless, the scope for confusion when the terminology of creativity is used is strongly in evidence as the Creativity Agenda rises. Taylor perhaps puts this most eloquently as part of a consideration of the different forms of creativity that can be seen to make up the 'creative economy':

> The reality of the creative economy is such that it can only be understood as an assemblage, a conceptual palimpsest of layers, additions, erasures and conceptual elaborations, each of which implicitly and perhaps momentarily signifies the creative economy as such. However, such polyvalent elusiveness cannot be allowed to mask a number of deep ambiguities intimated by the creative economy concept in its practical discourse. (2015, p. 366)

This chapter aligns with arguments that such ambiguities raise the prospect of what Sefton-Green and Parker refer to as the potential for 'misinterpretation' (2006, p. 3) when creativity is discussed—that is, the possibility that the use of common language implies we are talking about a common idea or object, obscuring circumstances where this may not be so. This misinterpretation of meaning can then have implications for practice. Richards (2014, p. 121) notes that differing understandings of creativity will imply the take-up of different policies and practices, even though these differences are masked when positions are presented as though similar, or interchangeable.

This scope for misinterpretation, or at least a range of differing understandings, of the common terms considered below is very much in evidence in the literature on the subject, and it is hard to disagree that the utilisation of the common label of creativity serves to aid this lack of clarity. Consider, for instance, the range of viewpoints within the following statements:

- 'The 'creative class' is made up of those working in creative industries such as film, fashion and publishing' (Gibson and Klocker 2005, p. 95).
- 'The creative industries [...] the creative class and the creative economy (the nebulous notion that is an ideological coagulation of the two) are all *defined* by a creativity that adheres to a narrow

remit – namely an economic one' (Mould 2017a, p. 50, original emphasis).

- 'The creative class debate is not about the cultural industries or cultural production' (Pratt 2008, p. 111).
- 'In the "creative city", it is not only artists and those involved in the creative economy who are creative' (UN 2008, p. 19).
- 'By the end of world war II Adorno and Horkheimer (1947) had coined the term 'cultural industries' to refer to commercial cultural products, and in the late 1990s, the term 'creative industries', developed in the UK, further refined this idea' (London Development Agency 2008, p. 12).
- 'The creative industries announced a new kind of economy that drew on culture-inflected creativity within a (transformed) commercial sector that was as far away from Adorno's Culture Industry as one could possibly imagine' (Oakley and O'Connor 2015, p. 3).
- 'Both [the creative industries and the creative class] involve the mobilisation of what is generally understood as culture for economic and social development purposes' (Prince 2014, p. 94).
- 'The benefits that are generated from either the provision of direct cultural interventions, or from having members of the 'cultural' class living in an area, have little to do with culture per se' (Gray 2009, p. 578).
- 'The conflation of culture with creative industries since 1997 has harmed both cultural policy and creative industries policy in the UK' (Bakhshi and Cunningham 2016, p. 3).

Despite the fact that the Creativity Agenda was on the rise in the period in which all these statements were made, it seems there is much disagreement about the nature of the concepts under discussion, and it certainly seems possible from the above statements for research into creativity to use identical language to take a range of differing, and often contradictory, positions.

As noted above, however, from some perspectives this state of affairs can be seen as beneficial. Gray (2009, p. 576), for instance, notes how the range of practices which can be given the common label 'cultural' gives policymakers significant latitude in choosing potential methods of intervention. Similarly, Grodach (2013) points to the flexibility available for policymakers when it comes to 'creativity', with the concept providing scope for a range of interventions all radiating from an apparently common core. Importantly, though, he also notes that the actual activities engaged in, or prompted by policy, can, as a result of this flexibility, end up being antithetical to the theories drawn on, arguing simultaneously that the 'creative city model' primarily derives from the idea of the 'creative class' originating in the work of Florida (discussed further below) (2013, p. 1749), but that due to the scope it allows, 'the creative city concept is used to promote strategies *at odds with* Florida's advice' (p. 1756, emphasis added). Given that there is scope for such paradoxical enactment of the Creativity Agenda, and given that understanding of key terms remains inconsistent even after this agenda has been in place for many years, it is thus important to consider further the nature of the creativity being promoted.

Creative Industries

As noted in Chapter 2, cultural policy has become increasingly justified politically in terms of the potential *economic* benefits of cultural practice (e.g. O'Connor 2005, p. 47). Prominent discussion of the economic role of the creative industries is important to squaring the problematic circle wherein the value of culture is seen as predominantly non-economic. From the 1990s, however, increasingly it seems as though we can have both *le beurre* and *l'argent du beurre* with the rise of arguments that 'art and culture are real social and economic mechanisms' which 'are responsible for thousands of jobs, billions of dollars in revenue' (Currid 2007, p. ix). As noted above, in such a context creativity and the creative economy are positioned as integral to 'competitive advantage' and it is argued that 'at the heart of the creative economy are the cultural or creative industries' (Throsby 2008a, p. 147). Although these have been mentioned many times so far, what these industries actually *are*, and the manner in which they are creative, is something that requires further interrogation.

Whilst the creative industries have now been an object of study and attention for so long that we can see what are now historic questions as to whether there is a possibility of entering an era 'after the creative industries' (Banks and O'Connor 2009), policy shows a continued engagement with this terminology (e.g. HM Government 2018) despite many valid concerns regarding its usage. Given the continuation of boosterist narratives around the potential of these creative industries, it therefore remains necessary to unpack the terminology in use, and so to also unpack what continue to be regularly taken for granted notions that, for instance, the operation of these industries is palpably beneficial, and indeed that these industries constitute a discernible and discrete mode of activity in the first place.

Issues of definition and boundary setting regarding the creative industries are often raised as the Creativity Agenda rises (e.g. Throsby 2008b; Banks and O'Connor 2009; Campbell 2011) and, as Chapter 5 will discuss further, the issue of definition remains contentious. To understand the rise of this aspect of the Creativity Agenda, however, it is necessary to understand the roots of this terminology, and the common criteria upon which membership of the creative industries is granted. To this end, it is instructive to trace a brief history of the development of terminology regarding the interaction between economic processes, culture and creativity. Understanding this process of development, or perhaps, rather, of mutation, is important in appreciating the ideological position which the creative industries continue to occupy.

Firstly, we can note that the creative industries narrative has always had, and continues to have, a strong emphasis on artistic, or culturally expressive activities. To take the most recent political statement of their importance, we see the nomination of a handful of specifically cultural activities aligned to economic success:

> The creative industries – including film, TV, music, fashion and design, arts, architecture, publishing, advertising, video games and crafts – are an undoubted strength of our economy; indeed, they are at the heart of the nation's competitive advantage. (HM Government 2018, p. 2)

In academic circles, activity in many of these sectors would historically be placed (at least by some scholars) under a slightly different label:

'the culture industry' (Adorno 1991). To spend time considering the differences between the 'culture industry' and the 'creative industries' may on the surface seem to be absurd. Absent any familiarity with their usage, it may seem like we are dealing with extremely similar, and perhaps identical, ideas. Yet, as the bulleted list of statements in the previous section demonstrates, some see the similarity in these terms as a process of gradual development from one to the other, whereas others see them as being in total opposition. When discussing creativity, then, small terminological differences matter.

By tracing how the specific language of creativity comes to prominence in this case, we can get a clearer sense of the potential for divergent understandings to be attached to similar labels, why the specific language of creativity achieves such prominence in this period, and the particular ends to which it is being put. The increasing prominence of the specific language of the 'creative industries' should therefore be understood not simply as a 'rebranding'—old wine in a new bottle—but rather a gradual process of development and reinterpretation of what certain activities are, and what they mean. This can be understood in terms of a changing attitude to, or an attempted repositioning of, the relationship between expressive activity and industrial activity. This begins with total opposition in the discourse of the 'culture industry', and evolves towards the currently entrenched position which attempts some form of synthesis. Indeed, such attempts at synthesising a range of positions is characteristic of the wider usages of the terminology of 'creativity' considered here.

The 'Culture Industry'

O'Connor (2007, p. 12) emphasises the importance of *scale* when considering the mid-twentieth-century idea of the 'culture industry'. This can be placed in the context of comparatively recent technological changes in the realm of culture. For most of human history, to hear music, see images, encounter performance and so forth required a physical proximity to the activity in question. Even the loudest instrument in the largest concert hall has a fundamentally limited audience. Adam Smith argued towards the end of the eighteenth century that cultural work such as that engaged in by 'players, buffoons, musicians, opera-singers, opera-dancers, &c.' is 'unproductive' as it 'does not fix or realize itself in any permanent subject, or vendible commodity which endures after that labour is past' ([1784] 1818, p. 235). Indeed, until the late nineteenth century this part of Smith's assessment remained accurate, as it was not technically possible to 'fix' sound or moving images in an 'enduring' manner for wider dissemination. Once such methods of recording became possible, the link with physical and temporal proximity was broken, and thus the path to mass production opened up, with the possibility of economies of scale and exponential rates of profit in areas such as the film, television and music industries mentioned as part of the list of 'creative industries' above. Whilst the situation in the twentieth century is thus radically different to any preceding era, it is perhaps instructive when considering the timing of developments in this field traced in Chapter 2 to briefly recall that in the UK context, for instance, at the beginning of the 1980s, whilst many would have the means of hearing recorded music on vinyl, cassette or radio, there remained only three terrestrial television channels (which ceased broadcasting overnight), consumer camcorders had only recently come to market, and purchasing or viewing film on home video remained rare. This provides a somewhat useful context to bear in mind in understanding the timing of the rise of the Creativity Agenda being considered here. Nevertheless, cultural commodities were common enough in the 1940s for Adorno and Horkheimer to write in the 'Dialectic of Enlightenment' on what they term the 'culture industry'.

As is implied by its singular title, this is understood to be something of a monolithic structure which produces films, magazines, music, radio broadcasts, arts and entertainment commodities. In the work of Adorno and Horkheimer, a strong value judgement on such commodities is explicitly stated, directly linked to their mass commodity status. For the authors, the work which is produced by the culture industry is knowingly 'rubbish' (1979, p. 121) and this modern method of production affects the cultural commodities produced thus: 'what is new is not that it is a commodity, but that today it deliberately admits it is one' (p. 157). The mass produced cultural commodity celebrates its position in the market. Adorno clarifies this in later writing on the culture industry which argues that cultural artefacts previously,

> sought after profit only indirectly, over and above their autonomous essence. New on the part of the culture industry is the direct and undisguised primacy of a precisely and thoroughly calculated efficacy in its most typical products. (1991, p. 99)

The premeditated accrual of profit, therefore, is the *sine qua non* of the products of the culture industry of the twentieth century. Profit is not a secondary by-product of the main activity of cultural and artistic achievement or expression; cultural outputs are to be understood here only in terms of the profit motive, operating just as any other business, and this new relationship is in no small part brought about by the technological developments discussed above. Prior to the twentieth century, it was simply not technically possible to reproduce audio-visual material in a way that would facilitate such 'industrialisation', and so it is this particular set of circumstances that allows the growth of the culture industry although, clearly, the emergence of such technology does not occur in a vacuum and must be situated in prevailing economic and ideological circumstances. Once this industrialisation occurs within such circumstances, however, the cultural object can become a product, and potentially nothing more than a product. For Adorno and Horkheimer, 'the technology of the culture industry is no more than the achievement of standardization and mass production' (1979, p. 122).

Clearly this is a damning assessment of the nature of these commodities that are at the heart of mass cultural engagement. Such commodities nevertheless continued to be ever more popular in the years following this theorising. Indeed, at the beginning of the twenty-first century, the activities which make up Adorno's 'culture industry', or their latter-day equivalents, and the commodities they produce are more popular and economically successful than ever, permeating society in an ever-expanding interconnected web, in ways which would have been almost unimaginable at the time Adorno was writing, and which would no doubt horrify him. Although the novel capacity for the mass production and reproduction of cultural goods opens up an increased *possibility* of standardisation within the cultural realm, however, it must be considered whether the analysis briefly traced here truly provides a nuanced picture of the realities experienced when these commodities are encountered or produced. At the very least, though, what is fundamentally clear is that the idea of 'the culture industry' is not an optimistic or celebratory one. A political discourse which emphasises the beneficial value of 'creative industries' is thus operating on a very different ideological basis to that presented by Adorno, even though apparently similar objects and processes are under consideration.

'Cultural Industries'

To further understand the development of the terminology of creative industries, it is thus important to consider changes in perspective on the interaction between industry and culture as the twentieth century continues. From these alternative perspectives, the position of the cultural commodity can be seen as being less problematic, yet more complicated than that conceived of within the idea of the 'culture industry': more complicated in that cultural commodities operate in ways other commodities do not, but less problematic in that the evidence for all cultural production becoming in effect a monolithic machine for propaganda and stupefaction is not as strong as Adorno indicates.

This dual transition marks the start of a process of reassessment of the economic role of cultural activity and eventually results in the emergence of wider discourse in which this cultural activity is also conceived of as being 'creative' in a number of forms. In terms of a move away from the 'culture industry', Garnham makes it clear that the cultural commodity need not *necessarily* support the dominant ideology (1990, p. 34), and Garnham's contemporary, Miège, is an important figure when it comes to problematising the views of Adorno, whose general position is summarised as follows:

> Reference to the 'cultural industry' – in the singular – misleads one into thinking that we are faced with an unified field, where the various elements function within a single process [...] The same model is said to be

at work quickly levelling out the different modes of creativity and imposing common standards. There is no need to take the analysis very far to discover that this postulate is false. (1989, p. 10)

Here we see not only an introduction of the terminology of creativity, but Miège arguing for an understanding which takes into account the complex, non-standardised, nature of the production of cultural commodities and artefacts. As such, he seeks to shift analysis towards 'the cultural *industries*'—plural. Whilst we are still dealing with a grouping unified by the production of cultural products, this output is no longer seen as being characterised by such an overarching unity. To emphasise the scope for misapplication which is made almost inevitable by the closeness of this terminology, however, it is worth pointing out that one can locate in the literature a number of authors pointing to Adorno's work on the 'cultural industries' (e.g. McKee 2013, p. 760; Richards 2014, p. 123).

The move to cultural industries takes us a step closer to the arrival of 'creative industries'. In addition to admitting plurality into considerations of cultural commodities, later work also introduces a different take on the nature of these commodities. Scott (2007, p. 321) argues that there is no reason to assume that a process of commodification *necessarily* leads to reduced aesthetic or artistic value as Adorno would have it, and the complex reality of the relationships involved in the cultural market is neatly defined by Garnham:

The cultural market [...] cannot be read either as a destruction of high culture by vulgar commercialism or as a suppression of authentic working-class culture, but should be read as a complex hegemonic dialectic of liberation and control. (1990, p. 164)

By attempting to understand the cultural sector in a more nuanced way, and by focussing on the centrality of the cultural industries to the London economy, Garnham was influential in policy development work situated at the Greater London Council (GLC) in the UK in the 1980s, which played a large role in shifting the terms of policy debate regarding culture away from the previously dominant approach in which cultural industries were 'the "other" against which cultural policy react[s]' (Hesmondhalgh and Pratt 2005, p. 3), attempting rather to integrate them within this policy. Space was thus opened up at this point for commercial activity to be dealt with more directly by cultural policy and, aligned to the idea of an emergent 'new economy' discussed in Chapter 2, studies of the cultural realm at this point demonstrate a sense that intervention in this area is prudent preparation for an inevitable economic future. Evans, for instance, notes of studies in the late 1970s and early 1980s that some,

> focused on subsidised arts facilities or art forms (e.g. theatre), others on cultural industries and visitor economy, but all stress that this area was both growing and likely to continue growing as other employment sectors faltered and declined. (Evans, G. 2001, p. 139)

In such circumstances, it may seem only sensible for policy to attempt to capitalise more directly on this expected growth. Direct applications of the cultural policy of the GLC cannot be studied in practice due to its disbanding in the mid-1980s, but the influence of the approaches explored at this time, and the space opened up to promote the development of cultural activity aligned to the market continues, even as the terms of the analysis of the interplay between culture and economy develop once more in the shift towards the specific usage of 'creative' industries. What should be noted, however, is that despite the embrace of cultural *industries* in policy, the influence of the GLC position was not exclusively concerned with economic development or promoting high-growth businesses. O'Connor argues that in addition to being the first local-level cultural industries strategy, the GLC's work was also an attempt to sketch 'contemporary democratic cultural policy' (2007, p. 23). In so doing, it,

> embraced new forms of popular culture, new gender, ethnic and sexual identities, and took a positive view of small-scale cultural (and indeed social) enterprises whose operation within the market had previously excluded them from the field of 'art' [...] Support for a dynamic local cultural industries sector was not just about economic growth but also about

a more democratic, participatory, diverse cultural policy, and both were
wrapped up in a new vision for the post-industrial city. (O'Connor 2013,
pp. 378–379)

This approach was influential in the early interventions in this field
seen in Chapter 2 such as the Sheffield Cultural Industries Quarter
(Hesmondhalgh et al. 2015, p. 125). Despite the *potential* for the two
labels to mean the same thing, therefore, and despite their clear similarity, we should be careful to draw a line between the goals of 'cultural
industries' and 'creative industries' approaches, even though they may
focus on similar activities.

'Creative Industries'

The shift towards the language of creativity in the nomenclature of
the 1990s diminishes the more directly social concerns of the 'cultural
industries' position and intensifies its economic ones. It also effectively
wipes this earlier language out (Miller 2009, p. 88), becoming the more
widely used term both within the UK and across the globe (Banks
2017, p. 10). As noted previously, much discussion of these terms has
a teleological bent. At a policy level there is a clear sense that the future
importance of the creative industries is all but assured: on reviewing
the situation at an international scale, Van Heur finds that 'all policy
documents on the creative industries are structured by [...] the assumption that creativity *will become* increasingly important' in the emergent
new economy (2010, p. 129, original emphasis). Being a term that, at
least initially, arises from, and is preponderantly associated with, the discourse of government policy and advocacy, we should perhaps not be
surprised that the creative industries are most often discussed in terms
celebrating their positive attributes and potential, and so even though
the language is in many ways very similar, at this point there are very
clear breaks away from the ideological position regarding the role of the
'culture industry' as conceived by Adorno.

The shift towards a language of 'creativity' does not, however, merely
alter the emphasis of 'cultural industries' thinking. It also means that

this grouping can, and does, encompass a broader range of activities than either the culture industry or cultural industries concepts discussed thus far allow for. As noted at the outset, whilst the referent of 'culture' can be extremely difficult to pin down, as per Williams' oft-cited definition of culture as 'one of the two or three most complicated words in the English language' (1983, p. 87), the sense in which it is used above in reference to expressive, artistic, symbolic content disseminated via recorded still or moving audio-visual materials, or text, is a fairly clear one. Such activities all become part of the 'creative industries' in practice, but so do other activities, the unifying principle of which is less clear.

The emergence of the new terminology of 'creativity' is seen by Pratt (2005) as being in some ways a distancing technique on the part of the incumbent Labour administration of the late 1990s who did not wish to be linked with the earlier work of the disbanded GLC discussed above. Certainly many authors have noted how creative industries policy diverges from this 'cultural industries' position. As Oakley et al. point out, for instance, in comparison to the cultural industries approach, the politics of the creative industries,

> is entirely different [...] replacing a concern to reconstruct the market along socialist lines, with a largely neoliberal focus on the economic growth of the (now-dubbed) 'creative' industries and on their effects on the wider economy in terms of innovation. (2018, p. 10)

Small differences in terminology thus continue to matter, as apparent synonyms can mask deep ideological and practical divisions. The language of 'creativity' thus signifies a closer alignment with the trends identified in Chapter 2 towards neoliberal ideology and economic primacy, away from other possible understandings of cultural practices, and this shift also allows a closer alignment with the broad range of 'new economy' thinking outlined previously. Garnham (2005), for instance, sees this shift in terminology as a more problematic and obfuscatory tactic, enabling a broad tent to be drawn over a wide variety of activities, obscuring their lack of commonality. That said, whilst the reason behind the creative industries grouping is questionable, their identification in policy is quite clear. On its emergence in the UK, the term is given a clear definition, which persists to a large degree over time and, as we have seen, is internationally influential, although other definitions are also in use (e.g. UN 2008). This existence of a clear definition enables the process of evidence gathering, identified as increasingly important in Chapter 2, to proceed with a clear object in mind. This process will be considered in more detail in Chapter 5, but for the overall life of the concept, the creative industries have largely had a stable definition, usually encompassing work in 'Advertising, Architecture, Art and Antiques Markets, Computer and Video Games, Crafts, Design, Designer Fashion, Film and Video, Music, Performing Arts, Publishing, Software, Television and Radio' (e.g. DCMS 2010).

In this definition of the sector, 'creative' is thus still *predominantly* being used to describe the cultural and arts-related activity we would be considering if still concerned with 'the culture industry'. Although concerns such as Adorno's have effectively been erased, and the broader concerns of the cultural industries approach are not present (Volkerling 2001), as Throsby (2008b, p. 220) has it, 'virtually all of the 13 industries included in the DCMS classification could be seen as "cultural"'. Indeed, some have argued that the shift in language from culture to creativity involved 'little to no change to the actual industrial production' falling under these definitions (Mould 2017a, p. 34). Relatedly, Taylor notes how it is the arts sector who most enthusiastically take up this new label and its associated evidence base (2006, p. 12). Indeed, due to the primacy of cultural activity, leveraging the economic success of the creative industries becomes one of the ways by which the 'culture-led regeneration' encountered previously is argued to take place.

The Overlap of Culture and Creativity

Given the change of terminology, it is instructive to return to Williams, and to briefly trace the long history he gives of the concept of creativity. Prior to the sixteenth century, Williams notes a prevailing view that humans cannot create in the truest sense, as the human being *is* a creation of the divine creator. We can work only with elements that have already been created. Williams traces a transformation during the period of the Renaissance towards a sense that humans *can* create in certain senses, particularly in imaginative, poetic work, and he notes an alignment especially with the notion of 'art' in the eighteenth century. Following this,

> the decisive development was the conscious and then conventional association of **creative** with *art* and thought. By [the early nineteenth century] it was conscious and powerful; by [the mid-nineteenth century] conventional. (1983, p. 83, original emphasis)

By this point then, we can see how certain senses of 'cultural' could be essentially synonymous with certain senses of 'creative'. In the late twentieth century, however, Williams identifies how the term slips loose of these moorings:

> The difficulty arises when a word once intended, and still often intended, to embody a high and serious claim, becomes so conventional, as a description of certain general kinds of activity, that it is applied to practices for which, in the absence of the convention, nobody would think of making such claims. Thus any imitative or stereotyped literary work can be called, by convention, **creative writing**, and advertising copywriters officially describe themselves as **creative**. (1983, p. 84, original emphasis)

The extension of this convention thus also helps us to understand the shift towards a terminology of 'creativity' in the period under consideration in this chapter, and the scope for the referent of this term to be increasingly unclear. Williams here directly demonstrates how it is that the creative industries can have 'advertising' as an appropriate constituent member, which would likely warrant more scepticism were we still to be using a language of 'culture' or 'art'. From the wider development of the term, we can also see how, for instance, architecture can also come under this heading. The manner in which we *could* interpret such an industry as being a 'creative' one is plain, even though it may involve activities quite different from the operations of the film or music industry. This broadening range, then, presents some conceptual difficulties. If these industries could be seen as creative, could not others also? Looking back to the earliest stages of the Labour government's attempts to make headway with this issue in the late 1990s, Hewison states the problem succinctly:

> [The DCMS Creative Industries Task Force] was immediately confronted by a practical problem. No one had decided what the creative industries were. (2014, p. 41)

Establishing a Task Force before establishing its object might help to explain the fact that in tandem with the persistence of the Creativity Agenda, we also see the persistence of questioning over what activities it is appropriate to include as 'creative industries', and of the coherence of any definition in use. Indeed, this can be identified all throughout the period in which the creative industries have maintained their dominance (e.g. Comedia 2004, p. 11; Galloway and Dunlop 2007, p. 28; Tremblay 2011, p. 290; Oakley et al. 2013, p. 21; O'Brien 2014, p. 6; Last 2016, p. 13). We can, however, at least point to *claims* of coherence. Firstly there is a consistent emphasis on the importance to creative industries of the exploitation of intellectual property, which becomes central to claims of the economic value of these industries. As Schlesinger has it, at the outset of Labour policy on creative industries,

> the key move was to *aggregate* 13 distinct fields of cultural practice, to *designate* these as "industries", and so to *constitute* a new policy object whose central purpose was – and remains – to "maximise economic impact…at home and abroad". Moreover, by making the exploitation of intellectual property so crucial, the complexity of cultural value was subordinated to economic value. (2017, p. 77, original emphasis)

A key report commissioned by DCMS also takes on the issue of coherence thus:

> The 13 creative industries which have developed against this background are often perceived to have as many differences as similarities […] However, the truth is that each creative industry has a core business

model in common. All originate ideas of expressive value which they commercialise. 'Ideas of expressive value' can range from the humblest pleasing song or appealing advert to the latest interpretation of Shakespeare or new design for a car. They create new insights, delights and experiences; they add to our knowledge, stimulate our emotions and enrich our lives. (The Work Foundation 2007, p. 19)

Despite apparently broadening out to any business activities which 'enrich our lives', we see a predominance of the 'traditionally' cultural here too—songs and Shakespeare. Throsby argues that the terminology of creativity may be implicitly problematic here given that it 'may be imposed by a particular policymaking agenda rather than evolving from definitional first principles' (2008b, p. 217). What is clearly being focussed on here, however, is the potential economic benefits of developing activity which *can* be labelled as creative, with a clear lineage arising from the culturally inflected understandings of the term traced above, albeit with a changing set of justifications. An increasing economic focus, however, is ironically one of the reasons the issue of definition is so important. As Connolly emphasises (2013, p. 172), and as is discussed further in Chapter 5, the issue of where the boundary for inclusion is set around the creative industries grouping can have a transformative effect on the economic claims made for the sector, and so definition is vital to any overarching economic justification.

The Creative Economy

What Chapter 5 also considers is an increased move towards the language of a 'creative economy' in generating evidence of the value of creativity. Whilst also in use in a range of senses in earlier periods, this language currently shifts emphasis away from discrete *industries* to work deemed to be creative in *any* sector of the economy. This in part originates from work measuring the 'Creative Trident' in Australia, later imported into the UK (Higgs et al. 2008; Throsby 2008a, p. 152). This influences official statistical data gathering, seeking to measure (i) those working in creative occupations inside creative industries, (ii) those working in other occupations inside creative industries, and

(iii) those working in creative occupations *outside* creative industries. This shift in terminology is also seen as having broader implications. Hesmondhalgh et al. argue that the increasing use of this term reflects 'the increasing importance of digitalisation and information technology in government cultural agendas' (2015, p. 45, see also Faggian et al. 2013), and points to a move towards the splitting of 'culture' from 'creativity' (2015, p. 196). Nevertheless, the language of creative industries remains prominent, with some noting the enlarged 'creative economy' definition but choosing nevertheless to retain the long-standing terminology of creative industries instead (e.g. Straw and Warner 2014, p. 8).

The issues raised by this shift will be considered in more detail in Chapter 5, but what can be concluded here is that whilst explicable, the shift towards a language of creativity is not necessarily one that offers greater clarity, although we can nevertheless garner a reasonably clear sense of what industries are being discussed and why. The Creativity Agenda also draws in a range of wider usages, however. These are similarly broad ranging, similarly successful, but also raise similar prospects for a lack of clarity.

A Creative Class

Whilst the role of the creative industries is vital to the promotion of the Creativity Agenda, Florida's theory of the 'creative class' (2003, 2004, 2005) is perhaps equally important. Comunian et al. note that at the same time as the creative industries concept was gaining prominence in the UK, the concept of the creative class was gaining prominence in the USA (2010, p. 391), and with similar speed. Grodach, for example, points to the explicit reference to Florida's work in policymaking in 2003 in Austin, Texas (2013, p. 1758), and outside the USA, in Toronto, in the same year (p. 1753). The creative class thesis also quickly became influential in the UK (e.g. Stevenson et al. 2010, p. 167), and Europe (e.g. Heinze and Hoose 2013). Indeed, Florida's work is argued by some to have done more than any other to disseminate the Creativity Agenda around the globe (Brouillette 2014, p. 5), and to be the 'most pervasive economic argument' around the idea of creativity as fundamental to economic success in 'new' economic times (Gainza 2017, p. 954). The creative class thesis has been influential internationally in the context of 'culture-led regeneration' (Potts and Cunningham 2008) as it seemingly delineates a clear mechanism by which culture-based programmes can serve the intertwining economic, social and cultural goals of such regeneration policies. An appropriate cultural infrastructure will serve to develop or attract the emergent 'creative class' who are central to the success of cities across these multiple domains. To this end, Florida makes the following claim, which is instructive in the goal of differentiating the range of meanings being applied to 'creativity' in this period:

> All members of the Creative Class [...] share a common creative ethos that values creativity, individuality, difference and merit. For the members of the Creative Class, every aspect and *every manifestation of creativity* – technological, cultural and economic – *is interlinked and inseparable.* (2004, p. 8, emphasis added)

The members of the creative class exercise a form of labour that is creative, and so due to this interlinkage, are presented as also having a broadly unified 'creative' set of tastes and practices outside of this work. Florida's earlier work draws the link thus:

> The presence of a significant bohemian concentration signals a regional environment or milieu that reflects an underlying openness to innovation and creativity. (2002, p. 56)

If the city landscape can provide appropriate cultural and 'creative' attractions, therefore, people who are 'creative' and thus embody the innovatory and entrepreneurial capacity seen as increasingly necessary for stimulating economic development, particularly within the creative industries at the forefront of the emergent new economy, will be attracted or retained, and the benefits associated with their presence can be reaped. Creative consumption and production thus form a virtuous circle. As Florida succinctly puts it, 'supporting lifestyle and cultural institutions like a cutting-edge music scene or vibrant artistic community [...] helps to attract and stimulate those who create in business and technology' (2004, p. 55). In this way, the creative class can be seen as being broadly similar in character to figures such as Gans' 'cosmopolite' (1968)—professionals with few ties, free to seek out areas in which they can live and experience the cultural facilities available in the city. The exemplary member of the creative class also fits neatly into prevailing political circumstances. Florida states that those within the creative class thrive on their individualistic creative expression and so, 'acknowledge that there is no corporation or other large institution that will take care of us – that we are truly on our own' (2004, p. 115); a particularly harsh but nevertheless clear evocation of the prevailing neoliberal ideology discussed in Chapter 2.

In the UK context specifically under consideration here, we can identify not only a leveraging of ideas similar to Florida's in cultural policy of this period, but also explicit references in national policy documents relating to the role of 'culture-led regeneration'. The influential DCMS report 'Culture At The Heart of Regeneration', released soon after Florida's work came to prominence, argued that 'cultural regeneration can bring economic benefits by providing employment and generating revenue. It also attracts people and businesses' (2004, p. 5), and made reference to,

> strong international advocacy of the importance of culture and creativity to economic and social growth. For example, Richard Florida in his acclaimed book, The Rise of the Creative Class, argues that cities will only thrive if they are able to attract the new breed of creative, skilled people who want to live in places with high quality cultural facilities. (2004, p. 8)

Indeed, Oakley noted contemporaneously that Florida's theories were accepted by policymakers in many areas within the UK (2004, p. 70), and Foord explains that Florida has 'had a major impact on creative enterprise policy' (2008, p. 97). Just as with the concept of the creative industries, then, we can see how the notion of the creative class aligns with a cultural policy environment increasingly concerned with economic growth, albeit from this perspective it is not necessarily those in the cultural field *themselves* who are at the centre of growth, but rather those their work attracts. One of the key props of the discursive structure on the value of culture-led regeneration is that cultural activity will act as a magnet for people who will proceed to set up skilled, creative businesses. Culture is presented as being able to attract the creative class by making a city into 'a more desirable place to live and work, and, subsequently, for businesses to invest' (DCMS 2004, p. 37). Just as the referent of 'creative' in 'creative industries' can be seen to have a predominantly cultural core, but with a somewhat blurred external boundary, so this is the case with the 'creative class', albeit in a different form.

Inclusion in the range of statistics produced regarding the role and nature of the creative class is allocated by Florida on the basis of occupation. As such, one may initially expect to mainly encounter those working in the creative industries within these statistics. From the broad indicators used to evoke the milieu of the creative class, one is certainly left with the impression that the primary interest is again in domains which are concentrated on arts-related production and culturally expressive forms of activity. Florida alludes to 'the Left Bank in Paris or New York's Greenwich Village' (2004, p. 15) as suitable settings for the members of the creative class, whose membership would include prominent figures such as 'Steve Jobs, Jimi Hendrix, Gertrude Stein, Paul Allen, Billie Holiday or Andy Warhol' (2004, p. xiv). Certainly, this mixture of the expressive and artistic with development of information technology maps closely to the listing of 'creative industries' considered above. Despite such similar markers, however, Florida's conception of creativity is quite different, being based on the 'the idea that *every human being is creative*' which Florida characterises as the 'single most important' element of his thesis (2005, p. 3, original emphasis).

The issue of drawing boundaries for the purpose of gathering statistical evidence again becomes relevant here. That Florida's conception of creativity extends well beyond the broadly culture-based definition which is mostly alluded to when it is discussed can be seen in the fact that the 'outer layer' of the creative class—the 'creative professionals'—as defined by Florida for the purposes of generating a range of numerical indices comprises 'management occupations, business and financial operations occupations, legal occupations, healthcare practitioners and technical occupations, [and] high-end sales and management' (2004, p. 328). Such a definition obviously takes us far beyond any previous conception of creative industries to the extent that it raises the question of how different this conception of 'creative professionals' is to one merely of 'professionals'. On this issue, McGuigan argues that, 'the Creative Class, then, is largely what would otherwise be called routinely "the professional-managerial class"' (2009, p. 293). Even in the most concentrated 'inner layer' of the creative class—the so-called Super-Creative Core—those who care to review the categories included for the purposes of data gathering will find those working in 'computer and mathematical occupations' and 'education, training and library occupations'. The creativity of the creative class, then, is explicitly *not* centred solely on artistic or expressive values. Florida suggests, rather, that the crux of creativity here is working in an occupation involving independent thought (2004, p. 69).

In the 'creative industries', we see creativity being used to refer to predominantly arts-based activity, with some extra activities added (although, as noted, why *these particular* activities get added to arts-based work to make up the 'creative industries' is the object of some contention, and will be considered further in Chapter 5). What 'creative' means when it comes to the 'creative class', however, proves more contentious. Whilst strident critiques of the work of Florida have been made, even from relatively early on in the concept's history (Peck 2005), this particular deployment of the idea of creativity has also proved extremely persistent. This is arguably not in spite of, but rather, *because* of the very mutability of the referent of 'creative' in this work, taking us closer to the notion of 'catachresis' introduced at the outset. This must, however, be given some caveats. Although broad ranging, the issue is not so much that 'creative' can mean almost *anything* in the work on the 'creative class', but rather that there is recurrent shift of focus whereby the 'creative class' is often talked about *as though* it largely represented arts-based, expressive practitioners when it is expedient to do so, thus sweeping up all the positive connotations of such activity, but simultaneously allowing a range of quite different activities along for the creative ride. Such an overlap is seen from Florida's position not to be problematic, but rather fruitful. Whilst it is argued that the members of the creative class approach both their work and their leisure in a similar, 'creative', manner according to a generally unified set of tastes and practices, to suggest a strong cultural affinity even for the handful of high-profile creative class members identified above, not to mention the third of the population which apparently constitute its full membership, is questionable at best (recent assertions of Paul Allen's apparent similarity to Jimi Hendrix aside [Marchese 2018]). Yet Florida contends that the creative class, for example, are united in 'the desire to be "always on", and make life a broad-ranging quest for experience' (2004, p. 195). The basis for such claims is not always made entirely clear. Although there is similar terminology in use, there is not necessarily a clear logic as to why, for example, the creative class would, or should, be associated closely with the operation of creative industries, yet these elements are repeatedly aligned as though close cousins. Once again, similar terminology raises the prospect of potential confusion, and small differences in usage continue to be important.

Whilst the growth of the creative class would be of clear interest to those seeking 'regeneration', it may be thought that any policy which sought to engender the promotion of creativity on such a broad basis would necessarily be different in character to one specifically geared towards the promotion or attraction of the creative industries, or of arts organisations, unless all the divergent possible meanings of the term 'creativity' were considered to be in some sense related due to their co-labelling. Whilst the importance of attracting outsiders to one's locale for economic prosperity has been the most influential impact of Florida's work, the dissemination of this conception of unity is arguably just as important; the process of linguistic association by which any policy around culture and the arts can radiate outwards to success in a multitude of 'creative' fields is one which characterises the Creativity Agenda (Campbell 2011). As has been noted previously, Florida's work also emphasises the notion that to ignore creativity is to be left behind: he asserts that 'the creative economy is reshaping nearly every aspect of economic development as we know it' (2005, p. 49), and so those who do not engage with this development risk losing out in the global competition for success. What we can certainly say, though, is, in agreement with Pratt's point above (2008, p. 111), that the creative class thesis is not concerned with creativity in the same sense as the term is used in the 'creative industries'. Given the similarity in both their terminology and their mutual evocation of artistic, expressive activity, it is not difficult to see how such confusion could easily occur, and result in ambiguous or contradictory policy positions.

Creative Innovation and Entrepreneurship

It is clear in Florida's work that an 'openness' to creativity in the cultural realm is seen to signal an openness to broader innovation and entrepreneurial activity. Whilst discussion often focusses specifically on cultural practice, we can thus see a blurring of boundaries whereby this creativity is 'inseparable' from the wider innovation and entrepreneurship that is increasingly valued in this era. Other influential positions in this era continue this alignment. It is argued, for instance, that not only will creative industries form the basis of a new economic order, but their predominantly entrepreneurial, creative character provides a model for how other industries will also eventually come to operate within this new order (Leadbeater and Oakley 1999, p. 13). There is thus a sense that the creation of a business and, for instance, the composition of a piece of music are two versions of the same act, with the same ultimate root. In the era under consideration, some make this link explicit, going even further than Florida regarding the ultimate unity of different forms of creativity. In Florida's work, one is left with the ultimate sense (be this accurate or not) that 'creative' entrepreneurs are attracted by 'creative' cultural environments, yet despite a sense of a common root—and Florida's assertion that these are 'interlinked and inseparable'—these manifestations of creativity are not presented as necessarily *identical*. Whilst a 'vibrant artistic community' will enable local administrations 'to attract and stimulate those who create in business' (Florida 2004, p. 55), there is the sense that there is some difference between these constituencies, despite an assertion of a close relationship. In his expansive consideration of the role of the urban environment in the gestation of key cultural and technological developments, however, Hall argues more strongly for the ultimate commonality of creative processes:

> Twentieth-century society has demanded phones as well as philosophy, bathrooms as well as opera; indeed, it gets most of its opera from the domestic CD player rather than the opera house. Yet these new technologies arise from the same creative spark: the same rules apply to art and culture as to that more mundane but equally momentous kind of creativity, which results in major technological advance and thus in new objects, new industries, new modes of production. (1998, p. 5)

To take some of the examples Hall considers in greater detail in this work we may well be left asking, *do* the same rules apply to, for example, the creation of impressionist art as to the creation of the motor car? Here, though, the answer is 'yes'—not only can these acts be described by the same *language* of 'creativity', but this common *language* is also a reflection of a fundamentally common *root*.

As the Creativity Agenda develops, Van Heur argues that one of the overarching themes of policy regarding creative industries is the importance of the role performed by entrepreneurs (2010, p. 135, see, for instance, European Parliament 2016, p. 8), and Potts and Cunningham argue that entrepreneurship is the dominant mode of growth within creative industries due to the prevalence of smaller firms (2008, p. 245). This overlapping manifestation of creativity is stated by some in particularly stark terms:

> Given the fact that creative people are more inclined to independence in general and to economic independence in particular it seems to be plausible that they have a higher propensity to start a company than non creatives. [...] Talented people are more creative than the rest of the population, they are more entrepreneurial. (Acs et al. 2008, p. 5)

There is thus a natural fit between the creation of a new business and creativity within that business. Indeed, for some in this era, cultural and/or creative work is (or can be) an ideal model of innovation (Nesta 2008, p. 2; Bakhshi et al. 2009; EICI 2012); they are 'overlapping concepts' (The Work Foundation 2007, p. 16), and thus the cultural and creative field presents ideal Schumpeterian opportunities for economic transformation and development.

It has been noted by some, however, that the actual role for creative industries in driving innovation has not actually been established (RSA 2013), and that the literature on culture, creativity and innovation is characterised more by assertion than by evidence (Throsby 2008b, p. 229; Oakley 2009, p. 407; Trip and Romein 2014, p. 2490). Nevertheless, such assertions regarding the alignment of all forms of creativity also persist. It has for instance recently been argued that 'culture and the creative economy are by definition driven by innovation and new knowledge' (Holden 2017, p. 3). From such a position, it is suitable for policy to seek to engender a climate suitable for creative activity in any sense of the term, as all outcomes essentially radiate from a common core. Promoting creative innovation and entrepreneurship will also assist in the regeneration of cities by enhancing 'the quality of all our lives' (DCMS et al. 2008, p. 1) and furthering 'social cohesion' (Leadbeater and Oakley 1999, p. 17). Such positions clearly link to wider neoliberal discourse around the value of 'enterprise' in and of itself, and a stress on the individual's responsibility for their own economic conditions (e.g. Morris 1991), but also echo positions first explored in discussion of the 'cultural industries'. Miège for instance argues that 'small businesses are better equipped to respond to changes in social demand and to renew creativity' (1989, p. 44). We thus see the notion of a particularly innovative, and small scale, form of creativity deployed in relation to the cultural realm, albeit one which risks being subsumed into broader discussions of innovation widely conceived (Banks and O'Connor 2009, p. 366). This unified sense of creativity leads to circumstances in which, as Böhm and Land explain,

> The assumption seems to be that 'creativity' is a transferable skill, and that developing the population's artistic creativity will deliver creativity and innovation in other sectors. (2009, p. 80)

We can certainly refer to both of these things as 'creative', but similarities in terminology need not imply similarities in substance, and so it would be appropriate to be sceptical regarding claims such as these.

The Creative City

Mould (2017a, p. 2) notes how this link between innovation, economic growth and competitiveness is also made in relation to discourse around the need to develop the 'creative city'. This is perhaps the most broadly applied label of those considered in this chapter, being attached in this period to almost any situation involving the forms of creativity considered above. For instance, despite his work focussing explicitly on a 'creative class' of individuals with creative occupations, tastes, dispositions and so on, many refer to Florida's work as being specifically on the idea of the 'creative city' (e.g. Bakhshi et al. 2013, p. 58; Munro 2016, p. 45). Again, we see how the deployment of similar terms allows a blurring of boundaries and definitions.

Whilst there are many overlaps, however, the intentions of the most prominent theorising around the creative city are at heart somewhat different to those encountered thus far. Key to the promotion of the 'creative city' is the work of Landry who fundamentally argues that the future success of any city depends on the quality of 'creative' solutions to urban problems. Scott (2014, p. 567) refers to Landry's 'landmark manifesto' on the creative city from 2000 as 'an all-azimuths call for the investment of creative energies in virtually every aspect of urban existence'. This thesis, much like the backdrop to the creative industries agenda, is based on a notion of fundamental transformation or implicit newness in the status of cities at the turn of the twenty-first century, and the necessity for their responses to their transformed conditions to be similarly novel. This, according to Landry (2006), requires breaking out of established forms of governance and traditional approaches. We can identify how this focus on creativity, broadly conceived, at the level of a city administration is aligned with the increasing prominence of a new form of governance in this era:

> Entrepreneurialism, the mode of urban governance which has emerged from the crisis of managerialism, is predicated on a competitive quest for new sources of economic development, in response to a collapsing manufacturing base and a growing internationalisation of investment flows. (Griffiths 1998, p. 42)

'New' economic times call for new political measures, and the creative entrepreneurship of the creative worker can thus also be reflected in the entrepreneurship of the urban policymaker.

In spite of the blurring, or removal, of conceptual boundaries between various manifestations of creativity in Florida's work resulting in the emergence of a more unified, yet curiously loose, conception of 'creativity', a particular emphasis on the value of artistic creativity remains. In Landry's work on 'the creative city', however, the definition of 'creativity' broadens out much further, seemingly moving away from an expressive, artistic usage much more explicitly. Nonetheless, there are once again elements of opacity and overlap regarding the nature of creativity both in the work of Landry itself, and in its subsequent adoption. Landry is initially clear about this distinction, stating that 'many cities now use the brand 'creative city', usually when referring to their arts strategy. The creative city is not an arts strategy; instead it seeks to embed a culture of creativity everywhere in the city' (Landry 2003, p. 17). Similarly, in his earliest work defining the term, Landry takes what we have seen to be a persistent line regarding the inevitable emergence of certain 'new' economic circumstances, making statements such as: 'the industries of the 21st century will depend increasingly on the generation of knowledge through creativity' (Landry and Bianchini 1995, p. 4). Whilst the creativity being referred to here is somewhat opaque, it may be a broad version of the 'imaginative' form of creativity discussed by Williams above, and this imaginative activity will 'generate knowledge', presumably useful to the city of the future not least in the operation of an emergent 'knowledge economy'. Initially, therefore, Landry is explicitly not proposing that the industries of the twenty-first century will depend predominantly on creativity in an expressive, cultural sense—neither the arts, nor the 'creative industries', should therefore be understood to play a central role in the creative city (Landry 2000, p. 52).

Here, then, creativity achieves its widest definition, akin to a general sense of openness to change, diversity and new ideas. The creative city is not limited by old problems, as it can be 'creative' in finding new solutions through the creative skills of its 'urban professionals'. This creativity thus involves the disruption of established forms of governance, and so does not necessarily involve any specific role for the arts or culture. Landry invites us to open our minds to new perspectives and to ponder, for example, 'how often do strategic urban plans start with the words "beauty", "love", "happiness", or "excitement"...' (2006, p. 2). The deployment of 'love' and 'beauty' in urban strategies is certainly rare, and whilst some have argued that such creative governance is not as utopian as it appears (Healey 2004), it certainly seems like a novel approach. What is perhaps emblematic of the concepts under consideration, however, is that, having initially established that the creativity of the creative city is not directly related to artistic activity, Landry states in later work that there *is*, in fact, a specific role for the arts in this broader creativity:

> Turning imagination into reality or something tangible is a creative act, so the arts, more than most activities, are concerned with creativity, invention and innovation. Reinventing a city or nursing it through transition is a creative act, so an engagement with or through the arts helps. (2006, p. 250)

This is an emblematic statement for the Creativity Agenda. For this statement to make sense, one must subscribe to a sense of creativity that unifies anything that can be so named. Whilst many things *can* be deemed creative, we are left with the persistent question of whether such common labelling helps or hinders. It certainly seems to aid the proliferation and application of the label, but potentially at the expense of clarity of meaning. Wherever applied, though, we never seem to be too far from the use of cultural activity as an anchor for the meaning of 'creativity'.

What we can certainly see is that regardless of intent, the creative city concept quickly becomes tangled up with the specifically cultural, rather than being deployed to promote the wider creativity that the concept initially seems so concerned with. Throsby, for instance, argues that in the creative city, 'the marriage of cultural policy and the cultural industries is finally consummated' (2008b, p. 229), and Markusen notes the centrality of arguments on the role for arts and culture in community and economic development in debates regarding the 'creative city and creative placemaking' (2014, p. 568). In this increasingly blurred range of applications, any 'creative' intervention, such as creative industries development programmes, or the staging of a cultural festival, may be assumed to automatically bring about the benefits associated with all other kinds of 'creativity'. What is certainly the case is that there is a central role for the arts and culture in the adoption of the creative city agenda in practice (e.g. Grodach 2013; Richards 2014).

Regardless of its coherence, or perhaps because it can speak to multiple agendas, just as the notions of the creative industries and the creative class have been globally successful, so it is the case with the creative city. Heartfield (2006, p. 82) points to a range of locations across the globe that have adopted Landry's idea, and Banks and O'Connor (2017) argue for the idea's wider influence:

> While in many ways Landry was responding opportunistically to a process already in train, it is hard to overestimate how far the idea of the 'creative city' came to influence thought about the creative industries more generally and how it continues directly and indirectly to shape academic and policy thinking internationally. (2017, p. 644)

Indeed, emphasising the idea of persistent creativity, Mould refers to the creative city as an idea that, after two decades of application, 'simply won't go away' (2017b).

Conclusion

This chapter has demonstrated the persistence of an agenda around creativity since the turn of the twenty-first century. This agenda achieved a rapid, global dominance by emphasising the role of creativity in succeeding in new economic times. The route by which the dominant concept of 'creative industries' arrived partly explains the central role for cultural activity in this conception, and cultural activity also remains important in the notion of the 'creative class' thesis that became prominent during this period. What is also clear is that both of these concepts move beyond specifically cultural conceptions of creativity, as does the notion of the 'creative city', but nevertheless this creativity is often discussed as though cultural activity were the main, or indeed the only, object under consideration. Small differences in terminology have been shown to introduce the space for a wide and potentially contradictory range of understandings. Although a common language does not necessarily imply a common referent, we have also seen how some explicitly put forward a position that argues that all forms of creativity *are* indeed united, not just by a common language, but a common nature. We have also seen, though, that this commonality seems to be more easily asserted than demonstrated.

This state of affairs has, however, potentially assisted the rise of the Creativity Agenda rather than hindered it. As noted at the outset of this chapter, 'catachresis', or the misapplication of terminology, can serve to bridge contradictions in discourse and amplify its power. In the cases considered here, it certainly seems to have been no hindrance. If creativity has no clear or precise referent, it can be deployed by multiple actors towards multiple agendas, perhaps even contradictory ones, yet retain an apparent coherence. Existing activities can be recast with the new sheen of creativity and be positioned as speaking to this 'new' agenda even though little may have actually changed. Creativity thus has a power to mask, at least superficially, the contradictions of cultural policy (see Hewison 2014, p. 61). Regardless of what might be the most theoretically rigorous position, therefore, we must acknowledge Pratt and Jeffcut's point that,

> labels such as creative industries, cultural industries, creative economy [...] have all been used. Whilst academic cases can be made for a differentiation between them, the overwhelming policy discourse is one in which they are used interchangeably. (2009, p. 5)

If there are a range of different intentions in these terms and the theories behind them, however, there is a risk of incoherence in outcomes if policy uses such labels in an indiscriminate fashion.

This may, though, merely be seen as a problem of theory rather than practice. As has also been previously noted, there is an emphasis in this period on the importance of evidence gathering. As this must surely be evidence for, or in relation to, a *particular* proposition we may expect the room for ambiguity to lessen if we consider the evidence base in this area. It is therefore instructive to consider how the case gets made for the arts, culture and creative industries. If so much time has been spent preparing for an inevitable new economy with a culturally inflected form of creativity at its core, and this occurs in an era increasingly concerned with evidence making, what evidence is actually produced? Can we move beyond the mere assertion of linkages and commonality of all things creative as a result of this evidence? The way in which the case is made for art, culture and the creative industries is thus the subject of the following chapters.

References

Acs, Z., Bosma, N., & Sternberg, R. (2008). *The entrepreneurial advantage of world cities*. Jena: Friedrich Schiller University.

Adorno, T. W. (1991). *The culture industry*. London: Routledge.

Adorno, T. W., & Horkheimer, M. (1979). *Dialectic of enlightenment*. London: Verso.

Bakhshi, H., & Cunningham, S. (2016). *Cultural policy in the time of the creative industries*. London: Nesta.

Bakhshi, H., Desai, R., & Freeman, A. (2009). *Not rocket science: A roadmap for arts and culture R&D*. Retrieved from https://mpra.ub.uni-muenchen.de/52710/1/MPRA_paper_52710.pdf.

Bakhshi, H., Hargreaves, I., & Mateos Garcia, J. (2013). *A manifesto for the creative economy*. London: Nesta.

Banks, M. (2017). *Creative justice: Cultural industries, work and inequality*. London: Rowman & Littlefield.

Banks, M., & O'Connor, J. (2009). After the creative industries. *International Journal of Cultural Policy, 15*(4), 365–373.

Banks, M., & O'Connor, J. (2017). Inside the whale (and how to get out of there): Moving on from two decades of creative industries research. *European Journal of Cultural Studies, 20*(6), 637–654.

Bazalgette, P. (2009, May 11). Thinking for inside the box. *The Guardian*. Retrieved from https://www.theguardian.com/media/2009/may/10/future-television-industry-recession.

Bell, D., & Jayne, M. (2010). The creative countryside: Policy and practice in the UK rural cultural economy. *Journal of Rural Studies, 26*(3), 209–218.

Bertacchini, E. E., & Borrione, P. (2013). The geography of the Italian creative economy: The special role of the design and craft-based industries. *Regional Studies, 47*(2), 135–147.

Bilton, C., & Leary, R. (2002). What can managers do for creativity? Brokering creativity in the creative industries. *International Journal of Cultural Policy, 8*(1), 49–64.

Böhm, S., & Land, C. (2009). No measure for culture? Value in the new economy. *Capital & Class, 33*(1), 75–98.

Brouillette, S. (2014). *Literature and the creative economy*. Stanford: Stanford University Press.

Campbell, P. (2011). You say 'creative', and I say 'creative'. *Journal of Policy Research in Tourism, Leisure and Events, 3*(1), 18–30.

Catachresis. (n.d.). *Oxford English dictionary*. Retrieved from http://www.oed.com.

CBI. (2014). *The creative nation: A growth strategy for the UK's creative industries*. Retrieved from http://www.cbi.org.uk/cbi-prod/assets/File/pdf/cbi_creative_industries_strategy__final_.pdf.

Chapain, C., & Lee, P. (2009). Can we plan the creative knowledge city? Perspectives from Western and Eastern Europe. *Built Environment, 35*(2), 157–164.

Chatterton, P. (2000). Will the real creative city please stand up? *City, 4*(3), 390–397.

Chenyan, W. (2014). *Training program to boost China's creative industries*. Retrieved from http://www.vtibet.com/en/news_1746/china/201405/t20140519_198297.html.

Comedia. (2004). *Culture and regeneration: An evaluation of the evidence*. Nottingham: Comedia.

Comunian, R., Faggian, A., & Li, Q. C. (2010). Unrewarded careers in the creative class: The strange case of bohemian graduates. *Papers in Regional Science, 89*(2), 389–410.

Connolly, M. G. (2013). The 'Liverpool model(s)': Cultural planning, Liverpool and Capital of Culture 2008. *International Journal of Cultural Policy, 19*(2), 162–181.

Conservative and Unionist Party. (2017). *Manifesto 2017*. Retrieved from https://www.conservatives.com/manifesto.

Currid, E. (2007). *The Warhol economy: How fashion, art, and music drive New York City*. Princeton: Princeton University Press.

DCMS. (2004). *Culture at the heart of regeneration*. London: DCMS.

DCMS. (2010). *Creative industries economic estimates: Technical note*. London: DCMS.

DCMS, BERR, & DIUS. (2008). *Creative Britain: New talents for the new economy*. London: DCMS.

De Propris, L., Chapain, C., Cooke, P., MacNeill, S., & Mateos Garcia, J. (2009). *The geography of creativity*. London: Nesta.

EICI. (2012). *European Interest Group on Creativity and Innovation e.V.* Retrieved from http://www.creativity-innovation.eu/european-interest-group-on-creativity-and-innovation-e-v/.

European Parliament. (2016). *Report on a coherent EU policy for cultural and creative industries*. Retrieved from http://www.europarl.europa.eu/sides/getDoc.do?pubRef=-//EP//NONSGML+REPORT+A8-2016-0357+0+DOC+PDF+V0//EN.

Evans, G. (2001). *Cultural planning*. London: Routledge.

Evans, G. (2009). Creative cities, creative spaces and urban policy. *Urban Studies, 46*(5–6), 1003–1040.

Evans, M. (2001). The economy of the imagination. *Locum Destination Review, 5*, 45–50.

Faggian, A., Comunian, R., Jewell, S., & Kelly, U. (2013). Bohemian graduates in the UK: Disciplines and location determinants of creative careers. *Regional Studies, 47*(2), 183–200.

Fahmi, F. Z., Koster, S., & van Dijk, J. (2016). The location of creative industries in a developing country: The case of Indonesia. *Cities, 59*, 66–79.

Flew, T., & Cunningham, S. (2010). Creative industries after the first decade of debate. *The Information Society, 26*(2), 113–123.

Florida, R. (2002). Bohemia and economic geography. *Journal of Economic Geography, 2*(1), 55–71.

Florida, R. (2003). Cities and the creative class. *City & Community, 2*(1), 3–19.

Florida, R. (2004). *The rise of the creative class*. New York: Basic Books.

Florida, R. (2005). *Cities and the creative class*. London: Routledge.

Foord, J. (2008). Strategies for creative industries: An international review. *Creative Industries Journal, 1*(2), 91–113.

Gainza, X. (2017). Culture-led neighbourhood transformations beyond the revitalisation/gentrification dichotomy. *Urban Studies, 54*(4), 953–970.

Galloway, S., & Dunlop, S. (2007). A critique of definitions of the cultural and creative industries in public policy. *International Journal of Cultural Policy, 13*(1), 17–31.

Gans, H. (1968). *People and plans: Essays on urban problems and solutions.* New York: Basic Books.

Garnham, N. (1990). *Capitalism and communication: Global culture and the economics of information.* London: Sage.

Garnham, N. (2005). From culture to creative industries. *International Journal of Cultural Policy, 11*(1), 15–29.

Gibson, C., & Klocker, N. (2005). The 'cultural turn' in Australian regional economic development discourse: Neoliberalising creativity? *Geographical Research, 43*(1), 93–102.

Gray, C. (2009). Managing cultural policy: Pitfalls and prospects. *Public Administration, 87*(3), 574–585.

Griffiths, R. (1998). Making sameness: Place marketing and the new urban entrepreneurialism. In N. Oatley (Ed.), *Cities, economic competition and urban policy* (pp. 41–57). London: Paul Chapman.

Grodach, C. (2013). Cultural economy planning in creative cities: Discourse and practice. *International Journal of Urban and Regional Research, 37*(5), 1747–1765.

Hall, P. (1998). *Cities in civilisation.* London: Weidenfeld & Nicolson.

Healey, P. (2004). Creativity and urban governance. *Policy Studies, 25*(2), 87–102.

Heartfield, J. (2006). A business solution for creativity, not a creativity solution for business. In M. Mirza (Ed.), *Culture vultures: Is UK arts policy damaging the arts?* (pp. 71–92). London: Policy Exchange.

Heinze, R. G., & Hoose, F. (2013). The creative economy: Vision or illusion in the structural change? *European Planning Studies, 21*(4), 516–535.

Hesmondhalgh, D., & Pratt, A. C. (2005). Cultural industries and cultural policy. *International Journal of Cultural Policy, 11*(1), 1–13.

Hesmondhalgh, D., Oakley, K., Lee, D., & Nisbett, M. (2015). *Culture, economy and politics: The case of New Labour.* Basingstoke: Palgrave Macmillan.

Hewison, R. (2014). *Cultural capital: The rise and fall of creative Britain.* London: Verso.

Higgins, C. (2013, March 19). New chair of Arts Council England warns against cuts to culture. *The Guardian.* Retrieved from https://www.theguardian.com/culture/2013/mar/19/arts-council-england-peter-bazalgette-cuts.

Higgs, P., Cunningham, S., & Bakhshi, H. (2008). *Beyond the creative industries: Mapping the creative economy in the United Kingdom.* London: Nesta.

HM Government. (2018). *Industrial strategy: Creative industries sector deal.* Retrieved from https://www.gov.uk/government/uploads/system/uploads/attachment_data/file/695097/creative-industries-sector-deal-print.pdf.

Holden, J. (2017). Foreword. In K. Hewlett, K. Bond, & S. Hinrichs-Krapels (Eds.), *The creative role of research: Understanding research impact in the creative and cultural sector.* Retrieved from https://www.kcl.ac.uk/Cultural/culturalenquiries/171020-TheCreativeRoleOfResearch-WEB2.pdf.

House of Commons. (2013). *Culture, Media and Sport Committee: Supporting the creative economy—Third report of session 2013–14* (Vol. I). London: The Stationery Office.

Jäger, S., & Maier, F. (2009). Theoretical and methodological aspects of Foucauldian critical discourse analysis and dispositive analysis. In R. Wodak & M. Meyer (Eds.), *Methods of critical discourse analysis* (2nd ed., pp. 34–61). London: Sage.

Keane, M. (2009). Creative industries in China: Four perspectives on social transformation. *International Journal of Cultural Policy, 15*(1), 431–443.

Landry, C. (2000). *The creative city.* London: Comedia.

Landry, C. (2003). The creative city: Aspiration and reality. In H. Ford & B. Sawyers (Eds.), *International architecture centres* (pp. 14–17). Chichester: Wiley-Academy.

Landry, C. (2006). *The art of city making.* London: Earthscan.

Landry, C., & Bianchini, F. (1995). *The creative city.* London: Demos.

Last, B. (2016). *Connecting creativity, value and money.* Retrieved from https://zenodo.org/record/55754/files/CREATe-Working-Paper-2016-10.pdf.

Leadbeater, C., & Oakley, K. (1999). *The independents.* London: Demos.

Lee, K.-S. (2007). Questioning a neoliberal urban regeneration policy. *International Journal of Cultural Policy, 13*(4), 335–347.

London Development Agency. (2008). *London: A cultural audit.* London: LDA.

Lysgård, H. J. (2013). The definition of culture in culture-based urban development strategies: Antagonisms in the construction of a culture-based development discourse. *International Journal of Cultural Policy, 19*(2), 182–200.

Marchese, D. (2018). *Conversation: Quincy Jones.* Retrieved from http://www.vulture.com/2018/02/quincy-jones-in-conversation.html.

Markusen, A. (2014). Creative cities: A 10-year research agenda. *Journal of Urban Affairs, 36*(s2), 567–589.

McGuigan, J. (2009). Doing a Florida thing: The creative class thesis and cultural policy. *International Journal of Cultural Policy, 15*(3), 291–300.

McKee, A. (2013). The power of art, the power of entertainment. *Media, Culture and Society, 35*(6), 759–770.

Miège, B. (1989). *The capitalization of cultural production.* New York: International General.

Miller, T. (2009). From creative to cultural industries. *Cultural Studies, 23*(1), 88–99.

Morris, P. (1991). Freeing the spirit of enterprise: The genesis and development of the concept of enterprise culture. In R. Keat & N. Abercrombie (Eds.), *Enterprise culture* (pp. 21–37). London: Routledge.

Mould, O. (2017a). *Urban subversion and the creative city.* London: Routledge.

Mould, O. (2017b). *Why culture competitions and 'artwashing' drive urban inequality.* Retrieved from https://www.opendemocracy.net/uk/oli-mould/why-culture-competitions-and-artwashing-drive-urban-inequality.

Munro, E. (2016). Illuminating the practice of knowledge exchange as a 'pathway to impact' within an Arts and Humanities Research Council 'Creative Economy Knowledge Exchange' project. *Geoforum, 71*, 44–51.

Nesta. (2008). *Beyond the creative industries: Making policy for the creative economy.* London: Nesta.

Oakley, K. (2004). Not so cool Britannia: The role of the creative industries in economic development. *International Journal of Cultural Studies, 7*(1), 67–77.

Oakley, K. (2009). The disappearing arts: Creativity and innovation after the creative industries. *International Journal of Cultural Policy, 15*(4), 403–413.

Oakley, K., & O'Connor, J. (2015). The cultural industries—An introduction. In K. Oakley & J. O'Connor (Eds.), *The Routledge companion to the cultural industries* (pp. 1–32). London: Routledge.

Oakley, K., O'Brien, D., & Lee, D. (2013). Happy now? Well-being and cultural policy. *Philosophy and Public Policy Quarterly, 31*(2), 18–26.

Oakley, K., Ball, M., & Cunningham, M. (2018). *Everyday culture and the good life* (CUSP Working Paper No. 9). Guildford: University of Surrey.

O'Brien, D. (2014). *Cultural policy: Management, value and modernity in the creative industries.* London: Routledge.

O'Connor, J. (2005). Creative exports: Taking cultural industries to St. Petersburg. *International Journal of Cultural Policy, 11*(1), 45–60.

O'Connor, J. (2007). *The cultural and creative industries: A review of the literature*. London: Arts Council England.

O'Connor, J. (2013). Intermediaries and imaginaries in the creative industries. *Regional Studies, 49*(3), 374–387.

Olma, S. (2016). *In defence of serendipity: For a radical politics of innovation*. London: Repeater Books.

Peck, J. (2005). Struggling with the creative class. *International Journal of Urban and Regional Research, 29*(4), 740–770.

Potts, J., & Cunningham, S. (2008). Four models of the creative industries. *International Journal of Cultural Policy, 14*(3), 233–247.

Pratt, A. C. (2005). Cultural industries and public policy. *International Journal of Cultural Policy, 11*(1), 31–44.

Pratt, A. C. (2008). Creative cities: The cultural industries and the creative class. *Geografiska Annaler: Series B, Human Geography, 90*(2), 107–117.

Pratt, A. C., & Jeffcut, P. (2009). *Creativity, innovation and the cultural economy*. London: Routledge.

Prince, R. (2014). Consultants and the global assemblage of culture and creativity. *Transactions of the Institute of British Geographers, 39*(1), 90–101.

Richards, G. (2014). Creativity and tourism in the city. *Current Issues in Tourism, 17*(2), 119–144.

Rindzevičiūtė, E., Svensson, J., & Tomson, K. (2016). The international transfer of creative industries as a policy idea. *International Journal of Cultural Policy, 22*(4), 594–610.

RSA. (2013). *New project in collaboration with Arts Council England*. Retrieved from https://www.thersa.org/fellowship/fellowship-news/fellowship-news/new-project-in-collaboration-with-arts-council-england.

Schlesinger, P. (2007). Creativity: From discourse to doctrine. *Screen, 48*(3), 377–387.

Schlesinger, P. (2009). *The politics of media and cultural policy*. Retrieved from http://www.lse.ac.uk/media-and-communications/assets/documents/research/working-paper-series/EWP17.pdf.

Schlesinger, P. (2017). The creative economy: Invention of a global orthodoxy. *Innovation: The European Journal of Social Science Research, 30*(1), 73–90.

Scott, A. J. (2007). Cultural economy: Retrospect and prospect. In H. Anheier & Y. R. Isar (Eds.), *The cultural economy* (pp. 307–324). London: Sage.

Scott, A. J. (2014). Beyond the creative city: Cognitive-cultural capitalism and the new urbanism. *Regional Studies, 48*(4), 565–578.

Sefton-Green, J., & Parker, D. (2006). Foreword. In S. Banaji, A. Burn, & D. Buckingham (Eds.), *The rhetorics of creativity: A review of the literature*. London: Arts Council England.

Smith, A. ([1784] 1818). *An inquiry into the nature and causes of the wealth of nations*. Hartford: Cooke & Hale.

Stevenson, D., McKay, K., & Rowe, D. (2010). Tracing British cultural policy domains: Contexts, collaborations and constituencies. *International Journal of Cultural Policy, 16*(2), 159–172.

Straw, W., & Warner, N. (2014). *March of the modern makers: An industrial strategy for the creative industries*. London: IPPR.

Taylor, C. (2006). Beyond advocacy: Developing an evidence base for regional creative industry strategies. *Cultural Trends, 15*(1), 3–18.

Taylor, C. (2015). Between culture, policy and industry: Modalities of inter-mediation in the creative economy. *Regional Studies, 49*(3), 362–373.

The Work Foundation. (2007). *Staying ahead: The economic performance of the UK's creative industries*. London: The Work Foundation.

Throsby, D. (2008a). The concentric circles model of the cultural industries. *Cultural Trends, 17*(3), 147–164.

Throsby, D. (2008b). Modelling the cultural industries. *International Journal of Cultural Policy, 14*(3), 217–232.

Tremblay, G. (2011). Creative statistics to support creative economy politics. *Media, Culture and Society, 33*(2), 289–298.

Trip, J. J., & Romein, A. (2014). Creative city policy and the gap with theory. *European Planning Studies, 22*(12), 2490–2509.

UN. (2008). *Creative economy report 2008: The challenge of assessing the creative economy—Towards informed policy-making*. Retrieved from http://unctad.org/en/Docs/ditc20082cer_en.pdf.

Van Heur, B. (2010). *Creative networks and the city*. London: Transaction Publishers.

Vasiliu, O. (2014). *Romanian creative industries to have their own festival*. Retrieved from http://business-review.eu/featured/romanian-creative-industries-to-have-their-own-festival-68944.

Volkerling, M. (2001). From cool Britannia to hot nation: 'Creative industries' policies in Europe, Canada and New Zealand. *International Journal of Cultural Policy, 7*(3), 437–455.

Wang, J. (2004). The global reach of a new discourse: How far can 'creative industries' travel? *International Journal of Cultural Studies, 7*(1), 9–19.

Williams, R. (1983). *Keywords*. New York: Oxford University Press.

4

Making the Case for Art and Culture: Persistent Challenges

The promotion of creativity holds out the promise of a range of beneficial, potentially 'regenerative', outcomes. In the context of the circumstances outlined in Chapter 2, however, there is an increasing emphasis in the period in which this Creativity Agenda comes to prominence on the need to *demonstrate* such beneficial outcomes. As such, this chapter considers further aspects of 'persistence' in the discourse around creativity: the persistence of the specific terminology of regeneration, the persistent focus on the need to demonstrate the outcomes of cultural practice, but also the persistence of a range of challenges in making the case for arts and culture. Although many problems are identified with the extant evidence base, it will be argued that this does little to curb the promotion of the Creativity Agenda discussed thus far. Indeed, where evidence is seen as lacking, the responses seem to emphasise the continuing need for *more* evidence. This raises the question of whether this evidence base is being used in part, as per the pithy phrase attributed to Andrew Lang regarding the drunkard and the lamppost, 'more for support than for illumination'. This chapter will consider these issues in light of research carried out as part of the AHRC's Cultural Value project, looking in particular at the methods used by researchers

© The Author(s) 2019
P. Campbell, *Persistent Creativity*, Sociology of the Arts,
https://doi.org/10.1007/978-3-030-03119-0_4

primarily in the UK over the period 2006–2014 to create an evidence base regarding the 'regenerative' role that arts interventions can play in specific sites. The key areas this evidence focusses on, the challenges in producing appropriate evidence in this period, and potential explanations for this, are thus discussed.

The Quest for Evidence and the Rise of Regeneration: A Brief History

Although some early attempts at developing an evidence base regarding the outcomes of arts and cultural practice were encountered in Chapter 2, it was seen that these were relatively limited and subject to some critique. Considering the development of the role of evidence in the cultural policymaking process, Selwood argues that prior to the election in the late 1990s of the Labour administration most associated with the promotion of the Creativity Agenda, the prevailing position regarding cultural activity in the UK was that 'performance measurement was generally considered inappropriate and was effectively avoided' (2006, p. 35). At the level of local government, for instance, it was noted by the UK's Audit Commission in the early 1990s that local authorities often made little effort to ascertain what was achieved as a result of their grants for provision of the arts (1991, p. 6). Schuster (1996, p. 254), however, notes an increasing concern with statistical indicators and measures of 'accountability' throughout the 1990s, and it is clear that there was an unprecedented rise in activity seeking to establish 'evidence-based policy' in this field, as in others, during the tenure of the Labour Party from 1997 onwards (Oakley 2008; Hesmondhalgh et al. 2015).

Alongside these developments, for this Labour administration, the emergent idea of a role for culture in regeneration became especially prominent and broad-ranging (Hewison 2014, p. 6), and this chapter will focus on evidence for the 'regenerative' power that culture is seen to wield, especially in light of the potential beneficial outcomes of the various 'creative' practices described in Chapter 3.

Given that demonstration of persistent patterns is one of the key concerns of this book, it is thus necessary to pause briefly to establish the continuation of the regeneration narrative around culture whose roots were first considered in Chapter 2. By the early 2000s, for example, Evans could state that 'the designation of the cultural city and the use of the arts and entertainment as tools in urban regeneration is now *a universal phenomenon*' (2003, p. 417, emphasis added). Similarly, in 2005 Miles and Paddison could convincingly argue that the use of culture to drive economic growth and competitiveness constituted a 'new orthodoxy' (2005, p. 833). Having established such prominence, projects seeking to establish some form of regeneration on this basis continued into the 2010s. Whilst Evans was able to conclude in 2011 that 'in terms of cultural and community development, the regeneration project and event city looks both tired and dated', nevertheless, 'the culture and regeneration phenomenon […] rolls on, as does the impact study and 'evidence-based policy' regime' (2011, p. 15). As the 2010s continued, one could point to prominent stakeholders in the UK continuing to emphasise how culture is 'increasingly acknowledged to play a role in regeneration' (Arts Council Northern Ireland 2014, p. 13) or, echoing earlier positions, is at the 'heart of regeneration' in many parts of the country (Conservative and Unionist Party 2017).

The period in which the promotion of the Creativity Agenda becomes prominent is, perhaps unsurprisingly, also one in which the role for culture in regeneration is increasingly taken as read, and this has happened in an era in which the role of evidence in substantiating policy is argued to be increasingly important. One may therefore presume that the rise of this position occurs in concert with the collation of an increasingly convincing evidence base on this topic. Whilst we can see that the role attributed to evidence in making the case for culture is noticeably more prominent in this era than the ones that precede it, though, this prominence often takes the form of a continuing emphasis on the unsuitability of the current evidence base, and the need for its development. Reeves (2002, p. 17), for instance, points to a 1999 report by the Department for Culture, Media and Sport (DCMS) which identifies 'a lack of hard information on the regeneration impact of arts' as a key issue requiring policy attention and concludes at the turn of the twenty-first century that there was,

> widespread consensus among commentators that there is a lack of robust evaluation and systematic evidence of the impact of arts projects, or cultural services, more broadly, despite a wealth of anecdotal evidence. (2002, pp. 31–32)

As attempts to leverage cultural activity to achieve regeneration continued from this point, Lees and Melhuish show that the position of DCMS in 1999 regarding a lack of robust evidence persists. A similar position 'was restated in 2001, and the lack of evidence to date noted. The same situation was recorded again in [2004]' (2015, p. 253).

Over at least the earlier period of the rise of the Creativity Agenda, then, we should be sensitive to the fact that, despite this being an era of 'evidence-based policy', this rise occurs with at least significant question marks over the nature of the evidence available to substantiate some of the positions outlined. Nevertheless, given the entrenchment of the ideological positions outlined in Chapter 2, the solution to a problematic evidence base is often given as the gathering of further evidence. Johanson et al. (2014, p. 47), for instance, cite Mercer in 2003 arguing the case for 'more numbers, more facts, more indicators, more benchmarks', and in 2004, García concludes that it is 'critical' to 'develop techniques to evaluate cultural impacts' as 'there is a lack of convincing evidence about cultural and social impacts', leading to a reliance solely on economic and physical factors when regeneration is assessed (2004, pp. 324–325).

Despite such issues being raised with the available evidence base, the idea of culture being linked to regeneration had gained major traction by this point, and in 2004, Evans and Shaw produced their much-cited review for DCMS, 'The Contribution of Culture to Regeneration in the UK'. García succinctly notes of this report that Evans and Shaw reiterate some of her concerns above and 'note important weaknesses due to the lack of evidence about long-term legacies and the limited understanding of social and, particularly, cultural impacts' (2005, p. 842). Indeed, DCMS themselves note the need for 'a stronger and more sophisticated longitudinal evidence base' (2004, p. 43), as do other prominent voices in the field at this point (e.g. Comedia 2004, p. 7). In their review, Evans and Shaw (2004) identify three key areas in which culture is seen as playing a role in regeneration: an economic role (evidenced using data regarding, e.g., visitor spend, cultural and creative industries employment or levels of inward investment); a role in physical regeneration (demonstrated using data, e.g., on the reuse of buildings or the level of new buildings, public art and clusters of creative businesses) and a socially regenerative role (which may be evidenced using data on, e.g., changed perceptions or increased social capital). They do, however, also point to a number of gaps in the evidence base available regarding, for instance, the lack of specific cultural outcomes in key regeneration programmes and a lack of long-term monitoring. Indeed, Evans argues that there is a long-standing literature pointing to issues with evidence gathering in this field, despite 'growing demands for evidence-based policy evaluation' (2005, p. 960).

We thus see a position as the Creativity Agenda develops whereby the importance of evidence regarding the role of culture is continually noted, as too is the limited availability of appropriate evidence to date. Nevertheless, the idea of cultural activity achieving a range of 'instrumental' outcomes, including those specifically linked to some form of economic or social regeneration, gains increasing traction. As the Creativity Agenda continues to spread, evidence production continues apace and some argue that later attempts to substantiate the role of the arts and culture are an improvement on historic practice and may offer 'precisely the kind of evidence that had been lacking' previously (O'Brien 2014, p. 95). We can therefore consider if this later period of evidence gathering shows notably improved practice.

The Quest for Evidence Continues

Immediately following Evans and Shaw's comprehensive review of 2004, it seemed there was little cause to assume that the gaps identified in the evidence base regarding the role of culture were being addressed. Selwood was able to note by 2006 a 'common criticism that cultural rigorous policy research is scarce, and that evaluation is regarded as under-developed and is poorly documented' (2006, p. 45). This point was reinforced by Bailey's assessment of the lack of rigour in data collection regarding cultural practice (2006, p. 3) and by Gray's summation that the cultural sector remained unable to 'demonstrate how and why it is important at anything other than an anecdotal level', arguing that governments were committed to 'inappropriate forms of policy evaluation' in the sector (2006, p. 111). Belfiore concluded, however, that a lack of appropriate evidence was doing little to stem a 'growing trend towards instrumentality' in the sector at this point (2006, p. 239).

In 2007, the appointment of James Purnell as Secretary of State for Culture seemed to signal a potential shift in the dominant position regarding evidence and measurement in the cultural sector, with prominent statements made about the need to 'trust our artists and organisations' and to free 'cultural organisations from [...] burdensome targets' which can stifle creativity (McMaster 2008, p. 4). These declarations came in a DCMS report subtitled 'From Measurement to Judgement'. The predominant focus on measurement, however, did not halt at this point. Purnell held the Culture Secretary role for only seven months, and 'measurement' practices—and their critiques—subsequently showed no noticeable decline. In 2009, for example, DCMS, in partnership with the UK's Research Councils, produced a report on 'Capturing the Value of Culture, Media and Sport', which discussed the continuing operation of the 'Culture and Sport Evidence Programme' (CASE) (ESRC 2009). At this point in time, Belfiore questioned the curious persistence of evidence gathering practices specifically in light of comments by Purnell's predecessor Tessa Jowell on the need to 'keep proving' that engagement with culture can have beneficial outcomes:

> If it had been possible to demonstrate incontrovertibly a causal link between arts participation and educational attainment or crime reduction, then surely, there would be no pressing need to *keep proving it*. The problem is that, for all the evaluation and performance measurement requirements imposed on the sector, such incontrovertible evidence of impact simply is *not* there. (2009, p. 351, original emphasis)

Contemporaneously, Gray pointed to the lack of clear measurement criteria in consideration of the role of culture and regeneration (2009, p. 578).

This general position regarding a lack of appropriate evidence continued into the 2010s. At the opening of this decade, and referring to some of the key strands of the ever-rising Creativity Agenda, Markusen and Gadwa noted that 'amid the buzz on the creative city and cultural economy, knowledge about what works at various urban and regional scales is sorely lacking' (2010, p. 379). Similarly, Flew (2010, p. 87) argued that the general literature regarding the idea of 'creative cities' is often characterised by being light on evidence. Although 2010 saw the arrival of a new government in the UK, similar criticisms persisted. Lees and Melhuish, reflecting back on the recent Labour administration, and the positioning of the arts and culture as having a particular role to play in urban regeneration by dealing with 'social exclusion', noted that,

> throughout New Labour's three terms in office, little or no substantive evidence was gathered in support of this position, despite a proliferation of statements relating to the importance of evaluation and a number of initiatives to implement evaluation methods. (2015, p. 243)

They also point out that this dearth of evidence seemingly continued as the party in government changed, highlighting that a report on the value of engagement in culture and sport released after the end of Labour's tenure concluded that it 'cannot present any evidence for, or conclusions on, the long-term benefits relating to community cohesion, and that further work needs to be carried out in this area' (2015, p. 243).

As the 2010s continued, these positions were echoed in assessments using the increasingly prominent language of creativity. Richards, for instance, argued at this point that an 'absence of hard evidence has [...] stimulated criticism of creativity-based development strategies' (2011, p. 1243), and a report from 2013 found little 'hard' evidence demonstrating a role for arts in social inclusion (Hull 2013, p. 9). Despite this apparently intransigent lack of progress, quite substantial work attempting to consider the evidence base around the economic impact of culture emerged in 2014, but this too drew attention to the limited nature of available evidence. The 2014 'What Works Centre' report considering international practice regarding economic impact evaluation reports related to both sports and culture ranked 556 reports against the 'Maryland Scientific Methods' scale, which ranks methods of evaluation. This scale considers how clearly the role of any 'intervention' can be established from the evidence available, ranging from 'level 1' (no 'untreated' comparison group, no use of control variables in statistical analysis to adjust for differences between 'treated' and 'untreated' groups) to 'level 5' (explicit randomisation into treatment and control groups, such as Randomised Control Trials). Of all reports considered, 520 failed to meet the minimum 'level 3' threshold for review, and of the remaining 36 reports, only three related to culture. The general tenor of these reports was summarised thus:

> The paucity of evaluations on cultural projects is in part a result of the methodologies deployed in the studies evaluating them (often simply surveys of attendees, asking them about spend, motivation for visit etc.). In the absence of a suitable control group, studies focusing on tourist surveys alone, were not included in this review. (What Works Centre for Local Economic Growth 2014, p. 20)

This year also saw substantial work from Arts Council England, with the publication of a review of evidence on 'The Value of Arts and Culture to People and Society' based on research published after 2010. This review noted a lack of longitudinal or comparative studies, in addition to a lack of evidence in key areas such as the role for creative industries in innovation (2014, p. 4). In 2015, Belfiore argued that after 25 years of 'economic value discourse', making the case for cultural spending remained a difficult task (p. 102), and despite gains in other areas, a 2015 review of the social impacts of culture and sport found, for instance, a 'lack of substantial evidence on arts and social inclusion' (Taylor et al. 2015, p. 85) and characterised evidence of the impact of the arts on well-being as 'quite weak and subjective' (p. 76). Another recent review of this issue concluded that 'many evaluations of arts projects [related to health and wellbeing] have been less than rigorous'

(APPG 2017, p. 5). The 2016 Culture White Paper produced by the UK government argued that understanding around the impact of culture 'is strongest for economic development' but that 'for personal well-being, educational attainment, life chances and soft power, more work is needed to refine how we measure the specific impact that culture makes' (DCMS 2016, p. 58).

It thus seems fair to argue that there continues to be an emphasis on the need for more evidence, but that the evidence produced does not actually seem to substantially improve as time passes. It is important to consider, therefore, why this may be.

Considering Recent Evidence for 'Regeneration'

Given the consistent identification of a lack of robust evidence from a range of research practices, in 2014 a review was conducted of evidence gathered regarding the role of the arts and culture in the process of 'culture-led regeneration' in the period following Evans and Shaw's report (2006–2014) as part of the AHRC's 'Cultural Value' project. Material was gathered in relation to cultural policy interventions that were explicitly described as 'regenerative', or which belonged to a 'type' of intervention routinely described as 'regenerative', by searching academic sources and grey literature, and through consultation with the cultural sector. The review focussed mainly on data from the UK, but also drew on practice further afield, including significant European cultural regeneration programmes. In total, 151 relevant sources from the period 2006 to 2014, covering reports from cultural organisations, commissioned research, policymakers, local government, academics and media sources, were identified and analysed.

Firstly, it should be noted that the three key areas for evidence gathering noted by Evans and Shaw in 2004 of economic, physical and social regeneration were closely echoed in this period, albeit in a manner more closely aligned with the burgeoning Creativity Agenda. Detail on the specific methods found to be in use is available elsewhere (Campbell and Cox 2017), but the evidence gathered in this period was found to relate to three broad outcomes:

1. *Evidence of sector development in cultural and creative industries*
   Evidence was gathered based on the implicit assumption that cultural activity would stimulate creative industries or creative skills. This has clear links to both the 'creative industries' and 'creative class' positions, and the broader overlapping senses of creativity, outlined in Chapter 3. From such a position, any activity conceived as 'creative', including cultural activity, is useful in stimulating regeneration, even if at its most instrumental cultural activity only acts as a 'sideshow that in turn attracts the workers, which attracts the hi-tech investors' (Pratt 2008, p. 108).

2. *Evidence of increased public profile of, and levels of engagement with, cultural activity*
   Evidence was also gathered based on related, but slightly different, assumptions. These were that cultural activity could involve new, or enhanced, activities or use of infrastructure in a given location. These may lead to higher land value, improved resident experience, increased tourism, increased activity in wider supply chains and improved external profile. This second position, like the first, is closely associated with *economic* outcomes and the wider justifications which come to predominate in this period. Analyses of the economic 'impact' of tourism and related spending have proved consistently popular and proliferate particularly in media reports of the effects of cultural programmes (e.g. Cavendish 2008; BBC 2009; Gosling 2010; *The Economist* 2012; Brooks-Pollock 2013; Edwards et al. 2013), and not only here. Tourism is often specifically linked to particular *physical* infrastructural developments, via the so-called Bilbao effect (Plaza 2006; Plaza et al. 2009) of 'iconic' cultural centres but also via the association of cultural festivals with wider physical change. As well as simply considering the development of new cultural practice or buildings, though, it should be noted that some interventions seek to utilise the arts to render wider processes of physical regeneration more 'creative' in some way, in a manner analogous to the 'creative city' idea encountered in Chapter 3. The Commission for Architecture and the Built Environment (CABE 2008, pp. 3–4), for instance, refers to 'join[ing] forces with Arts & Business and Public Art South West [...] to inject creativity into

development' and to 'include artists in determining the future look and feel of our towns and cities' (p. 6). The Creativity Agenda is thus leveraged in these processes in many of its forms.

3. *Evidence of specifically social effects, such as social inclusion and skills development*

Finally, evidence was gathered in this period regarding the potential social effects of cultural activity, with the underlying assumptions seeming to be that cultural activity may provide opportunities to develop transferrable skills and to engage communities, contributing to wider social outcomes in ways that may ameliorate potential negative effects of regeneration programmes. This third position moves beyond the economic or at least links the economic with wider concerns. The particularly social impacts of cultural activity continue to be emphasised in evidence gathering, with cultural engagement being seen to have the potential to alleviate not just economic deprivation but also to transform a social, or perhaps even spiritual, poverty (O'Brien 2014, p. 41). Böhm and Land (2009, p. 77) date this increasing attention to the 'less tangible benefits' of cultural activity as a later development in the discourse, and this may account for the fact that the propositions made for potential social outcomes are amongst the least well defined covered in the review of evidence-gathering practices. Just as Evans and Shaw note in 2004 that gathering evidence of social regeneration is a 'new field' in which much literature can be characterised as 'advocacy and promotion' (p. 28) so, for instance, is it noted many years later that 'the evidence base on the 'social' impacts of cultural regeneration remains relatively thin' (Colomb 2011, p. 81).

Persistent Challenges

Given that evidence gathering can be seen to coalesce around a fairly clear set of desired outcomes over this period, and these are closely aligned to those for which evidence has been sought over a longer period, we must thus return to the question of why research persistently points to the lack of a well-established evidence base in these domains.

Firstly, it should be noted that the outcomes above are characterised as being based on 'implicit assumptions' in the research examined. This is due to the fact that clear propositions, logic models or theories of change are seldom stated explicitly in research in this field, and thus, it is often unclear what it is that the evidence being produced is expected to be evidence *of*, or why. As noted in Chapter 3, the potential lack of clarity in the Creativity Agenda raises challenges. If research begins from a position where the unity of creativity is taken as read, then it will be only logical to, for instance, expect cultural activity to result in the development of creative skills and for there to be no explicit statement, or testing, of this assumption. That said, it is not merely the lack of clarity around the propositions being tested that can be seen to cause problems for evidence gathering in this period. Evidence is also often drawn from less than ideal sources. There is a continued reliance, for instance, on proxy data from outside the cultural sector, or on research which establishes its case based on perception data from convenience samples. In many cases, the very existence of a project is posited as evidence of a successful outcome. More broadly, a number of persistent explanatory factors can be suggested to account for the steadfast nature of the critiques of evidence-gathering practice in this period.

Short-Term Data Will Not Establish Long-Term Outcomes

In an era in which policy must be 'evidence-based', and in which outcomes must be demonstrated as 'objectively' as possible, methods are often employed on behalf of those organising a cultural event to enable 'impact' to be demonstrated to funders and other stakeholders. This is usually a short-term necessity, and so, research evidence is most often generated alongside specific programmes or events and in close proximity to their operation. Once data has been generated, 'evidence' has done its job (for certain parties, at least). The goal of urban regeneration, however, must almost by definition occur (if it ever does) long after such schemes or events take place. There is thus a mismatch between the timescale of methods used and evidence sought.

Referring to a range of developments around new cultural venues over the course of a decade, Hyslop argues that 'in most cases it is too early to judge the success of the long-term impact of these projects on the economic and social development of their communities' (2012, p. 153, see also Barnardo's 2005, p. 16; CABE 2008, p. 5; Ela Palmer Heritage 2008, p. 30). In many cases, therefore, evidence is only available regarding an event or activity itself, and not on its wider effects. Ennis and Douglass pointedly state the necessity for longer-term study, and the production of longitudinal data, without which 'it may not be possible to determine conclusively whether culture-led regeneration, or indeed any regeneration, works' (2011, p. 2). Whilst there is much that is specific about regeneration programmes using culture, this deficit therefore applies much more broadly. Indeed, a report produced in this period for the Department of Communities and Local Government focussing on the economic value of all kinds of regeneration initiatives notes the paucity of evidence available (Tyler et al. 2010, p. 21).

Despite long-standing identification of this problem (Reeves 2002, p. 104; Evans and Shaw 2004, pp. 8, 57), it is notable that long-term study remains rare. In their review of the history of the European Capital of Culture programme, for instance, García and Cox find virtually no research into the long-term effects of the programme, and of the small amount of research which does exist, note that 'the quality and consistency of claims and evidence about medium to long-term effects varies considerably' (2013, p. 24). At the very least, we may expect studies hoping to provide evidence of change to seek to establish some form of baseline from which this change can be gauged. The 2013 Centre for Economics and Business Research report to Arts Council England and the National Museum Directors' Council finds, however, that this is often not the case:

> Many studies do not comprehensively evaluate the underlying state of an area before the arts and cultural investment or only report on the impact of the project for a short period after its completion. This poses problems for assessing the longer-term impacts that the arts and culture can have on a given geographic location. (CEBR 2013, p. 88)

This lack of long-term analysis is particularly problematic as short-term responses to cultural projects can be very different to long-term ones and potentially more optimistic. Sharp (2007, p. 286), for instance, discusses how enthusiasm around the potential impact of projects can initially be very high, but that this can also easily change dramatically in a relatively short period of time. Similarly, García and Cox (2013, p. 133) demonstrate that developments in physical infrastructure can be well used during a major cultural programme and that tourism levels can be boosted in the short term, but that both of these changes can prove unsustainable. These factors will remain unexamined or obscured in short-term studies. This is not to say that long-term study does not present difficulties (THRU 2013, pp. 10–13), not least as reference points in secondary data can fluctuate over time (Brennan 2010, p. 5; CEBR 2013, p. 113), but it can at least attempt to tackle these important issues. Such potential complexity is, for some stakeholders, 'helpfully' reduced by brief studies which focus largely on initial 'good news', and which may inappropriately inflate the role that culture plays in broader regeneration. Once this evidence of 'success' has been achieved, often there is no political impetus to consider effects over the longer term. Evans succinctly describes how this kind of practice will not enable us to adequately contextualise the size and nature of the role that cultural programmes may play in urban settings:

> The culture and regeneration story requires a historical analysis that also maps change and effects over a much longer time period, within which events form only a relatively small (financial and strategic) part. Investment in housing, retail, transport, education and local amenities are likely to have a more lasting legacy and impact. This will also be important in order to consider how culture might better contribute to the regeneration process, as opposed to simply being corralled into a "festival event" or "year". (2011, p. 6)

Limited Resources

One of the reasons for a lack of such longitudinal data is likely to be the expense of carrying out longitudinal research. It is clearly less onerous to carry out a single cross-sectional piece of research than to return to a research site year-on-year to track any potential changes. Many rightly note the complexity and cost of long-term assessment (e.g. Evans and Shaw 2004, p. 58; Ennis and Douglass 2011, p. 10), and this is likely to be beyond the capabilities of all but the very largest institutions (Ela Palmer Heritage 2008, p. 30). Evans and Shaw's conclusions from 2004 specifically regarding economic impact thus remain applicable:

> The level of primary survey research required to measure economic and distributive effects outside of the cultural project itself (and even here, distributive data is hard to capture) is felt to be prohibitive and hard to justify, unless motivated by a funding or other imperative – longitudinal studies of effects even more so. (2004, p. 21)

To adequately back up the claims made for culture takes financial resources which, increasingly, the cultural sector does not have (Lees and Melhuish 2015, p. 256). Besides limited financial resources, we can also consider how limitations in terms of other forms of resource influence evidence gathering practices. Generating evidence of regeneration is an inherently difficult task, but it is also only one task amongst many for those working in the cultural field, and for many cultural organisations this kind of activity is also likely to be significantly outside the skills and capacities of the governance and administration of the organisation. Hesmondhalgh et al. describe not only a proliferation of performance management indicators, auditing and monitoring over recent years, but also the fact that those in the cultural sector 'often lacked the skills and resources to provide the kind of evidence that was being required of them' (2015, p. 92). Newsinger and Green, for instance, point to the mismatch between the resources allocated to evaluation and the outcomes expected from these evaluations, and a general scepticism from those in the sector to standard evaluation techniques (2016, p. 388), and in a discussion of the deployment of statistical modelling in relation to the cultural realm, Oman and Taylor argue that such models may be 'impenetrable to many in the sector' (2018, p. 229).

The kinds of evidence sought regarding 'regeneration' can also often relate to outcomes that are not necessarily a fundamental part of core operational or charitable objectives. Whilst evidence which can be used for advocacy purposes may seem worth generating, evidence which cannot may seem to be more limited in value to many organisations. Given limited resources (e.g. O'Connor 2007, p. 44) and a range of competing pressures (Selwood 2006, p. 41), it is therefore perhaps unsurprising to see the persistent critiques of evidence-gathering practices discussed above. It may also be instructive to consider the point made by General Public Agency (2008, pp. 8–9) regarding the competing pressures which apply not just to cultural organisations, but to potential external partners in research:

> The evaluation methodology was predicated on involving local authority data collection officers in gathering the quantitative data. Despite extensive efforts it proved impossible to ensure the involvement of the officers in gathering data to demonstrate the role of culture within regeneration. If Arts Council England is to pursue an emphasis on 'hard evidence' it may wish to consider making funding conditional on the involvement of such officers.

The resources which evaluation can draw on to establish a firm case may, therefore, continue to be limited in a number of senses. Vickery (2007, p. 21) notes in the context of local authority practice how culture is a relatively low priority, and, whilst it is certainly true that many recent regeneration initiatives have found a role for arts and culture as part of wider investment programmes, one key continuity in recent practice is the somewhat marginal position of cultural activity in such programmes. In this period, initiatives which can be identified as positing a role for culture in processes of regeneration include: the Single Regeneration Budget, which helped, for instance, to fund public art (Gateshead Council 2006; Public Art Leicester 2005), community music projects (Dhamak Beats 2012), and artists' studios (ACAVA 2014); the European Regional Development Fund, which has invested in the renovation and construction of new cultural facilities (European Commission 2013), and business assistance for cultural enterprises (DCLG 2013); the New Deal for Communities, which, in certain areas, used arts and culture-related activities to attempt to tackle mental health inequalities (Blank et al. 2004); and the Housing Market Renewal scheme, which helped fund artists' studios (NFASP 2010), public art (Pendle Borough Council 2014), and artist-led participatory projects (Arts Council England 2009; Media and Arts Partnership 2008). Whilst such initiatives fund cultural projects and so propose that these may contribute in some way to wider regeneration goals, the peripheral position of this activity proves problematic in dealing with the persistent evidence gap outlined above, as there is typically little or no discussion of the role of culture in relation to overall findings regarding regeneration from these programmes (e.g. Audit Commission 2011; DCLG 2007, 2009, 2010; Leather et al. 2012). So long as culture remains a low priority in urban policy broadly speaking, we can therefore expect the evidence base available to reflect this. It should also be noted that, even when a programme's focus is entirely cultural, such as in the case of the European Capital of Culture, the scale of investment is often small in comparison with these wider regeneration programmes (Cox and O'Brien 2012, p. 97).

A Lack of Clarity on the Terms of Research

Even if resources were not a barrier to research, however, one of the major obstacles encountered in the review of practice in this period is a lack of clarity about what research is actually attempting to achieve. Often the starting point of research is to position cultural activity as a known benefit with known effects, already revealed by previous evaluation practice, which can thus be continued. If, though, cultural activity aims to promote 'creative industries', for instance, what is the mechanism by which this will occur? As noted, for some this question almost does not arise as all forms of creativity are seen as being inherently linked. For evidence gathering to be useful, however, questions such as these must be clearly addressed. Knell and Oakley (2007, p. 21) note on this particular example that whilst discussion of creative industries has become prominent, funding of arts activity has often carried on in much the same manner as it did prior to this prominence, with any linkages being assumed rather than made explicit. As is commonly noted in many areas of research, though, correlation does not imply causation, and simply monitoring what happens at the same time as a cultural event does not necessarily provide us with evidence for what this event itself has achieved. On this subject, specifically in relation to the recent years of the European Capital of Culture programme, García and Cox (2013, p. 142) point out a continued articulation of an assumed relationship between this programme and the development of creative industries, rather than any kind of clear planning to promote such a relationship. Again, when evaluating the achievements of cultural activity, a search for 'good news' rather than an attempt to establish solid evidence seems to characterise practice. Without the articulation of a mechanism by which culture plays a role, evidence gathering can involve a 'sweeping up' of any available information that can add weight to the argument for the beneficial role of culture, veering away from research and towards advocacy. For instance, a general residents' survey around a cultural intervention may furnish reports of higher perceptions of safety or greater feelings of self-confidence, but if most residents have no direct experience of the intervention, or this is not at least questioned, it may not be appropriate to attribute any improvement to the scheme under evaluation.

Nevertheless, a cultural programme's presence is often perceived as (and indeed could be) a 'catalyst' for wider transformation (García and Cox 2013, p. 132), but disambiguating the role for culture is often impossible in short-term research, and extremely difficult even in long-term research (THRU 2013). Whilst this problem with establishing clear terms of engagement is sometimes acknowledged by those producing evidence (e.g. Labadi 2008, pp. 59–60), this lack of clarity may leave us in a position where a role for culture is asserted (e.g. New Economy 2013, p. 27), suspected (THRU 2013, p. 259), or where research proves to be merely descriptive rather than analytical (Markusen and Gadwa 2010, p. 382). By contrast, where a relationship seems to be established in a more concrete fashion—for instance, between the concentration of cultural institutions and house prices—the direction and nature of this relationship are not necessarily clear (CEBR 2013, p. 113).

In considering this issue of clarity with regards to developments in physical infrastructure, Vickery notes that policy often assumes that cultural developments will have beneficial outcomes in forging civic identity, but asks 'what is civic identity in an age of cultural hetero-geneity and the dissolution of historical civic virtues and authority of tradition? Is it even needed?' (2007, pp. 73–74). Evidence can be offered on the number of landmark buildings, their cost or their eco-nomic impact, but if an improvement in civic identity is expected, such evidence does not really address the core question and may be used as a proxy for data which is not available and, even if it were, may not be relevant. Whilst questions around issues such as the nature of civic identity are not amenable to HM Treasury's 'Green Book' providing guidance on robust evaluation practices, its guidance indicating the need for a clear rationale for evaluation, which clarifies how benefits will be achieved and the mechanism by which beneficiaries will receive these (2003, pp. 54–55), would nevertheless be a useful starting point for research to consider, as this may establish a clearer understanding of the forces at play.

This deficit in clarity is also not a new development. Reviewing gen-eral practice around gathering evidence on the impact of the arts in 2002, for instance, Reeves noted 'a lack of clarity by arts organisations about the intended outcomes of arts interventions' (p. 39), and this can also be identified in much earlier periods (see Evans 2005, p. 2), as well as more recently. Without clarity on how it is culture is expected to con-tribute to regeneration, and by what means, most evidence produced will be of little relevance beyond its own specific context. Evans astutely tackles this issue:

> Whilst there is no shortage of "evidence", techniques and methods, how these relate – if at all – to the governance and regeneration regime, and where power over which and whose culture is "invited to the festival" resides, is not apparent or at least not part of the evaluation or impact study process. The extent to which this accumulating evidence on the wider effects of hosting and delivering such mega-events has and may be used in the future to inform future events and both cultural and regenera-tion strategies, is at best marginal. (2011, p. 13)

Nevertheless, such accumulation continues to occur. Whilst it could be argued that many of the most important effects that cultural activity can have are difficult, if not impossible, to measure, with the reception of individual activities potentially varying drastically from individual to individual, or even within a single individual over time, this does not mean that there is no room for improvement in practice. In a review of evaluations by English 'Regional Development Agencies' concerned with culture and regeneration, Ennis and Douglass find that whilst evidence which is related to economic outcomes, such as the number of 'safeguarded jobs', can be firmly established, other areas are left to 'qualitative judgment'. They continue, echoing the points above:

> These qualitative assessments are in some cases little more than hopeful statements, lacking the specific evidence that has long been needed. For example, countless evaluations point to improved perceptions of a neighbourhood, but do not demonstrate how this connects to the long-term goals of regeneration. Similarly, projects are said to improve confidence amongst residents, based on small surveys taken shortly after the completion of the project. Since evaluations are generally carried out shortly after completion, there are none showing the long-term impact that really matters most for regeneration. (2011, p. 8)

Labadi also notes that qualitative data on the impact of regeneration schemes can be tainted by 'optimism bias', referring to one study where,

> the six people who agreed to be interviewed and had overall positive opinion of the scheme were all deeply involved in the regeneration and therefore could not really have the necessary critical detachment. (2008, p. 107)

Again, for the reasons noted above, 'research' on regeneration impacts may veer too close to advocacy for cultural organisations for it to give an accurate picture of what has been achieved, seeking primarily to *demonstrate* positive impact rather than ascertain *whether* it exists (e.g. General Public Agency 2008, p. 11; DC Research 2011, p. 2; LARC 2011, p. 9). There are many ways in which such practice could theoretically be changed, but there is limited evidence that any such changes have occurred in recent years. In 2002 (p. 104), for instance, Reeves noted the lack of comparative studies, or the use of control groups to establish the effects of cultural activity. In examining more recent practice, no evidence of such studies was located, and broader problems with the evidence base on these issues have been noted (Belfiore 2006; What Works Centre for Local Economic Growth 2014). O'Brien notes of methods to assess the impacts of cultural engagement more broadly that 'there has been little progress over the past decade of evaluation and research' (2014, p. 47), and Lees and Melhuish (2015, p. 243) note repeated difficulties with evaluating arts projects linked to goals of social regeneration.

Selwood (2006, pp. 50–51) argues that the kind of evaluation that seems to be attempted in much of the research considered above ideally requires policymakers and funders 'to explain how, and to demonstrate that, individuals' transformational experiences can be, and indeed are, transferred from the individual to society'. Acknowledging that this does not happen in practice, she continues in a manner which mirrors much of the discussion above:

> That doesn't obviate the need for certain improvements: the desirability of rationalising DCMS and other agencies' data collections; of distinguishing between advocacy and research; of investing in long-term evaluation, rather than short-term assessments which are determined by funding rounds; of initiating a rather more considered and honest discussion about the 'transformatory' qualities of the arts. In short, to cut through the rhetoric would benefit the politics and the pragmatics of the sector immeasurably.

Part of such a pragmatism may entail what Vickery terms 'an acknowledgement of the non-visible and unquantifiable elements of experience' (2007, p. 16), and also perhaps an acknowledgement that the arts and culture are, as Gray (drawing on Gallie 1956) puts it, 'essentially contested concepts' (2008, p. 212). As predominant methods of evaluation seek rather to attempt to prove their case 'objectively' in line with the ideological developments traced in Chapter 2, this may therefore lead to an emphasis on identifying results in a single realm—the economic.

An Over-Emphasis on the Economic

Maria Miller, UK Culture Secretary from 2012 to 2014, argued that despite the fact that she had 'come in for a lot of stick for demanding that the arts promote their economic value', this was an appropriate position as economic measures constitute 'hard facts that make sense to everyone' (Miller 2013). This may certainly seem to be the case. Indeed, whilst non-economic impacts may be poorly established due to the difficulties outlined above, they may also be poorly established due to a lack of political interest in such matters. The goals of those commissioning and funding cultural activity may therefore not necessarily match those of cultural institutions or indeed those of the wider public (García 2005, p. 846; Holden 2007, p. 32; Shin and Stevens 2013, p. 644). In their discussion of the specific use of heritage-related programmes to achieve regeneration goals, for instance, Ela Palmer Heritage note a lack of evidence relating to social impact for these reasons:

> The lack of requirement for social impact evaluation has stemmed from a focus on the economic impacts of regeneration, mainly concentrated on market value, job creation and the desirability of the area for business. (2008, p. 30)

Once economic matters are dealt with, social impacts are seemingly either taken for granted, or expected to naturally 'trickle-down'. As with many of the propositions above, however, the mechanisms by which this would occur are unclear and so are questionable. Indeed, some research specifically argues that 'cultural investments do not trickle down to deprived and marginalised populations without strong, proactive forms of political and public intervention at various scales' (Colomb 2011, p. 77, see also Evans and Shaw 2004, p. 58). Justified scepticism over 'trickle-down' effects also exists with respect to broader regeneration programmes (Jones and Evans 2008, pp. 72–73).

Echoing the patterns identified above, even if data relating to the economic impact of specific cultural interventions is taken on its own terms, these impacts can be difficult to disentangle from the impacts of other investments and regeneration programmes (Cox and O'Brien 2012). Perhaps even more problematic, as O'Brien (2014, p. 12) points out, is that 'our choice of economic valuation methods may then lead us to actually miss the importance of what it is we are attempting to value'. That said, the prevailing circumstances resulting in a reliance on economic valuation methods continue to intensify. This does not mean that there is not room for improvement in the methods applied in this area, however. In her earlier review of methods used in this field, Reeves noted a reliance on economic indicators, but also the following problems:

— A reliance on narrow economic values and economic indicators considered inadequate for measuring 'difficult-to-quantify' outcomes
— failure to take account of displacement and leakage of spending from the local economy
— failure to distinguish between distributional effects and aggregate income effects of arts spending (2002, p. 46).

Similar criticisms can be identified long before this list of Reeves' (e.g. Hughes 1989, p. 38) and continue to characterise the research field. In considering a wide range of research relating to culture and creativity, in 2010 Markusen and Gadwa argue that many studies,

> are plagued with unwarranted assumptions and inference problems. These include: 1) not adequately demonstrating that the arts are an export base industry; 2) treating all spending as new spending, as opposed to factoring out expenditures that would otherwise have been made elsewhere in the local economy; 3) not acknowledging that non-profit arts expenditures are directly subsidized by the public sector through both capital and operations support; and, 4) failing to count the foregone tax revenues that non-profit status confers. (2010, pp. 380–381)

Similar points were found in consideration of specific studies reviewed in this period (e.g. Labadi 2008, pp. 28–29). Guidance on matters such as these has been offered, such as English Partnerships 'Additionality Guide' (2008), and guidance is also available in the UK government's 'Green Book' on evaluation regarding leakage, deadweight and displacement (HM Treasury 2003, p. 53), but importantly with the following caveat:

In some cases, the best source of information for assessing additionality may be from those who clearly have an interest in the outcome of the decision. In these circumstances, the information and forecasts should be confirmed by an independent source.

In cases relating to the cultural field in this period (e.g. GHK 2009, p. 28), it is often difficult to ascertain whether this has been attempted, but it seems rather that 'traditional' methods persist which do not heed such advice. Even studies which do take these issues into consideration somewhat may leave questions unanswered. For instance, although English Partnerships (2008, p. 14) caution against assuming zero deadweight when assessing interventions, this assumption can be seen to occur in practice (e.g. Roger Tym and Partners 2011, p. 27). More often, though, it seems issues such as these are simply not considered at all in extant research (CASE 2011, p. 63). As noted above, the evidence review by the 'What Works Centre' (2014) does not include any studies attributing economic impact to cultural interventions as a result of visitor numbers, on the basis that the available studies were insufficiently robust, particularly with regards to identifying the net benefits of such interventions. The lack of consideration of many of these issues can perhaps be accounted for at least in part by the points above regarding limited resources and conflicting priorities for organisations producing such research. These factors may also account for criticisms made of such studies regarding small sample sizes or a lack of primary research, leading some economic impact figures to be characterised as no more than 'wild guesses' (Labadi 2008, p. 34).

What should also be noted, however, is that even if such factors were considered there is also robust criticism of economic impact studies per se. Rushton (2015) argues that 'there are no insights to be gained, no policy implications' from such studies, which are 'expensive to produce, useless and forgotten as research'. Little, therefore, seems to have changed since Madden considered these techniques in detail in 2001 and found that, despite their proliferation, 'nearly every economist who reviews 'economic' impact studies of the arts expresses concern over the technological and practical limitations of the methodologies' (2001, p. 165). These concerns reflect the 'failures' noted above, but also more conceptual issues—namely that economic impact studies 'provide no argument for government funding' (p. 161) and, indeed, are not designed to serve such a purpose; they cannot indicate whether a sector 'is important or not important' (p. 165), and they often 'overstate the net financial impact on the local economy' (p. 168).

When it comes to the matter of what evidence can be used to make the case specifically for the role of *cultural* activity, the following point of Madden's is especially instructive:

> By their very nature, 'economic' impact studies are poor at accounting for intangibles. And it is worth pointing out that governments are prone to put intangible considerations before financial considerations. For example, governments often intervene to depress the drugs, prostitution and pornography industries despite their sometimes substantial financial flow-on effects. (2001, p. 1170)

To echo the points above, however, Madden concludes that despite being inappropriate in many ways for the uses to which they are put, economic impact studies of cultural activity 'can be seen as a perfectly rational response to political demand' (p. 174). To *understand* their usage is surely useful, but does not ameliorate the problems they present. Crompton (2006 cited in CASE 2011, p. 79) is instructive here, and in other areas of impact measurement, in arguing that 'most economic impact studies are commissioned to legitimize a political position rather than search for economic truth'. As with a range of methods, we may not be led to a more useful evidence base, but achieving such an evidence base may not be the dominant goal of evaluation practice. Bakhshi et al.'s later conclusions on the proliferation of such studies are helpful in this context:

> Funders in the UK's arts sector have been dazzled by the blizzard of economic impact studies, which use no consistent methodology and are of varying quality of execution. The poorest quality examples have dragged down how the better-executed ones are perceived and, in a variant of the Prisoners' Dilemma, organisations have felt obliged to commission economic impact studies because others have done so [...] Prisoners'

> Dilemmas can only be resolved by decisive leadership, which has to date been lacking. The dearth of rigorous economic valuation studies in the cultural area has left the arts open to judgments expressed in crude instrumental terms, of a kind that Keynes would have abhorred. (2013, p. 72)

Given their reduction of outcomes to brief figures regarding 'impact', such studies are also particularly susceptible to the generation of myths or legends (common in many areas of research, see Rekdal 2014), whereby a piece of data, often a figure or limited set of figures, becomes a 'known' truth which is then repeated in multiple sources, free of contextual information, and thus becomes a desired point of replication for future studies. For instance, as a very brief illustration of the potential disconnect between evidence and its provenance, Arts Council England (2014, p. 19) note the 'estimated £10 million' contribution to the local economy of the Hepworth Wakefield gallery but give limited contextual information on the derivation of this figure, which is sourced directly from a 2013 Local Government Association report. This second report also gives limited information on how this figure was derived (LGA 2013, p. 6), and no further reference to enable the source of this information to be followed up. Further, investigation, however, reveals to the curious that this figure seems to have been sourced from the gallery's annual report (Hepworth Wakefield 2012, p. 80), which notes that the figure is based on '511,781 visitors' spending 'an average of £21' each in the local area during their visit. This headline figure of '£10 million', and other similar figures, are thus easily separated from context and can proliferate in a form which is not directly comprehensible, remaining subject to critiques such as those above.

The Distinction Between Economic, Cultural and Social Outcomes

Whilst economic impact analysis can be problematic, what is not under question is *whether* cultural activity has a wider economic impact, but rather how this can best be understood. That said, if evidence is increasingly focussed *only* on the economic, García sounds a warning on the use of economic indicators such as tourism levels as an indicator of the success of cultural activity. If attracting tourism is seen to be the main objective of cultural programmes, then a case could be made to instead invest in sports competitions or corporate events that could also bring in a significant number of high-spending visitors (2005, p. 863). Similarly, if the expectation that cultural provision may transform the *image* of a location is primarily valued for eventual economic outcomes related to increased tourism, Liu notes that marketing spend for cultural programmes, and city visits show only limited correlation and that:

> Image generation in itself does not ensure tourism inflow. In many cases, in fact, if the event is not sustained or followed-up by strategic marketing initiatives or valid investments, no significant medium- to long-term changes to local place image will stem even from a well-executed event. (2014, p. 506)

More broadly, in a reconsideration of the 'Bilbao effect' referred to above, Plaza et al. question the absence of a consideration of the cultural effects of new cultural infrastructure in the urban environment. Despite great attention being paid to the change in tourism levels and city image, 'nothing or very little has been said about the *artistic* effects of the [Guggenheim Museum Bilbao]' (2009, p. 1712, emphasis added). To return to the idea of 'instrumentalism' considered previously, as Vickery notes, in policy circles it is the 'intrinsic' benefit of cultural activity that is most likely to be neglected:

> There is an empirical case to be made for culture in the way it can attract more visitors and make a place look more interesting, but there's no conceptual 'driver' in the field of public policy asserting a strong argument for culture per se. (2007, p. 67)

That said, some arguments in this period align the specifically economic with broader social outcomes, emphasising the 'indivisible' model of creativity seen to characterise the Creativity Agenda. A 2009 DCMS report, for instance, argues that:

The creative industries are a significant source of employment and national wealth creation, as well as almost uniquely delivering cultural and social benefits. (DCMS and BIS 2009, p. 106)

The economic, social and cultural are thus increasingly presented as somehow fused (Stevenson 2004, p. 127). Connolly notes how in the period of the Creativity Agenda, cultural policy concerns move away from 'social justice' towards 'social inclusion'. This inclusion can be fostered by increased cultural engagement, and the ultimate evidence of inclusion is 'engagement with the economy' (Connolly 2013, p. 168, see also Warren and Jones 2015, p. 1741). Similarly, Stevenson (2004) notes how engagement with urban public space 'animated' by cultural activity is seen as a proxy for engagement with the public sphere and civic society more broadly.

As noted above, however, the lack of evidence on more social outcomes may also be accounted for by the fact that these are more difficult to evidence. For instance, Ela Palmer Heritage (2008, p. 7) state that:

There is little quantitative evaluation of the benefits of regeneration on social capital. This may be due to the difficulty of measuring the experience of a whole community. Therefore, the most successful evaluation of this type has been of participant numbers in smaller regeneration projects, for instance the level of local voluntary activity or civic action.

Whilst numbers of participants can be established relatively easily, establishing the social outcomes of such participation poses a greater challenge (Newsinger and Green 2016). As with the issue of economic impact, this also raises the broader issue of the specific value of cultural interventions. Looking at cultural policy more broadly, Gray points at the potential problem of evaluating such policy in a manner which 'would have no bearing at all on whether the policies involved actually are cultural policies or whether they are social inclusion policies manqué' and also argues that such social outcomes 'are often, by their nature, actually non-assessable in any straightforward, conventional, sense' (2006, p. 105). Also at this broader level, Oakley et al. raise the following warning regarding the assumption that cultural participation or volunteering can resolve social problems:

There appear to be well-being benefits from cultural participation, but they remain captured by those healthy, happy, and educated enough to participate in them in the first place. More disturbingly, research on activities such as volunteering, which are correlated with well-being benefits, seems to suggest that it is easier to improve the well-being of people who have relatively high levels of well-being to start with. (2013, p. 23)

Round and Round in Circles?

In the case of evidence for culture-led urban regeneration, we can thus see the persistence in recent years of the production of evidence in ways which continue to demonstrate the problems identified in the field historically. The limitations of evidence produced by methods utilised in the 1990s found by Reeves (2002, p. 102), and later echoed by Evans and Shaw (2004) and Vickery (2007), clearly persist in the evidence produced in more recent years. Indeed, near-identical critiques are consistently made regarding, for example the prevalence of ad hoc evaluations which cannot be drawn together to build a substantial evidence base (Ennis and Douglass 2011, p. 10), and evaluation which veers more towards advocacy and which thus cannot entertain the possibility of negative impacts (Belfiore 2006, p. 32). Whilst these findings are not brand new, then, given the manner in which the Creativity Agenda persists it is important to establish the continuation of these key patterns. As the underlying agenda shaping evidence gathering persists, so too do the kinds of evidence produced. Indeed, despite continued critique of the evidence base, it can be argued that the fact that evidence gathering proceeds on these same lines helps to entrench a certain position regarding what evidence 'should' be available, and which questions are most appropriate to ask. As noted above, the conclusion drawn from this evidence is more likely to be that insufficient evidence has yet to be gathered to convincingly demonstrate, for example, the role of cultural activity in promoting creative industry development and broader innovation, rather than that such evidence is not available, or that research would be better focussed on other topics. As such, this can usefully be considered in light of Law and Urry's theories on the role of methods in 'enacting the social' (2004). The role of culture is 'enacted' in certain ways by the methods in use, and the fact that these findings are not conclusive is secondary to the fact that they enable certain framings regarding what the value of culture and creativity *ought* to be to persist, at the expense of other framings.

To seek to create certain forms of evidence is thus to accept certain positions. Regardless of how convincing the evidence base produced may be, it can still have real effects. Oakley argues, for instance, that research which seeks to provide evidence of beneficial outcomes for the creative industries from cultural practice may help to make the case for funding cultural activity, but does so 'at the cost of collapsing several, carefully constructed arguments for public cultural funding into essentially one: it's good for the economy' (2009, p. 410). The methods in use help to substantiate this position and to resist others, even if the precise nature of the link between economic growth and such industries is open to question (see Hesmondhalgh 2007, p. 141 and Chapter 7). These methods thus help to constitute an object of study and a field of practice which, having been well established in the early 2000s and found to persist in the early 2010s, is likely to continue for the foreseeable future, and perhaps intensify in its drive towards quantification. Not surprisingly, given the ultimate goal of producing valuable and 'objective' evidence, there seems to be increasing enthusiasm (e.g. Markusen and Gadwa 2010, p. 382; Arts Council England 2014, p. 6) for the use of statistical analysis of secondary data to ameliorate some of the problems with evidence discussed above, perhaps inspired by recent enthusiasm for the concept of 'big data'. There is good reason to exercise caution here. The 2014 Arts Council review of evidence of the value of culture (p. 6) points to 'promising work using [...] logistic regression techniques', but the work referred to actually enables us to conclude relatively little from its statistical findings. Before methods move further in this direction, it may be wise to note Gorard's warning on the use of statistical analysis more broadly:

> The danger of spurious findings is a general one, and cannot be overcome by using alternative forms of regression [...] In fact, more complex

methods can make the situation worse [...] Complex statistical methods cannot be used post hoc to overcome design problems or deficiencies in datasets. (2006, pp. 82–83)

This issue also raises the question of what can realistically be known with available secondary data. Whilst utilising large secondary data sets can deal with some of the challenges for primary data gathering outlined above, the CASE report into this very issue (2011) concluded that currently available secondary data and related methods were primarily helpful when considering business- and property-related data (p. 71) and that current approaches often still do not effectively consider issues of economic displacement (p. 4), appropriate comparators (p. 17), or direct attribution to specific interventions (p. 80). When data is available to deploy such methods, which is rarely, only relatively large interventions can be adequately assessed. As such, this does not seem like a trajectory for research that will necessarily avoid the difficulties noted above.

In addition, given the conditions outlined above, it seems unlikely that broader factors constraining the production of robust evidence on culture's role in regeneration will disappear. What is perhaps more pressing is whether the very idea of culture-led regeneration is one which has now reached its peak (Evans 2011, p. 15; Lees and Melhuish 2015, p. 243). Even if no longer in the ascendant, however, the importance of establishing a robust evidence base around these issues continues to be prominently asserted, and arguments around culture's regenerative potential remain familiar both at a national level in England...:

There are five key ways that arts and culture can boost local economies: attracting visitors; creating jobs and developing skills; attracting and retaining businesses revitalising places; and developing talent [...] There is strong evidence that participation in the arts can contribute to community cohesion, reduce social exclusion and isolation, and/or make communities feel safer and stronger. (Arts Council England 2014, pp. 7–8)

...and at an international level, in assertions such as this:

Culture-based initiatives and industries have multiple roles to play in local and regional development, traditionally raising the attractiveness of regions, ensuring the socio-economic inclusion and development of rural and isolated areas, but also allowing for an integrated sustainable urban regeneration. (European Parliament 2016, p. 8)

We can thus see that both the arguments made around the value of culture and the critiques made of these arguments seem to have an impressive stability. Arts Council England's review of evidence gathering since 2010 finds that 'most of the studies reviewed cannot establish causality between arts and culture and the wider societal impacts' (2014, p. 8) and again highlights the need for longitudinal study. Nevertheless, such a document continues some of the circular reasoning which partially accounts for the lack of progress highlighted above. After stating that no causal relationship has been established between cultural activity and broader social impact, we find this statement:

We know that arts and culture play an important role in promoting social and economic goals through local regeneration, attracting tourists, the development of talent and innovation, improving health and wellbeing, and delivering essential services. (p. 11)

The Creativity Agenda continues even as it is being critiqued: we cannot establish the broader causalities suggested by policy rhetoric, but 'we know' that culture plays a role that it develops innovation, promotes regeneration, improves the economy and so on. Given the precursors to these positions considered in Chapter 2, it is clear that many have felt they 'know' such things for quite some time, but it is clear that this knowledge is not the result of the accumulation of a range of convincing evidence. Indeed, given the limitations outlined above, even if such evidence could be gathered, current conditions work against this. It is, though, unclear what role 'better', more fine-grained and/or longitudinal data could play in policy development if it arrived, the need to promote the Creativity Agenda being something that ultimately seems to be 'known' regardless.

Conclusion

On a basic sociological level, Schutz (1960, p. 214) argues that 'human activities are only made understandable by showing their in-order-to or because motives'. In considering how the case is made for the regenerative powers of culture and the arts, then, it could be argued that evidence is gathered in similar ways over time, despite the persistent challenges noted above, *in order to* support the narrative around the role culture can play in urban settings, *because* the generation of evidence is presented as being necessary. As noted above, a lack of resources means the research evidence ideally 'required' of the cultural sector can often not be gathered and so research follows previously established patterns, aligned with the increasing primacy of economic value traced in previous chapters. As such, there is an ironic *lack* of creativity in evidence-gathering practices over this period. Given the relatively weak role of cultural policy, and the limited resources available for evidence gathering, we can consider the broader structuring role of more intangible factors stated in Evans' persistent take on the field:

> Major culture-led regeneration schemes are not wholly grounded or rational-decision-based. (2005, p. 960)

> Host city decisions lack 'normal' rationality and are overridden by geopolitical and individual (commercial, politician, 'personality') imperatives and ultimately acts of blind faith, where contrary evidence is dismissed or offset by the larger gains at stake, particularly property, prestige and pride. (2011, p. 14)

Short-term projects, convenience samples and a focus on secondary data are understandable in this context, but will not bring about the robust longitudinal data long argued for, which may in any case be irrelevant if faith and prestige are the greater considerations in decision-making. Even if this decision-making process did aim to rest on a sober consideration of the evidence available, we can also point to the lack of 'institutional memory' in this field, and the disinclination to 'evaluate evaluation':

Relevant stakeholders do not have the inclination, the time, or the opportunity to assess the research they have commissioned or used, be it as an intellectual resource or a campaigning tool; there is no resource to reproduce evaluations and few researchers can identify their organisation's commissioned research over a long period. These absences enable research for advocacy, which is branded as legitimate, to become some of the major resources (and major uses of resources) of the cultural sector. (Oman and Taylor 2018, p. 239)

Given the persistent need for evidence to 'prove' the case for policy intervention, therefore, we are thus left in a position where evidence gathering is sometimes akin to a simulacrum of research, with questions unclear, premises unstated and little sense that an extant body of findings is known or can be built upon (Schuster 1996, p. 262). Without clear propositions to test, this situation is likely to persist, both in terms of the prevalence of certain evidence-gathering tactics and of their critique. More robust findings become increasingly unlikely in the context of a 'fast policy' environment (Peck 2002), in which 'rapid results', and positive results at that, are required (Van Heur 2010, p. 190). As such, it is likely that the continually growing evidence base will continue to be mostly unnecessary for those already convinced of the case for culture, and unlikely to persuade those who are not.

References

ACAVA. (2014). *Regeneration archive*. Retrieved from http://www.acava.org/regeneration/regeneration-archive.

APPG. (2017). *Creative health: The arts for health and wellbeing*. Retrieved from http://www.artshealthandwellbeing.org.uk/appg-inquiry/Publications/Creative_Health_Inquiry_Report_2017_-_Second_Edition.pdf.

Arts Council England. (2009). *The North West Housing Market Renewal arts partnership*. Retrieved from http://www.artscouncil.org.uk/media/uploads/publications/NW-Housing-Market-Renewal.pdf.

Arts Council England. (2014). *The value of arts and culture to people and society: An evidence review*. Manchester: Arts Council England.

Arts Council Northern Ireland. (2014). *Ambitions for the arts: A five year strategic plan for the arts in Northern Ireland 2013–2018*. Belfast: Arts Council Northern Ireland.

Audit Commission. (1991). *Local authorities, entertainment and the arts.* London: Her Majesty's Stationery Office.

Audit Commission. (2011). *Housing Market Renewal: Housing, programme review.* Retrieved from http://archive.audit-commission.gov.uk/auditcommission/SiteCollectionDocuments/Downloads/201103HMRprogrammereview.pdf.

Bailey, C. (2006). *Cultural values and culture led regeneration: The case of Newcastle-Gateshead.* Retrieved from http://www.fokus.or.at/fileadmin/fokus/user/downloads/acei_paper/Bailey.doc.

Bakhshi, H., Hargreaves, I., & Mateos Garcia, J. (2013). *A manifesto for the creative economy.* London: Nesta.

Barnardo's. (2005). *Art of regeneration: Evaluating the impact of the arts in a disadvantaged community.* Retrieved from http://www.dmss.co.uk/wp-content/uploads/2013/06/art_of_regeneration_report.pdf.

BBC. (2009). *City gears up for culture finale.* Retrieved from http://news.bbc.co.uk/1/hi/england/merseyside/7820243.stm.

Belfiore, E. (2006). The unacknowledged legacy: Plato, the *Republic* and cultural policy. *International Journal of Cultural Policy, 12*(2), 229–244.

Belfiore, E. (2009). On bullshit in cultural policy practice and research: Notes from the British case. *International Journal of Cultural Policy, 15*(3), 343–359.

Belfiore, E. (2015). 'Impact', 'value' and 'bad economics': Making sense of the problem of value in the arts and humanities. *Arts & Humanities in Higher Education, 14*(1), 95–110.

Blank, L., Ellis, L., Goyder, E., & Peters, J. (2004). *Tackling inequalities in mental health: The experience of new deal for communities.* Retrieved from http://extra.shu.ac.uk/ndc/downloads/reports/RR34.pdf.

Böhm, S., & Land, C. (2009). No measure for culture? Value in the new economy. *Capital & Class, 33*(1), 75–98.

Brennan, D. (2010). *A better place to live: 10 years of the new deal in Radford and Hyson Green.* Nottingham: Castle Cavendish Foundation.

Brooks-Pollock, T. (2013, October 12). Manchester International Festival created hundreds of new jobs in £38 m boost for city, report says. *Manchester Evening News.* Retrieved from https://www.manchestereveningnews.co.uk/news/greater-manchester-news/manchester-international-festival-created-hundreds-6173999.

CABE. (2008). *Artists & places: Engaging creative minds in regeneration.* Retrieved from http://www.liminal.org.uk/uploads/9/warwick_bar_masterplan_Artist_and_Places_2008-pdf.

Campbell, P., & Cox, T. (2017). 'Regeneration' in Britain: Measuring the outcomes of cultural activity in the 21st century. In V. Durrer, T. Miller, & D. O'Brien (Eds.), *The Routledge handbook of global cultural policy* (pp. 538–557). London: Routledge.

CASE. (2011). *The art of the possible—Using secondary data to detect social and economic impacts from investments in culture and sport: A feasibility study.* Retrieved from https://www.gov.uk/government/uploads/system/uploads/attachment_data/file/77608/CASE_The_Art_of_the_possible_2.pdf.

Cavendish, N. (2008). *Culture and money.* Retrieved from http://www.newstatesman.com/theatre/2008/06/festival-lift-economic/.

CEBR. (2013). *The contribution of the arts and culture to the national economy.* London: Centre for Economics and Business Research Ltd.

Colomb, C. (2011). Culture *in* the city, culture *for* the city? The political construction of the trickle-down in cultural regeneration strategies in Roubaix, France. *Town Planning Review, 81*(1), 77–98.

Comedia. (2004). *Culture and regeneration: An evaluation of the evidence.* Nottingham: Comedia.

Connolly, M. G. (2013). The 'Liverpool model(s)': Cultural planning, Liverpool and Capital of Culture 2008. *International Journal of Cultural Policy, 19*(2), 162–181.

Conservative and Unionist Party. (2017). *Manifesto 2017.* Retrieved from https://www.conservatives.com/manifesto.

Cox, T., & O'Brien, D. (2012). The "Scouse Wedding" and other myths and legends: Reflections on the evolution of a "Liverpool model" for culture-led regeneration. *Cultural Trends, 21*(2), 93–101.

DCLG. (2007). *The Single Regeneration Budget: Final evaluation.* Retrieved from http://www.landecon.cam.ac.uk/pdf-files/cv-etc/pete-tyler/SRB_RESEARCHSUMMARY_2007.pdf.

DCLG. (2009). *National evaluation of Housing Market Renewal Pathfinders 2005–2007.* Retrieved from webarchive.nationalarchives.gov.uk/201209191 32719/http:/www.communities.gov.uk/documents/housing/pdf/1362833.pdf.

DCLG. (2010). *The new deal for communities experience: A final assessment.* Retrieved from http://extra.shu.ac.uk/ndc/downloads/general/A%20 final%20assessment.pdf.

DCLG. (2013). *Investing in your future: Case study booklet—East Midlands European Regional Development Fund programme, 2007–2013.* Retrieved from https://www.gov.uk/government/uploads/system/uploads/attachment_data/file/147821/East_Midlands_ERDF_Case_Study_Booklet_Edition_1.pdf.

DCMS. (2004). *Culture at the heart of regeneration*. London: DCMS.

DCMS. (2016). *The culture white paper*. London: DCMS.

DCMS & BIS. (2009). *Digital Britain*. Norwich: The Stationery Office.

DC Research. (2011). *Economic value and impact of Yorkshire Sculpture Park*. Retrieved from http://www.ysp.co.uk/media/editor/file/YSP%20 Economic%20Impact%20Final%20Report%20Web%20251011%20CF. pdf.

Dhamak Beats. (2012). *About Dhamak*. Retrieved from http://dhamak.barefoot-hosting.com/wordpress/?page_id=11.

Edwards, A., Crossley, C., & Brooke, C. (2013, November 20). City of culture? It's a hull of a thought! £184 million boost for the area once derided as a dump. *Daily Mail*. Retrieved from http://www.dailymail.co.uk/ news/article-2510411/City-culture-Its-Hull-thought–184million-boost-area-derided-dump.html.

Ela Palmer Heritage. (2008). *The social impacts of heritage-led regeneration*. London: Ela Palmer Heritage.

English Partnerships. (2008). *Additionality guide: A standard approach to assessing the additional impact of interventions*. Retrieved from https://www.gov. uk/government/uploads/system/uploads/attachment_data/file/191511/ Additionality_Guide_0.pdf.

Ennis, N., & Douglass, G. (2011). *Culture and regeneration—What evidence is there of a link and how can it be measured?* London: GLA.

ESRC. (2009). *Not only…but also: Capturing the value of culture, media and sport*. Swindon: ESRC.

European Commission. (2013). *Housing investments supported by the European Regional Development Fund 2007–2013: Housing in sustainable urban regeneration*. Retrieved from http://ec.europa.eu/regional_policy/sources/docgener/studies/pdf/housing/2013_housing_study.pdf.

European Parliament. (2016). *FEFF report on a coherent EU policy for cultural and creative industries*. Retrieved from FEFF http://www.europarl. europa.eu/sides/getDoc.do?pubRef=-//EP//NONSGML+REPORT+ A8-2016-0357+0+DOC+PDF+V0//EN.

Evans, G. (2003). Hard-branding the cultural city—From Prado to Prada. *International Journal of Urban and Regional Research, 27*(2), 417–440.

Evans, G. (2005). Measure for measure: Evaluating the evidence of culture's contribution to regeneration. *Urban Studies, 42*(5–6), 959–983.

Evans, G. (2011). Cities of culture and the regeneration game. *London Journal of Tourism, Sport and Creative Industries, 5*(6), 5–18.

Evans, G., & Shaw, P. (2004). *The contribution of culture to regeneration in the UK: A review of evidence*. London: DCMS.

Flew, T. (2010). Toward a cultural economic geography of creative industries and urban development: Introduction to the special issue on creative industries and urban development. *The Information Society, 26*(2), 85–91.

Gallie, W. B. (1956). Art as an essentially contested concept. *The Philosophical Quarterly, 6*(23), 97–114.

García, B. (2004). Cultural policy and urban regeneration in Western European cities: Lessons from experience, prospects for the future. *Local Economy, 19*(4), 312–326.

García, B. (2005). Deconstructing the city of culture: The long-term cultural legacies of Glasgow 1990. *Urban Studies, 42*(5–6), 841–868.

García, B., & Cox, T. (2013). *European Capitals of Culture: Success strategies and long-term effects*. Retrieved from http://www.europarl.europa.eu/RegData/etudes/etudes/join/2013/513985/IPOL-CULT_ET%282013%29513985_EN.pdf.

Gateshead Council. (2006). *The angel of the North*. Retrieved from http://www.gateshead.gov.uk/DocumentLibrary/Leisure/Angel/Angel%20Pack%20large.doc.

General Public Agency. (2008). *Art at the centre phase II—Final evaluation report 2005–2008*. London: General Public Agency.

GHK. (2009). *Economic impact of HLF projects, volume 1—Main report*. Retrieved from http://www.hlf.org.uk/aboutus/howwework/Documents/Economic_impact_HFprojects2009_Finalreport.pdf.

Gorard, S. (2006). *Using everyday numbers effectively in research*. London: Continuum.

Gosling, P. (2010, March 2). Economic future is bright for the city that's brimming with culture. *Belfast Telegraph*. Retrieved from http://www.belfasttelegraph.co.uk/news/campaigns/derry-culture-bid/economic-future-is-bright-for-the-city-thats-brimming-with-culture-28536848.html.

Gray, C. (2006). Managing the unmanageable: The politics of cultural planning. *Public Policy and Administration, 21*(2), 101–113.

Gray, C. (2008). Arts council England and public value: A critical review. *International Journal of Cultural Policy, 14*(2), 209–214.

Gray, C. (2009). Managing cultural policy: Pitfalls and prospects. *Public Administration, 87*(3), 574–585.

Hepworth Wakefield. (2012). *Annual review 2011–12*. Retrieved from https://ripassetseu.s3.amazonaws.com/www.hepworthwakefield.org/_files/documents/dec_12/FENT__1355235958_THW_Annual_Review_2011-12_LR.pdf.

Hesmondhalgh, D. (2007). *The cultural industries*. London: Sage.

Hesmondhalgh, D., Oakley, K., Lee, D., & Nisbett, M. (2015). *Culture, economy and politics—The case of new labour*. Basingstoke: Palgrave Macmillan.

Hewison, R. (2014). *Cultural capital: The rise and fall of creative Britain*. London: Verso.

HM Treasury. (2003). *The Green Book: Appraisal and evaluation in central government*. Retrieved from https://www.gov.uk/government/uploads/system/uploads/attachment_data/file/220541/green_book_complete.pdf.

Holden, J. (2007). *Publicly-funded culture and the creative industries*. London: Arts Council England.

Hughes, G. (1989). Measuring the economic value of the arts. *Policy Studies, 9*(3), 152–165.

Hull, D. (2013). *Examining social inclusion in the arts in Northern Ireland*. Belfast: Northern Ireland Assembly.

Hyslop, D. (2012). Culture, regeneration and community: Reinventing the city. *Gateways: International Journal of Community Research and Engagement, 5*, 152–165.

Johanson, K., Glow, H., & Kershaw, A. (2014). New modes of arts participation and the limits of cultural indicators for local government. *Poetics, 43*, 43–59.

Jones, P., & Evans, J. (2008). *Urban regeneration in the UK*. London: Sage.

Knell, J., & Oakley, K. (2007). *London's creative economy: An accidental success?* London: The Work Foundation.

Labadi, S. (2008). *Evaluating the socio-economic impacts of selected regeneration heritage sites in Europe*. Retrieved from http://www.encatc.org/pages/fileadmin/user_upload/Forum/Sophia_Labadi_2008CPRA_Publication.pdf.

LARC. (2011). *Liverpool Thrive programme final report*. Retrieved from http://www.larc.uk.com/wp-content/uploads/2013/06/Thrive-Final-Report.pdf.

Law, J., & Urry, J. (2004). Enacting the social. *Economy and Society, 33*(3), 390–410.

Leather, P., Nevin, B., Cole, I., & Eadson, W. (2012). *The Housing Market Renewal programme in England: Development, impact and legacy*. Retrieved from http://www.inta-aivn.org/images/cc/Habitat/background%20documents/HMR%20legacy%20paper%201%2012.pdf.

Lees, L., & Melhuish, C. (2015). Arts-led regeneration in the UK: The rhetoric and the evidence on urban social inclusion. *European Urban and Regional Studies, 22*(3), 242–260.

LGA. (2013). *Driving growth through local government investment in the arts*. London: Local Government Association.

Liu, Y.-D. (2014). Cultural events and cultural tourism development: Lessons from the European Capitals of Culture. *European Planning Studies, 22*(3), 498–514.

Madden, C. (2001). Using 'economic' impact studies in arts and cultural advocacy: A cautionary note. *Media International Australia Incorporating Culture and Policy, 98*, 161–178.

Markusen, A., & Gadwa, A. (2010). Arts and culture in urban or regional planning: A review and research agenda. *Journal of Planning Education and Research, 29*(3), 379–391.

McMaster, B. (2008). *Supporting excellence in the arts: From measurement to judgement*. London: DCMS.

Media and Arts Partnership. (2008). *Housing Market Renewal*. Retrieved from http://www.maap.org.uk/sholver/.

Miles, S., & Paddison, R. (2005). Introduction: The rise and rise of culture-led urban regeneration. *Urban Studies, 42*(5–6), 833–839.

Miller, M. (2013, June 20). I argued for the arts—And won. We will keep the philistines from the gates. *The Guardian*. Retrieved from https://www.theguardian.com/commentisfree/2013/jun/20/argued-for-arts-and-won-philistines-economic-case.

New Economy. (2013). *Beyond the arts: Economic and wider impacts of the Lowry and its programmes*. Retrieved from http://www.thelowry.com/Downloads/reports/The_Lowry_Beyond_the_Arts.pdf.

Newsinger, J., & Green, W. (2016). The infrapolitics of cultural value: Cultural policy, evaluation and the marginalisation of practitioner perspectives. *Journal of Cultural Economy, 9*(4), 382–395.

NFASP. (2010). *Developing affordable artists' studios in a Housing Market Renewal area*. Retrieved from http://artspace.org.uk/download-file/downloads/Manor-Oaks-CS.pdf.

Oakley, K. (2008). Any answer as long as it's right: Evidence-based cultural policymaking. In L. Andersen & K. Oakley (Eds.), *Making meaning, making money* (pp. 18–41). Newcastle Upon Tyne: Cambridge Scholars.

Oakley, K. (2009). The disappearing arts: Creativity and innovation after the creative industries. *International Journal of Cultural Policy, 15*(4), 403–413.

Oakley, K., O'Brien, D., & Lee, D. (2013). Happy now? Well-being and cultural policy. *Philosophy and Public Policy Quarterly, 31*(2), 18–26.

O'Brien, D. (2014). *Cultural policy: Management, value and modernity in the creative industries*. London: Routledge.

O'Connor, J. (2007). *The cultural and creative industries: A review of the literature*. London: Arts Council England.

Oman, S., & Taylor, M. (2018). Subjective well-being in cultural advocacy: A politics of research between the market and the academy. *Journal of Cultural Economy, 11*(3), 225–243.

Peck, J. (2002). Political economies of scale: Fast policy, interscalar relations, and neoliberal workfare. *Economic Geography, 78*(3), 331–360.

Pendle Borough Council. (2014). *Housing Market Renewal*. Retrieved from http://www.pendle.gov.uk/galleries/gallery/5/housing_market_renewal_hmr/.

Plaza, B. (2006). The return on investment of the Guggenheim Museum Bilbao. *International Journal of Urban and Regional Research, 30*(2), 452–567.

Plaza, B., Tironi, M., & Haarich, S. (2009). Bilbao's art scene and the "Guggenheim effect" revisited. *European Planning Studies, 17*(11), 1711–1729.

Pratt, A. C. (2008). Creative cities: The cultural industries and the creative class. *Geografiska Annaler: Series B, human geography, 90*(2), 107–117.

Public Art Leicester. (2005). *Cultural mapping public art programme Leicester*. Retrieved from http://www.leicester.gov.uk/culturalmapping/index.html.

Reeves, M. (2002). *Measuring the economic and social impact of the arts: A review*. London: Arts Council England.

Rekdal, O. B. (2014). Academic urban legends. *Social Studies of Science, 44*(4), 638–654.

Richards, G. (2011). Creativity and tourism: The state of the art. *Annals of Tourism Research, 38*(4), 1225–1253.

Roger Tym & Partners. (2011). *Economic impact of the Liverpool Arts Regeneration Consortium*. Retrieved from http://www.larc.uk.com/wp-content/uploads/2011/10/LARC-Economic-Impact-Final-Report.pdf.

Rushton, M. (2015). *On the return to public investments in Museums*. Retrieved from http://www.artsjournal.com/worth/2015/03/on-the-return-to-public-investments-in-museums/.

Schuster, J. M. (1996). The performance of performance indicators in the arts. *Nonprofit Management & Leadership, 7*(3), 253–269.

Schutz, A. (1960). The social world and the theory of social action. *Social Research, 27*(2), 203–221.

Selwood, S. (2006). A part to play? The academic contribution to the development of cultural policy in England. *International Journal of Cultural Policy, 12*(1), 35–53.

Sharp, J. (2007). The life and death of five spaces: Public art and community regeneration in Glasgow. *Cultural Geographies, 14*(2), 274–292.

Shin, H., & Stevens, Q. (2013). How culture and economy meet in South Korea: The politics of cultural economy in culture-led urban regeneration. *International Journal of Urban and Regional Research, 37*(5), 1707–1723.

Stevenson, D. (2004). "Civic gold" rush—Cultural planning and the politics of the third way. *International Journal of Cultural Policy, 10*(1), 119–131.

Taylor, P., Davies, L., Wells, P., Gilbertson, J., & Tayleur, W. (2015). *A review of the social impacts of culture and sport.* Retrieved from https://assets.publishing.service.gov.uk/government/uploads/system/uploads/attachment_data/file/416279/A_review_of_the_Social_Impacts_of_Culture_and_Sport.pdf.

The Economist. (2012). Art the conqueror. Retrieved from http://www.economist.com/node/21550291.

THRU. (2013). *Townscape heritage initiative schemes evaluation—Ten year review report.* Oxford: Townscape Heritage Research Unit, Oxford Brookes University.

Tyler, P., Warnock, C., Provins, A., Wells, P., Brennan, A., Cole, I., ..., Phang, Z. (2010). *Valuing the benefits of regeneration.* Retrieved from https://www.gov.uk/government/uploads/system/uploads/attachment_data/file/6382/1795633.pdf.

Van Heur, B. (2010). Small cities and the geographical bias of creative industries research and policy. *Journal of Policy Research in Tourism, Leisure and Events, 2*(2), 189–192.

Vickery, J. (2007). *The emergence of culture-led regeneration: A policy concept and its discontents.* Warwick: Centre for Cultural Policy Studies.

Warren, S., & Jones, P. (2015). Local governance, disadvantaged communities and cultural intermediation in the creative urban economy. *Environment and Planning C: Government and Policy, 33*(6), 1738–1752.

What Works Centre for Local Economic Growth. (2014). *Evidence review 3: Sports and culture.* Retrieved from http://www.whatworksgrowth.org/public/files/Policy_Reviews/16-06-15_Culture_and_Sport_Updated.pdf.

5

The Persistent Case for the Creative Industries

The previous chapter demonstrated a range of persistent challenges raised when seeking to demonstrate the value of the arts and culture. We may, however, expect the drive to produce evidence to be somewhat less problematic in making the case for the creative industries. Here it may be presumed that there is a clearer object for evidence-gathering processes to work with: the number of people working in specific occupations, for instance, can be estimated, and statistics on the economic output of given industries can be sought from the work of national statistical bodies. This chapter will demonstrate, however, that things are not quite so simple by outlining the way in which such statistics are formed and used to drive the Creativity Agenda forward. Firstly, the means by which a narrative regarding the economic success of a set of culturally-focussed creative industries is entrenched over the first decade of the Creativity Agenda are discussed. Then, in a consideration of the key role that definition plays in data gathering, the way in which statistics from the Department for Culture, Media and Sport (DCMS) undergo revisions that undermine this dominant narrative in the early 2010s is shown. From this point, the role of external bodies in quickly 'repairing' these statistics is traced, and links to the broader Creativity

© The Author(s) 2019
P. Campbell, *Persistent Creativity*, Sociology of the Arts,
https://doi.org/10.1007/978-3-030-03119-0_5

Agenda traced in Chapter 3, and pre-existing thinking about the emergence of 'new' economic times established in Chapter 2, are considered. The chapter will conclude by reflecting on the resulting state of creative industries data, which, despite decades of data-wrangling, sees many of its unresolved tensions persist.

Stage One: The Creative Industries Are Shown to Be Economically Important (1998–2011)

Key to the persistent position regarding the current and future importance of creative industries first encountered in Chapter 1 are statistics regarding their exceptional economic performance, and the work of the UK government in establishing a set of methods to gather these statistics has helped the concept of the creative industries to proliferate internationally, as seen in Chapter 3. DCMS definitions in this period have been referred to as a 'de facto world standard' (Bakhshi et al. 2013, p. 3), and DCMS notes its influence in describing a brief history of its own practices in this field:

> From 2001 DCMS has produced annual estimates of the size of the creative industries in the UK economy. DCMS uses data from the Office for National Statistics (ONS) to estimate their contribution to UK employment, Gross Value Added (GVA) and exports. The DCMS approach has gained an international precedent for measuring the contribution of the creative industries. (2007, p. 2)

For the majority of this period, DCMS produced a series of 'Creative Industries Economic Estimates' (CIEE) reports outlining the performance of the creative industries, and the key headline figures produced in these documents were quickly taken up by academics, policymakers, consultants, the media—indeed, seemingly anyone interested in discussing the nature of the creative industries. In this chapter, headline figures regarding employment and GVA ('Gross Value Added' which 'measures the contribution to the economy of each individual producer, industry or sector' [ONS 2006, p. 25]) from these reports are considered, following

Throsby's explanation that these are the two most important variables to consider when assessing economic contribution (2015, p. 64).

The CIEE reports build on earlier 'Creative Industries Mapping Documents' produced in 1998 and 2001. Pratt argued early on in this process of data gathering that the statistical information in such documents was,

> crucial in establishing a legitimacy for the 'creative industries', notably with regard to the Treasury. It is this establishment of legitimacy in terms of their economic weight that has helped to reinforce the economic interpretation of the creative industries. (Pratt 1999, pp. 155–156, cited in Volkerling 2001, p. 445)

Indeed, other authors reflecting back on this period argue that the magnitude of the economic statistics presented in such documents 'allowed the sector to be taken seriously by finance ministries' both in the UK and beyond (Banks and O'Connor 2017, p. 645). To take just one example of the international influence of these statistics, Rindzevičiūtė et al. note that the status of creative industries in Lithuania became of interest to government 'when we presented them the data on how much income the creative industries brought to national and local budgets in the UK' (2016, p. 600) and a 'National Association for Creative and Cultural Industries' was subsequently established in Lithuania, following UK definitions of the sector, and producing its own similar data (2016, p. 604). As well as having a national and international role, the economic picture presented by these mapping documents was also central to the adoption of creative industries policy at a sub-national level, being 'seized upon by creative industry advocates as important and authoritative statements' (Taylor 2006, p. 8). As well as outlining their current importance, these statistics also play a role in making the case that creativity will become ever more important in the future (e.g. Bazalgette 2017, p. 7). What pattern, then, do such statistics show?

Both the broader uptake of the DCMS statistics and the pattern they reveal over this period can be quickly established by listing a series of typical statements from a range of stakeholders covering the first decade of data gathering:

- '[The Creative Industries Task Force] established the creative industries as a central plank of the United Kingdom's "postindustrial" economy, observing that the sector accounted for 5 percent of total national income in 1998, employed 1.4 million people, and was growing at about double the rate of the British economy as a whole' (Flew and Cunningham 2010, p. 113).
- 'A statistical bulletin issued by the UK Department of Culture, Media and Sport in July 2003 revealed that the creative industries accounted for 8.2 percent of Gross Value Added of the UK economy in 2001' (Montgomery 2005, p. 340).
- 'The Creative Industries accounted for 8% of UK Gross Value Added (GVA) in 2002 [and] grew by an average of 6% per annum between 1997 and 2002 compared to an average of 3% for the whole of the economy' (Comedia 2004, p. 12).
- 'In 2004 the creative industries accounted for 8% of UK Gross Value Added, compared to 4% in 1997; The creative industries grew by an average of 5% p.a. between 1997 and 2004, compared to an average of 3% for the economy as a whole; The creative industries employ 1.8 million people in the UK' (Holden 2007, p. 1).
- '[Creative Industries] now make up 7.3 per cent of the economy, and are growing at 5 per cent per year (almost twice the rate of the rest of the economy). Including those working in related creative occupations, the creative economy employs 1.8 million people' (Jowell in The Work Foundation 2007, p. 6).
- 'Within the UK, the Creative Industries sector contributes over 6.4% of UK Gross Value Added and is growing at a faster rate than the economy as a whole. In 2007, total Creative Industries revenues amounted to some £67.5bn' (Technology Strategy Board 2009, p. 7).

Although the difference between the figures stated here is not unimportant, and will be considered further below, we can at least see the general picture which dominates over this period, and therefore, it is understandable that in 2007 Jones and Wright draw this broad conclusion:

We know well enough by now that the creative and cultural industries are a vital part of our economy. We tell the story of our success in the creative industries with the oft-quoted statistic that they account for 8 per cent of our GDP and are one of the fastest growing parts of our economy. (2007, p. 40)

Similarly, we can understand why the first paragraph of the UK government's cross-departmental 'Creative Britain' report referred to in Chapter 1 reads thus:

Britain is a creative country and our creative industries are increasingly vital to the UK. Two million people are employed in creative jobs and the sector contributes £60 billion a year – 7.3 per cent – to the British economy. Over the past decade, the creative sector has grown at twice the rate of the economy as a whole (DCMS et al. 2008, p. 6)

From this very brief consideration of the first ten years of data gathering, one is thus left with the impression of a group of industries employing somewhere close to two million people, that accounts for a rising proportion of total UK GVA, moving from 5% to somewhere closer to 8%, which translates to a figure close to £60 billion, and that is growing twice as fast as the economy as a whole. At least at the level of such headlines, the creative industries certainly seem to be of legitimate economic interest and able to demonstrate their economic role with the kind of 'hard facts that make sense to everyone' claimed as particularly important by ex-Culture Secretary Maria Miller (2013), as noted in the previous chapter.

Whilst some sources point to concerns or difficulties regarding the nature of these headline statistics, the dominant approach in this period is to quote the available figures as clear evidence of how these industries are integral to a burgeoning new economy and how vital they are, or will be, to economic success in any given location. Foord (2008, p. 92) gives evidence that this state of affairs is characteristic not only of the UK case, but is the predominant way in which creative industries are presented internationally. Such statistics thus represent one of the key 'knowledges' contained in broader discourse on the creative industries (Jäger and Maier 2009, p. 34) and by their repetition constitute a key justification for the promotion of the Creativity Agenda. The persistent collation of this data can be seen as being in sympathy with the general turn towards 'evidence-based policymaking' noted in this era: Oakley, for instance, notes that once they emerge as an object of significant political attention, any discussions around creative industries are 'always accompanied by a stress on evidence' (2008, p. 21).

Aligning Data with Culture

Key to any data-gathering exercise is the issue of definition. The development of the definition of the creative industries was first considered in Chapter 3, where it was noted that, despite its expansion into other areas, the majority of activities included can be considered to overlap with the earlier grouping of the 'cultural industries'. This centrality of cultural activity is reflected when the economic figures above are being discussed in this period, with 'creative industries' and 'culture' often being treated as essentially synonymous. To consider a handful of prominent statements towards the end of this period, for instance, then First Secretary of State Baron Mandelson noted that as well as 'driv[ing] much of our economy', creative industries 'ensure that Britain punches above its weight on the global cultural stage' (2009). Taking up the general theme of economic importance, in March 2010, a consortium of 17 major UK cultural organisations released the 'Cultural Capital' report, subtitled 'investing in culture will build Britain's social and economic recovery', which restated figures such as those above with the following justification, emphasising how a teleological understanding of the economic role of 'creativity' had intensified after the 2008 financial crisis:

> Creativity is the key to economic recovery. Public investment in the arts and heritage helps to generate the cultural capital that feeds the creative industries [...] the creative and cultural industries have grown faster than the rest of the economy, and account for 6.2% of Gross Value Added. (Arts Council England et al. 2010, p. 7)

When specific activities are picked out to exemplify the creative industries, these are similarly cultural in nature. Data-gathering projects, for instance, note that the value of the creative industries is derived in part from products such as 'new books or movies' (Stoneman 2009, p. 4), and the Chief Executive of Arts Council England reports that 'it is commonly acknowledged that the arts are the bedrock of the creative economy' (Davey in Fleming and Erskine 2011, p. 1). In the context of a decline in UK students registering to study arts subjects at this time, the then Chief Executive of Universities UK made this argument:

> Student fears about finding work in the arts need to be challenged. Chief executive Nicola Dandridge points out that the UK has "one of the largest and most successful creative sectors in the world" which, after a boom in the past decade, now employs 8% of the country's workforce (Davis 2011)

Similarly, media reports relating to Arts Council England funding cuts at this time point to artists discussing the apparent ignorance of the 'return on investment' being foregone:

> If we look at the arts as a whole (both subsidised and commercial) the return is immense compared to other industries – while arts funding represents about 0.07% of GDP, the creative industries contribute 7% to GDP. (Babani and Gerrard 2011)

We can thus see, even in this brief sketch, a sense not only of what the economic performance of creative industries is understood to be in this period, but that this economic performance is ultimately aligned to, or seen to radiate out from, artistic and cultural activity.

Setting Definitional Boundaries

Despite this alignment with specifically cultural activity, contention over the definition of the creative industries, and calls for a more rigorous definition of the term, date back to the very emergence of the concept in the 1990s (see Evans 2001, p. 274; Comedia 2004, p. 11).

Even in the midst of the 'Creative Economy Programme', a substantial data-gathering exercise commissioned by DCMS in 2006/7, we find somewhat coy statements to the effect that issues of 'definition and coverage both remain considerable talking points' (2007, p. 4), and towards the end of this period, Banks and O'Connor refer to the 'necessary (but seemingly interminable) debate' (2009, p. 366) over definition and measurement. The issue of definition is, however, obviously key to the derivation of the economic headline figures discussed above. It is thus important to examine in some detail how this definition is arrived at, and how measurement has been carried out.

Whilst a broad outline of the emergence of the terminology of the 'creative industries' was given in Chapter 3, it is necessary here to point to the debates in this period around the most appropriate object for this terminology, debates which, as will be seen below, continue to characterise this field. The definitional drift which occurs as a result of a change of focus from 'cultural' to 'creative' industries, and the potential difference between the two, is an important factor when it comes to drawing a logical boundary around this sector and in understanding the role of the industries contained therein. In this period, there are a number of conflicting approaches regarding what groups would be most appropriate to include under the novel grouping of creative industries, the extent to which these overlap with the cultural sector within a country or region, and the methodologies which can be used in either of these areas to achieve an accurate level of measurement once a definition is finally reached (any 'perfect' definition being of little use unless there is an accompanying data source to apply it to). Whilst the range of positions taken over this period cannot be outlined in its entirety here, the following discussion from DCMS, taken from a broader consideration of how the measurement of the cultural sector should be approached, serves to give a flavour of the historical and persistent nature of these debates, their geographical scope, and also provides a sense of the difficulty in achieving any form of consensus on this issue:

> In Europe there have been long running discussions on the constitution
> of the cultural sector and data collection [...] A Leadership Group (LEG)

reported on the possibility of harmonisation of cultural statistics in 1999, and a Working Party on Cultural Statistics continues to explore the issues. The LEG group [...] acknowledged the problem that definition is in part a matter of policy, and departed significantly from UNESCO's FCS [Framework for Culture Statistics] in terms of 'breadth', by establishing more limited parameters for the cultural sector. So, Sport, Environment, Advertising, Fashion, Languages and Games were excluded. (DCMS 2004, p. 8)

Such definitions are therefore inevitably and inherently political ones as, it can be argued, is the entire endeavour of 'evidence-based policy' (Oakley 2008). The discussion above, however, refers to measurement of the *cultural* sector. As established in Chapter 3, even though the two terms are potentially identical, this is a field in which small differences matter. If *cultural* practice, however defined, produces statistics showing a minimal rate of employment growth, but *creative* practice, alternatively defined, produces statistics showing exceptional growth, then these seemingly trivial semantic differences may result in significantly different policy responses. Indeed, despite the apparent difficulty of alighting on a sturdy definition, numerous attempts have certainly been made to delineate the difference between these terms. Again, to give a brief sense of the nature of the 'interminable' work around definition here, a study in this period for the European Commission identifies these two areas thus:

The "cultural sector":
- Non-industrial sectors producing non-reproducible goods and services aimed at being "consumed" on the spot (a concert, an art fair, an exhibition). These are the arts field (visual arts including paintings, sculpture, craft, photography; the arts and antique markets; performing arts including opera, orchestra, theatre, dance, circus; and heritage including museums, heritage sites, archaeological sites, libraries and archives).
- Industrial sectors producing cultural products aimed at mass reproduction, mass-dissemination and exports (for example, a book, a film, a sound recording). These are "cultural industries" including film and video, video-games, broadcasting, music, book and press publishing.

The "creative sector":

— In the "creative sector", culture becomes a "creative" input in the production of non-cultural goods. It includes activities such as design (fashion design, interior design, and product design), architecture, and advertising. Creativity is understood in the study as the use of cultural resources as an intermediate consumption in the production process of non-cultural sectors, and thereby as a source of innovation. (KEA European Affairs 2006, p. 2)

KEA were also responsible for authoring a paper for the European Commission considering 'The Impact of Culture on Creativity' wherein we discover that,

culture-based creativity helps to promote well-being, to create lifestyle, to enrich the act of consumption, to stimulate confidence in communities and social cohesion [...] It contributes to product innovation, to branding, to the management of human resources and to communication. (2009, p. 6)

Clearly, this chimes strongly with the broader Creativity Agenda encountered previously in highlighting the prospect of beneficial social and economic outcomes. What is also clear here, though, is that for an idea such as 'culture-based creativity' to make sense, this then entails culture and creativity as overlapping but somehow separate concepts. Based on the 2006 KEA report, the DCMS-commissioned Work Foundation report (2007, p. 4) posits a 'concentric circles' model with a central 'core' of creativity with 'a high degree of expressive value' radiating out into 'cultural industries' which 'involve mass reproduction of expressive outputs' and 'the commercialisation of pure expressive value' (pp. 103–104), such as the music or film industries, and then further out again into 'creative industries and activities' where the 'use of expressive value is essential' (p. 4). Whilst creativity and culture are separated somewhat by such a model, expressive activity of some form permeates the sector and is its principal characteristic. Expressive *creative* (but non-cultural) industries include the architecture, design and fashion industries. So, by this model, advertising is 'creative', whereas music is 'cultural'; design work is 'creative', and a computer game is 'cultural', but the cultural is in essence a more concentrated form of the wider expressive, creative sector. Such demarcations demonstrate the difficulties encountered when trying to separate these areas of activity in any simple or, perhaps, useful way when gathering data, especially given the often interchangeable application of terminology highlighted above.

Considering Creative Industries Statistics in Detail—The DCMS 13

Previous chapters discussed how the DCMS definition of creative industries becomes internationally influential and, whilst there are many modifications to the data-gathering process, the definition at the root of its Creative Industries Mapping Documents and CIEE reports remains fairly stable for around a decade. Below, the definition and statistics contained in the 2009 CIEE report will be examined in detail, as this represents the point at which this period of relative continuity starts to break down, with figures around the performance of the creative industries subsequently undergoing redefinition.

Although the scope and reliability of evidence produced in earlier periods have been questioned (Oakley 2004, p. 68; Schlesinger 2009, p. 13), in 2006/7 DCMS commissioned the 'Creative Economy Programme' to offer a more detailed understanding of the nature and contribution of creative industries, and potential policy responses (DCMS 2007). This programme produced a massive range of statistical outputs not mirrored since, exploring issues such as the size and scope of the creative sector, spillover effects and the role of multinational companies, based on the set of 13 sectors identified in the original Creative Industries Mapping Document of 1998. What it did not seek to do, however, was to question this definition. Rather, it re-employed these categories 'to maintain consistency' (2007, p. 4) with earlier work, and so these categories persist in a fairly stable form throughout the majority of the period under consideration here. It is, therefore, this list of sectors that are the basis for the headline figures noted at the outset of this chapter. A persistent trope of definition in this period is stated explicitly by DCMS: the key characteristic of these sectors is that they 'have their origin in individual creativity, skill and talent and [...] have a potential for wealth and job creation through the generation and exploitation of intellectual property' (2007, p. 4). Given the emphasis on the role of the individual, it is also clear that the role for a form of innovative entrepreneurship, key to the Creativity Agenda, is important here too. As noted above, though, the Work Foundation explains the criteria for the inclusion of any given industry thus:

> What is distinct about the creative industries is that their revenues are largely generated by commercialising 'expressive value' and that necessarily a greater part of their commercial turnover is attributable even more so than other parts of the knowledge economy to acts of genuine 'creative origination'. (2007, p. 96)

The 13 sectors which constitute the DCMS creative industries on the basis of these definitions are listed by 2009 (p. 9) as:

1. Advertising
2. Architecture
3. Art and Antiques
4. Crafts
5. Design
6. Designer Fashion
7. Video, Film and Photography
9. and 10. Music and the Visual and Performing Arts
11. Publishing
8. and 12. Software, Computer Games and Electronic Publishing
13. Radio and TV.

It is clear from this list how the notion expressed by Throsby of 'virtually all' (2008, p. 220) of these activities being 'cultural' comes about, and the role for 'expressive value' also seems fairly clear. Yet the creative industries concept as delineated here also seems to go beyond this: we may see 'computer games' as expressive or cultural, but all other 'software' production? This will be considered further below, but first we must also ask why these 13 sectors are listed by DCMS in 11 groups.

This returns us to the difficulty of measurement and the limitations of official data sources. It is noted that 'due to the structure of the official classifications used, it is necessary to combine "Interactive Leisure Software" with "Software and Computer Services" and "Music" with "Performing Arts"' when producing statistics (DCMS 2009, p. 3), and that it is particularly difficult to gather statistics upon groups 4 and 5 of 'Crafts' and 'Design'. Before considering the appropriateness of the activities included in this grouping, therefore, it is also necessary to consider the intimately related issue of how data is actually sourced, as inclusion in the creative industries grouping is also somewhat dependent on the availability of relevant data (e.g. OECD 2007, p. 41).

Data Sources: SIC Codes, SOC Codes, the ABI and the LFS

In addition to there being variation in the definitions of creative industries taken up between countries (OECD 2007, p. 48), all countries face issues with the appropriateness of data sources. KEA European Affairs state the following caveats in this period:

> Statistical tools do not enable the cultural & creative sector to be captured properly. At European and national level, statistical categorisations are often too broad. Data are rarely comparable. A considerable amount of cultural activity takes place in establishments whose primary classification is non cultural and therefore not recorded within existing classifications. Self-employed cannot be identified. (2006, p. 4)

Were the issues around definition resolved, therefore, the task of *how* to best gather data relating to this sector would still remain. On the issue of considering 'cultural activity' in 'non-cultural' businesses raised above, though, it is worth noting that statistics produced in UK in this period do to some degree engage with the 'creative trident' approach developed by Higgs et al. (2008) by attempting to capture the economic output of creativity both inside and outside the creative industries, although in so doing really only separate out two forks of this 'trident' by giving data on (i) total employment in creative industries and (ii) employment in creative occupations outside these industries. For the most part in this period, though, both policy discourse and statistical outputs mostly remain attached to the idea of a discrete set of creative industries that are outperforming other industries, rather than being concerned with a more generalised notion of creativity permeating throughout the economy. Where then do figures regarding these industries come from?

For the purposes of official data gathering, all industrial activity is assigned a 'Standard Industrial Classification' or SIC code. SIC codes provide an increasing level of specificity from 2 to 5 digit level and map to the European NACE (*Nomenclature statistique des activités économiques dans la Communauté Européenne*) system to the 4 digit level. From the list above, for example, in 2009, data on 'publishing' was created by the concatenation of data derived from this set of 4 digit SIC codes:

22.11—Publishing of books
22.12—Publishing of newspapers
22.13—Publishing of journals and periodicals
22.15—Other publishing
92.40—News agency activities (DCMS 2009, p. 9).

Due to its wide remit, only a proportion of activity in the 'other publishing' code was used, and this highlights part of the problem with using SIC codes for the purpose of producing data relating specifically to these creative industries. There are many areas where the match between the activity of interest and the activity captured by the codes available is partial or slight. This problem arises due to SIC codes being essentially unresponsive, a problem exacerbated by the creative sector being especially changeable and volatile (DCMS 2007, p. 2). Early discussion of the SIC system indicated that only 'extremely serious reasons' could result in any fundamental changes due to the 'great problems and costs' involved in any discontinuity in data (Government Statisticians Collective 1979, p. 140), and so as the SIC codes were first established in 1970, codes often map poorly to activities specifically in the 'new economy'.

The Organisation for Economic Co-operation and Development (OECD) gives some idea of the scale of the problem in this period, noting that 'a European Commission Leadership Group, working on a somewhat restricted definition of culture, listed 57 industry classes it considered to be culture related. Of this list, only *five* were considered to be *entirely* cultural' (2007, p. 64, emphasis added). Indeed, an international OECD survey of those responsible for statistical information regarding the cultural sector found that 'responses tend to confirm that countries find existing classifications not fit for purpose when applied to the culture sector' and that 'the culture sector is not well reflected in most existing general purpose classification standards' (2006, p. 2), adding that,

> all of these classifications underwent a significant revision process during the late 1980s and early 1990s. It was hoped at the time that the revisions would lead to a greater concordance among the various standards; in the areas relevant to culture, the success of this process was particularly limited. (2007, p. 11)

There have, however, been some updates in the twenty-first century. The 2009 statistics considered here are based on a list of SIC codes updated in 2003, and later periods considered below use the 2007 iteration of these codes. As noted, though, whilst there has been a slight improvement in the 'match' with creative industries possible with the latest 2007 codes, this is limited by the speed with which any change can occur. The 2007 revision (which remains in use in producing the figures discussed below published in 2018), for instance, was the result of a series of consultations started in 2002, carried out in concert with a major revision of the EU's industrial classification system (ONS 2009, p. 2), and data resulting from this reclassification first became available seven years after these first consultations. Clearly, with any reassessment potentially taking the best part of a decade, and remaining in use for a further decade, there is little scope for such codes to swiftly react to and reflect wider changes in the economy. As such, any figures 'should be considered as best estimates rather than definitive valuations' (The Work Foundation 2007, p. 194). Nevertheless, almost all statistical data is subject to some uncertainty, and this classification system remains the best available for the task at hand in producing national economic estimates.

Although the gathering of appropriate data to attain an accurate sense of the relative makeup of the creative sector thus has many attendant difficulties, it should be noted that even where activities designated as creative industries do not have their own *discrete* SIC code, they do at least have *somewhere* to sit, and we can therefore place some measure of confidence in this estimated data. That said, it is also accurately noted by many that certain activities characteristic of creative industries raise particular problems for data gathering as data sources mainly rely on VAT (Value Added Tax) and PAYE (Pay As You Earn) records, which will miss businesses operating below certain thresholds. In the UK in 2018, at the time of writing, VAT registration is compulsory for any business with an annual *turnover* in excess of £85,000 (up from £68,000 at the start of the decade) and voluntary for those with a lower turnover, and PAYE registration is dependent on many factors, including a business having at least one employee being paid in excess of £107 per week (up from £97 at the start of the decade). It must be borne in mind, then, that in official sources there is a,

> lack of data on self-employment and Small and Medium-Sized Enterprises (SMEs) – the ABI does not include data on self-employment (an important category in many parts of the Cultural Sector), and only uses a limited sampling of SMEs. Given that there is a well-documented preponderance of SMEs in the Cultural Sector – compared with the economy as a whole – the accuracy of the survey data is compromised. (DCMS 2004, p. 6)

Whilst this preponderance of smaller businesses involving self-employment is also noted in more recent years (e.g. Last 2016, p. 12), recent figures also show that 76% of businesses in the UK as a whole have no employees, and 96% are 'micro'-businesses with fewer than ten employees (Rhodes 2017, p. 5). As such, there is also clearly a preponderance of small businesses across the economy as a whole, so these challenges of coverage do not exclusively apply to the creative industries. Also, given that it is businesses with lower levels of turnover or employment which are not well captured by such records, we can be confident that a majority of the economic output of the creative industries will be captured by such data sources.

The 'ABI' referred to above is the 'Annual Business Inquiry', one of two main sources of information recommended by the DCMS Evidence Toolkit and used in the CIEE reports considered below (the other being the Labour Force Survey [LFS]). The ABI gives nation-wide data down to 4-digit SIC code level, and this data comes from a sampling of the Inter-Departmental Business Register (IDBR), a list maintained by the ONS of UK businesses, covering nearly 99% of UK economic activity (ONS 2010a). It not only covers VAT-registered businesses and businesses with employees registered for PAYE, as noted above, but also includes data from surveys sent to over a quarter of a million businesses.

Data on relevant employment types *outside* of specific industries is also sourced via the use of Standard Occupational Classification (SOC) codes, with data gathered from the LFS to give a sense of the number of creative workers employed outside the creative industries. To take the example of 'publishing' once more, the 2009 CIEE report identifies that the following SOC codes are used to generate statistics:

3431—Journalists, Newspaper and Periodical editors
5421—Originators, Compositors and Print preparers
5422—Printers
5423—Bookbinders and Print finishers
5424—Screen printers (DCMS 2009, p. 11)

As it is not based on companies, the LFS can capture less conventional employment patterns, as well as self-employment and smaller enter-prises, although again there are reservations expressed in this period about the ability of such data to cover the *entirety* of cultural work (DCMS 2004, p. 34). Despite the important caveats above, however, there is reason to have some measure of confidence that statistics regard-ing the creative industries can provide a reasonably informed view on the performance of its subsectors, and especially of their position in the economy, despite their clear limitations.

Data from the 2009 Creative Industries Economic Estimates

By 2009, seven annual CIEE reports had been produced, and the 2009 iteration is the basis of the figures considered below. Whereas those pro-moting the Creativity Agenda early on had to take a statement claiming that creative industries 'are where the wealth and the jobs of the future are going to be generated from' (Smith 1998, p. 31) on faith, by this point it was possible to look back on data covering a decade to look for signs of the emergence of this 'future' state. First, then, let us consider the headline figures stated above regarding economic contribution and employment. Figure 5.1 shows the proportion of total UK GVA attributable to creative industries based on the data available in 2009 for the period 1997–2006.

Whilst the reports of 8% of GVA being attributable to creative industries referred to above thus seem somewhat optimistic by this point, and whilst there is not a consistent year-on-year increase in the data, the proportion of total UK GVA attributable to creative industries does broadly rise over this period, and the average proportion of total GVA attributable to creative industries over this first decade of data is 6.3%. A similar picture can also be seen in terms of total creative employment, as shown in Fig. 5.2.

It must be emphasised that the figures given in the 2009 CIEE report are for *total* creative employment, that is all those employed within creative industries *plus* all those employed in creative roles in the wider

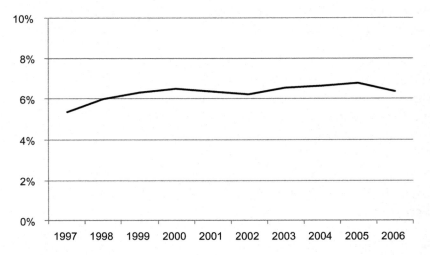

Fig. 5.1 Proportion of total UK GVA attributable to creative industries (2009 definition) (*Source* DCMS [2009])

economy. The average proportion of total UK employment attributable to this wider 'creative economy' over this first decade of data is 6.4%, and again, although not totally consistent, there is broadly a year-on-year rise in this period. It should be noted, however, that in any one year, only around 60% of the employment in this creative economy is specifically in the creative *industries* considered in Fig. 5.1, and so average creative industries employment in this period would likely be closer to 4% of the UK total.

However defined, it is clear that employment and GVA levels represent a not inconsiderable slice of the wider economy, but given the relative size of this sector in comparison with the economy as a whole, Figs. 5.1 and 5.2 do not enable comparative year-on-year growth to be easily seen. We can, however, look at this another way by taking 1997 as a baseline, treating levels in this year as representing '100%' and then comparing the growth shown by creative industries over this period in comparison with overall levels of growth. These patterns are shown in Figs. 5.3 and 5.4.

In Fig. 5.3, we can see that, although by no means growing at twice the rate of the economy as a whole as suggested in some of the headline reporting considered above, higher levels of growth in the creative industries in this period are clear. Whereas in 2006 the total UK GVA

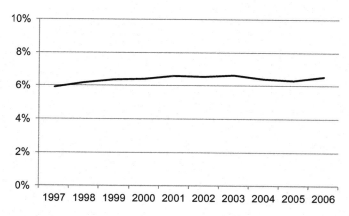

Fig. 5.2 Proportion of total UK employment attributable to the creative economy (2009 definition) (*Source* DCMS [2009])

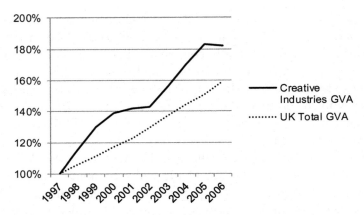

Fig. 5.3 Creative industries vs. total UK GVA growth—proportion of 1997 levels (2009 definition) (*Source* DCMS [2009])

figure was almost 60% higher than its level in 1997, creative industries GVA rose by just over 80%, with broadly consistent outperformance year-on-year. We could thus make a more modest claim of outperformance based on these figures that the creative industries are growing around 1.3 times as fast as the economy as a whole.

Whilst overall employment growth is lower than GVA growth, the solid creative economy line in Fig. 5.4 represents a rise in creative employment from over 1.5 million people to almost 2 million, again broadly in line with the headline figures quoted above, although again it should be emphasised that this is not the level of employment solely in creative *industries*, which is around 60% of this figure.

As such we can see that in reflecting back based on the data available in 2009, although some of the positions quoted above from earlier in this period seem overly optimistic, there is nevertheless some evidence here to substantiate an account of a successful set of industries performing well in comparison with the national economy as a whole. What then of the positions which clearly link this performance with culturally expressive activity which we saw also dominate in this period? Here a problem emerges. What is also clear from consideration of these figures is the extent to which they are dominated by one of the 13 creative industry sectors, namely 'software, computer games and electronic publishing'.

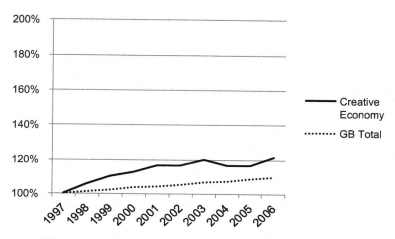

Fig. 5.4 Creative economy vs. total GB employment growth—proportion of 1997 levels (*Source* DCMS [2009])

The Emergence of the Software Problem

Given the consistent emphasis on cultural, expressive activities in determining what unifies the creative industries, the inclusion of 'software' in the overall definition, and in subsequent data gathering, has long been queried. Of the earlier DCMS Mapping Documents, Bilton and Leary argued that these gather up 'the usual suspects (music, the performing arts, television and radio) as well as some more contentious candidates (software and computer services)' (2002, p. 50). Mould similarly argues that these mapping documents are 'rather random' exercises, and that the inclusion of sectors such as software 'bloated the figures [collated] somewhat' (2017, p. 35). In 2005, Hesmondhalgh and Pratt referred to 'dubiously broad' definitions, resulting in 'inflated commentary' via processes such as 'software design of many kinds [being] blurred with [cultural activities such as] recording' (p. 8). In establishing why the industries included in the definition of creative industries might have ended up covering such a broad range of activities, beyond what would traditionally be considered 'cultural industries', Hesmondhalgh et al. refer to an interview with British film producer Lord Puttnam who is characterised as 'highly influential and respected in Labour circles' (2015, p. 51) during the period in which such data gathering occurs, and 'part of a network of industry activists who were seeking to exert influence on government by persuading them of the economic importance of industries such as film, music recording and so on' (p. 50). In this interview, figures such as those considered above are directly discussed:

> I think the very first number we ever coined for the value of the creative industries was about 2.2 per cent [...] of GDP. In conversations with Chris Smith and you need to talk to him, my memory is saying to me, he said we could drive that to 3.5 per cent, you know, we certainly could drive it to 3.5 per cent and maybe beyond that. We then started getting very excited talking about 5 per cent. I think the figure at the moment, not many people will argue [with the view] that it's probably a tad under 6 per cent. (Puttnam, cited in Hesmondhalgh et al. 2015, pp. 63–64)

Indeed, from the figures cited above, it seems that a figure of around 6% of both GVA and employment would be a suitable conclusion to draw. How, though, does one lift the figure from 3.5% of total economic output to 6%? Whilst the percentage figures are trifling, in the context of an entire economy, the difference in GVA will represent dozens of billions of pounds, and so is not inconsiderable. In effecting this rise, Hesmondhalgh et al. point to the necessity of taking a 'very inclusive definition of the creative industries that brought in the very large sectors of software and architecture' alongside the activities that would more usually be considered as cultural industries (2015, p. 64). Whilst one could argue for some form of culturally expressive activity in some forms of architecture, Hesmondhalgh's analysis of the appropriateness of the inclusion of 'software' in this grouping is stark:

> Developing [...] software is a very different activity from the artistic-expressive (or journalistic-informational) pursuits evoked by the term 'creative industries'. It is this artistic-expressive element – the aura of the 'artist' – that is in large part the source of the sexiness of the concept for politicians and other policymakers. (2007, p. 179)

Given this difference, Garnham argues that the inclusion of software explains the shift to a language of 'creativity'. Software production is not generally considered to be cultural in an expressive, artistic sense, and so will not easily fit as a 'cultural industry', but he argues it is only via the inclusion of software that it is 'possible to make the claims about size and growth stand up' (2005, p. 26), a point echoed by Banks and O'Connor, who argue that the new terminology of creativity is specifically designed to create this bridge from expressive cultural activities to software, and so align its economic performance to these more cultural activities, allowing the sector 'to be taken seriously by finance ministries and government accountants' (2017, p. 645).

What is concerning here is that although the importance of artistic and cultural activity to the creative industries is consistently argued for, these authors are correct that it is in fact this most unusual sector that is most important in creating the economic statistics produced in this period. It is also almost never mentioned when headline figures are reported. As such, in this period Taylor notes that the inclusion of particular codes relating to software in data gathering ultimately 'gives an impression of size that is unjustified' (2006, p. 9). Figure 5.5 shows how the proportion of creative industries GVA attributable to 'software,

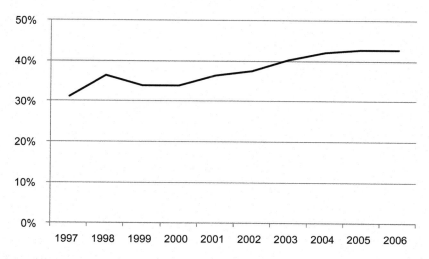

Fig. 5.5 Proportion of creative industries GVA attributable to software (2009 definition) (*Source* DCMS [2009])

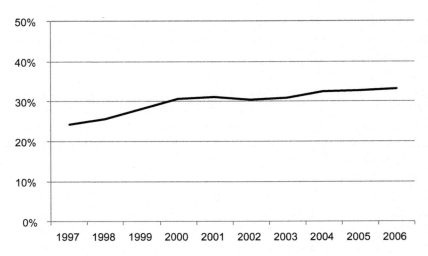

Fig. 5.6 Proportion of creative economy employment attributable to software (*Source* DCMS [2009])

computer games and electronic publishing' rises almost consistently year-on-year in this period, approaching half of the overall total. As it is with GVA, so it is, to a lesser extent, with levels of creative economy employment, as Fig. 5.6 shows.

At this point, it may be objected that to refer to the category 'Software, Computer Games & Electronic Publishing' just as 'software' is to ignore the cultural component that forms part of this category, and which *is* an appropriate sibling to the other expressive, cultural sectors listed. If publishing is appropriately creative due to its dissemination of expressive forms, why not *electronic* publishing also? Is it not simply a form of cultural elitism that considers computer games not to be an expressive form? It should be noted, therefore, that it is much wider activities than these which form the major part of this grouping. Whilst the development and encroachment of information technology and software into ever more areas of human existence have indeed been transformational within living memory, including in the cultural realm (e.g. Hesmondhalgh and Meier 2018), there seems no clear justification at this point for aligning this development with a group of industries based on artistic, cultural expression, nor for statistics to be based upon a position whereby *all* activity relating to software is considered to be expressively creative, other than for the inflationary motives outlined above. As noted above, certain SIC codes are seen as only partially representative of the creative industries when data is collated, and therefore, scaling factors are applied to these codes in an attempt to more accurately represent the creative sector. We may consider then what scaling factors are applied to this group, as at least *some* developments in software will surely be relevant to cultural practices. For the 'Software, Computer Games and Electronic Publishing' sector, however, SIC codes representing large swathes of employment and GVA are not scaled at all, and so are taken to be *wholly* 'creative'. In 2009, the constituent parts of DCMS group 8/12 were given by three separate SIC codes. A sense of the activities they cover and the proportion taken for data gathering in this period can be gleaned from official definitions:

22.33 Reproduction of computer media (25%)
This class includes: reproduction from master copies of software and data on discs and tapes

72.21 Publishing of software (100%)
This class includes: development, production, supply and documentation of ready-made (non-customised) software

72.22 Other software consultancy and supply (100%)
This class includes:

- analysis, design and programming of systems ready to use:
- analysis of the user's needs and problems, consultancy on the best solution
- development, production, supply and documentation of made-to-order software based on orders from specific users
- writing of programs following directives of the user
- web page design.

(HMSO 2002, pp. 77, 149–150)

A sense of the relative size of each of these codes is presented in Fig. 5.7 showing levels of employment within each of these areas in Great Britain in 2007.

Although the 2003 SIC codes do not enable computer games to be separated out, the 'electronic publishing' component of DCMS category 8/12 'Software, Computer Games and Electronic Publishing' is

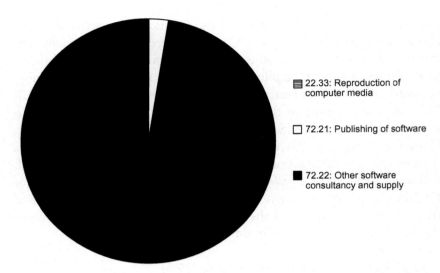

Fig. 5.7 Relative 2007 employment in SIC03 codes relating to software (*Source* ONS [2010b])

a negligible proportion of this grouping, so small as to be invisible in Fig. 5.7, and thus it is not unreasonable to refer to this group as 'software' as has been done above. Using this data from 2007, however, also enables this picture to be refined somewhat by considering the data which maps to these codes in the newer, more refined, 2007 SIC schema discussed above. This is shown in Fig. 5.8.

The overall pattern can here be understood in a more refined fashion: code 18.20 represents 'reproduction of recorded media', part of which is computer media which, again, is negligible; 58.21 is a new code for 'publishing of computer games' both online and offline, which is essentially invisible in Fig. 5.8; 58.29 represents 'other software publishing' (i.e. it does *not* include computer games), which forms a similar slice to 72.21 in Fig. 5.7; and the large 72.22 category now maps to three separate codes, officially defined as follows:

62.01 Computer programming activities
This class includes the writing, modifying, testing and supporting of software.

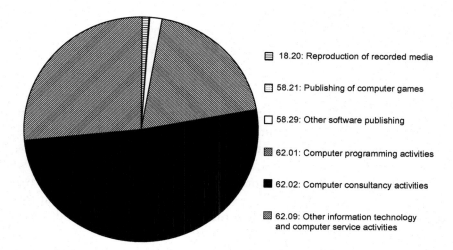

Fig. 5.8   Relative 2007 employment in SIC07 codes relating to software (*Source* ONS [2010b])

This class includes:
- designing the structure and content of, and/or writing the computer code necessary to create and implement:
  *systems software (including updates and patches)
  *software applications (including updates and patches)
  *databases
  *web pages
- customising of software, i.e. modifying and configuring an existing application so that it is functional within the clients' information system environment

62.02 Computer consultancy activities
This class includes the planning and designing of computer systems which integrate computer hardware, software and communication technologies. Services may include related users training.

62.09 Other information technology and computed service activities
This class includes other information technology and computer-related activities not elsewhere classified, such as:

- computer disaster recovery services
- installation (setting-up) of personal computers
- software installation services.

(ONS 2009, p. 189)

The majority of these activities clearly have very little to do with the expressive value or cultural forms posited as characteristic of the creative sector. Whilst employment is being treated in the figures above as a proxy for overall size, a sense of the minor role for computer games, for instance, is also given by work emerging from the DCMS Creative Economy Programme which suggests that computer games account for only 1% of employment and 3% of turnover of 'core' creative industries activity (Frontier Economics 2007, p. 119).

Over this period, we thus also begin to see arguments for the removal of these codes when gathering data to represent the performance of the creative industries. A Nesta report of 2006 takes direct issue both with the inclusion of software and with the 'creative economy' model of generating employment figures:

The "creative industries" is taken to include sectors and activities that would not commonly be regarded as creative. The most obvious example is the inclusion of software and computer services in the DCMS figures. This sector accounts for up to 37 per cent of GVA (£20.7 billion), 33 per cent of employment, and 43 per cent of the total number of businesses in the creative industries as a whole. Further, the frequently quoted figure of 1.8 million people employed in creative occupations consists of nearly 770,000 people who are employed outside of the creative industries. These jobs have not been generated by the creative industries, and so cannot be regarded as directly indicative of the economic significance of the creative industries. (Nesta 2006, p. 53)

There is also an indication in 2006 that data gathered by other bodies takes a different approach to that employed by DCMS:

The DCMS boosted employment by 500,000 and income by £36.4bn by adding in the UK's software sector – the biggest single contributor to employment and earnings, but precious little to do with the arts. (Pointedly, the DTI [Department of Trade and Industry] now excludes computer software from its estimate of the earnings of the creative industries, which in any case it refuses to see as a sector in its own right.) (Heartfield 2006, p. 77)

Indeed, Schlesinger also notes that inside the DTI (and later in its reconfigured form, 'BERR', the Department for Business, Enterprise and Regulatory Reform), figures relating to software were judged to have inappropriately inflated the case for creative industries (2009, p. 16), and in the wider literature, there is speculation as to what the impact on creative industries statistics would be if software categories were removed (White 2009, p. 341). Soon after this period, however, the need for such speculation ceases.

Stage Two: Changing Definitions (2011–2014)

In 2010, the regular DCMS CIEE report was produced for the first time using the newly available 2007 SIC codes. Although by this period the ABI was running as the Annual Business Survey (ABS), data sources remain comparable, but due to the introduction of these new data categories, disclaimers are included warning of the discontinuity with earlier periods. Whilst not directly comparable, though, the overall proportion of total UK GVA stated as attributable to creative industries in 2010 remains similar to the general run of figures seen in Fig. 5.1, albeit slightly smaller at 5.6%. Software also continues to act as the largest individual subsector, with the proportion of creative industries GVA and employment attributable to software being 45 and 33%, respectively. Also, a similar proportion of total 'creative economy' employment is specifically within the creative industries themselves in these figures (56%).

Whilst the overall picture is comparable, however, the slight reduction in overall GVA is attributed in the 2010 report to a refinement of measurement of the software sector made possible by the new SIC coding schema encountered in Fig. 5.8, explained thus:

The dividing up of code 72.22 from SIC 2003 has improved our ability to measure this sector considerably. 72.22 has been split up into 3 codes in SIC 2007: 62.01, 62.02 and 62.09. Using the definition from the 2001 creative industries mapping document, we were able to drop 62.09 (Other information technology and computer service activities) from our definition, as it was clear that this did not belong in the Creative Industries. Category 62.09 consists of the following types of business:

- Computer disaster recovery services
- Installation (setting-up) of personal computers
- Software installation services. (DCMS 2010, p. 30)

An explanation is also provided of how the inclusion of this code now excluded as inappropriate would have affected the overall statistical picture:

If we measured Software in the same way that we did in 2007 (i.e. included code 62.09), then our estimate of the GVA that the Creative Industries account for would be just under 7%, much higher than previously. Therefore our ability to measure the Creative Industries more accurately (and exclude those businesses whose main activities are not creative) has actually led to our estimates falling. (DCMS 2010, p. 30)

Obviously, a more accurate definition is to be favoured over a less accurate one, but here we see that most of the codes previously used to represent software (or, rather, the newer versions of these codes) are still seen as appropriately 'creative', and thus, overall figures change slightly, but by no means dramatically. Further revision, however, occurs in 2011 when more codes relating to software are removed in the name of accuracy and an appropriate capturing of creativity, described by DCMS thus:

SIC codes 62.02 and 62.01/2 were removed as the industries these captured were more related to business software than to creative software. (2011, p. 9)

It seems by this point in time as though critiques such as these outlined above have, after many years of data production, been heeded. As these software codes constitute such a major part of the statistics considered above, this further revision dramatically alters the overall statistical picture relating to the creative industries. The total GVA attributed to creative industries in the 2011 CIEE report is at half of its previous level—down from 5.6 to 2.8%, lower than any previous level (see Fig. 5.1). Total creative employment is also reduced to 65% of its previous level, at 1.5 million, or 5% of total employment, again lower than any previous level (see Fig. 5.2).

Given the primacy of economic narratives, this reduction would seem to pose some problems for the furthering of the Creativity Agenda encountered thus far, and there is speculation from interested parties that these amendments represent a response to external pressure. Jeremy Silver, a member of the UK Creative Industries Council, characterises the change as 'a revenge of the statistics nerds type scenario', speculating that rather than being appropriately labelled as creative industries, social media companies may be labelled as telecommunications companies, and 'maybe the statistical nerds are too afraid of an industry lobby group more alert to the value of metrics than the less numerate Creative Industries lobbyists' (2012). This may be the case, although it is also possible that those collating the statistics were attempting to respond to calls such as those made by the Technology Strategy Board at a time when Silver was the Board's 'lead specialist in creative industries' which argued for the inclusion of social media, but also argued that 'it would be helpful to remove the broader category of software development from the Creative Industries sector' (2009, p. 21). Similarly, Anamaria Wills, CEO of the Creative Industries Development Agency, argues that the redefinition seems to be DCMS 'cav[ing] in to Treasury contempt' (2013). In any case, after many years of data-gathering exploits, statistics which at least make a defensible case to be 'more accurate' definitions, capturing only the more culturally expressive activities which are positioned as central to the creative industries, result in a picture of a sector which is responsible for less than 3% of total GVA. It is therefore hard to see how the dominant position, positing a set of artistic and culturally expressive activities resulting in a fast-growing sector, approaching 10% of total GVA and central to future economic success, could persist. But persist it does, largely as a result of the presentation of the above 'crisis' point not as the gradual emergence of a more realistic picture of the position of the creative industries, but rather as a technical problem regarding definition, with an objective technical solution.

Repairing the Creative Industries Statistics

After the much reduced figures in the 2011 CIEE report, DCMS 'agreed with stakeholders' to cease publication of any further estimates until 'a new classification' was decided upon (2013a, p. 2). Why is any change needed? It cannot be that the numbers simply 'need' to be larger. Rather, DCMS argues in 2013 that the reason is that 'inconsistencies in the DCMS methodologies [...] have emerged with the passage of time' (2013b, p. 6) relating to both the areas of activity included and the SIC codes used to capture these. It seems, however, that these problems with methodology had been identified in some areas for a decade, yet had only become sufficiently problematic for action to be taken once they began to have a major impact on the magnitude of the statistics regarding economic performance.

Key to the 'repair' of the creative industries statistics in the UK is Nesta, an organisation originally established by New Labour in 1998, but operating on a quite different basis as a charity since 2012, as briefly noted in Chapter 1 (Oakley et al. [2014] give a detailed account of Nesta's history). Soon after the 2011 release, Nesta was quick to note that the newly reduced figures are ultimately the result of changing definitions, rather than any changes in actual activity (Bakhshi and Freeman 2012), and one year on, in early 2013, released a report proposing a new definition (Bakhshi et al. 2013). This rightly began by noting that, despite the continuing success of the concept, and years of data production, 'creativity' had never been explicitly defined by those responsible for such data (p. 6), and elsewhere noted that the 2011 redefinition above reveals that DCMS statistics are based on a 'pragmatic selection' of SOC and SIC codes, not a 'systematic methodology' (Bakhshi et al. 2015, p. 8). A new model is thus proposed to rectify this based on the concept of 'creative intensity': if a creative industry employs many workers in creative occupations, it has a higher 'intensity'. This is based on work carried out by Freeman in 2004 which found, for example, that in London in 2003 48% of those working in creative *industries* also had creative *occupations* (GLA Economics 2004, p. 7). By this model, we thus start to move more definitively away from a concern with particular industries, towards particular creative activities, and thus, the concerns expressed by Nesta in 2006 noted at the end of the previous section regarding this shift (albeit by different authors, under a different organisational structure) have by this point been put aside. We thus see an application of the more broad-ranging models of creativity considered in Chapter 3. Here in evidence gathering too, therefore, creativity proves to be a malleable concept, able to change shape depending on the task at hand.

By this new model, Bakhshi et al. argue that the SIC codes used to define creative industries by DCMS range from those with high creative intensity (e.g. 9003 'Artistic Creation', in which 90% of workers are in creative occupations) to very low creative intensity (e.g. 5829 'Other Software Publishing' in which 3% of workers are in creative occupations). The task, then, remains to define what appropriately counts as 'creative'. A first indication of the definition in Nesta's report is given in the following statement:

> The creative worker has a concept of what 'kind' of effect is desired, but is not told how to produce that effect in the same way that, say, an assembly line worker or even skilled technician is instructed. The creativity, in our view, consists in devising an original way of meeting a differentiated need or requirement that is not expressed in precise terms. (Bakhshi et al. 2013, p. 22)

Creative industries are thus characterised primarily by the 'creative talent' of their workforce: they are *not* distinguished by cultural outputs, or by innovation or originality, necessarily (p. 23). What makes a distinctively creative occupation then? This is defined as follows, echoing the text above:

> A role within the creative process that brings cognitive skills to bear to bring about differentiation to yield either novel, or significantly enhanced products whose final form is not fully specified in advance. (p. 24)

Here we have some problematic circularity. Whilst on the one hand it is accurately noted that historically there has been a lack of systematic definition, here we find that creative occupations involve 'a role within the creative process'—what, then, is the creative process? A further set of five criteria is offered to make things clearer. These, however, also demonstrate this circularity to some degree. Firstly, the creative role must achieve a goal in a novel way; even if an established process exists, the creative occupation exhibits 'creativity' at many stages in the process (p. 24). Secondly, creative roles must be resistant to mechanisation:

> The very fact that the defining feature of the creative industries is their use of a specialised labour force shows that the creative labour force clearly contributes something for which there is no mechanical substitute. (p. 24)

Whilst we may choose to *define* creativity as a quality resistant to mechanisation, this is not objectively clear. The third condition given is that creative roles are not repetitive, however, which helps to qualify this resistance to mechanisation. Fourthly, the role must make a 'creative contribution to the value chain' and the outcome must be 'novel or creative' regardless of context. Whilst this again may seem unhelpfully circular, an example is offered:

> A musician working on a cruise ship (a transport industry) is still creative while a printer working within a bank is probably operating printing technology and hence would be considered mechanistic and not creative. (p. 24)

Why is the musician creative? What is 'novel' about the musical output? As Becker argues specifically of the example of musicians in a different setting:

> We typically treat playing an instrument in a symphony orchestra as an extremely original and creative way of making a living, although many, if not most, symphony players testify that it is, in fact, extremely repetitive and boring work. How many times can you play the nine Beethoven symphonies "creatively"? (2017, p. 1580)

If the novelty is simply in the fact that any live performance is in some sense 'new', then presumably there may also be a small element of novelty to the specific outputs of the printer referred to. If the musician is creative because music is creative, then we get no closer to an actual definition of what this creativity is, above and beyond the definitions already in use. Finally, the creative role is also defined as involving 'interpretation, not mere transformation'. Again, an example is offered:

> A draughtsperson/CAD technician takes an architect's series of 2D drawings and renders them into a 3D model of the building. While great skill and a degree of creative judgement are involved, arguably the bulk of the novel output is generated by the architect and not by the draughtsperson. (Bakhshi et al. 2013, p. 24)

Again, then, we may ask of the hypothetical musician, are they 'creatively' interpreting the music they play, or translating a written score into sound, in a manner analogous to a drawing being rendered into a model? Again, if music is simply 'inherently' creative, we have not established here on what basis.

Whilst these criteria leave many areas open to further clarification, their delineation is concluded by a note that 'of course' they are problematic when considered in isolation, and 'do not offer hard and fast rules for determining whether an occupation is or is not "creative"' (Bakhshi et al. 2013, p. 25). In light of this, one may well question how far we have come in rectifying the problem of the prior absence of explicit definitions or systematic methodologies. Nevertheless, Bakhshi et al. proceed to use these five criteria to allocate each SOC code a score out of 5. Occupations scoring 4 or 5 out of 5 count as 'creative'. To give some examples, dancers and choreographers, artists, and musicians score 5 out of 5, as do librarians, IT strategy and planning professionals, and marketing and sales directors (p. 27). Elsewhere, Bakhshi refers to this as 'an inherently subjective exercise' (2016, p. 5). Given the importance of this definitional process, it is somewhat odd that comparatively little time is spent explaining it, and much more time is spent explaining its potential effects in a manner which, given its reference to statistical concepts such as type I and II errors and Bayesian priors, may be somewhat opaque to many within the creative sector. Still, following the application of a range of statistical methods to the subjective scoring exercise, the report argues that to consider any industry a 'creative' one requires more than 30% of its workers to be in roles scored as creative. The potential statistics that would result from the application of such a method are traced, and Bakhshi states that Nesta's goal is for 'the British government and the DCMS to adopt our methodology' (2013). This goal is essentially achieved, and this intensity measure is referred to as the basis of the CIEE reports as reintroduced in 2014, with the patterns revealed by this process characterised as 'robust' (DCMS 2014a, p. 4).

Given their centrality to the celebratory economic headlines prior to 2011, we may ask if the software industries previously judged to be inappropriate inclusions due to the judgement that they are predominantly concerned with business-related software make it above this 30% threshold for inclusion as creative. Then Culture Minister Ed Vaizey's update to the Creative Industries Council (CIC) from 2013, prior to the first publication by DCMS of revised estimates, is instructive (as is the use here too of the shorthand of 'software' to refer to these industries):

> DCMS was asked to provide an update on its consultation on classifying and measuring the creative industries: revised economic estimates were needed for the CI website and the upcoming strategy. [Vaizey] reported that the consultation outcome and estimates would soon be published. Software would be included. (CIC 2013a, p. 4)

In considering the 30% 'intensity' threshold, it is pertinent to note that SIC code 62.02, 'Computer Consultancy Activities', which makes up the majority of the large 'software' category, returns as it is calculated to have a 'creative intensity' of 32.8% (codes relating to libraries and museums are also included, despite having 'creative intensities' below 25%, 'after consultation' [DCMS 2014a, p. 27]). It is perhaps useful here to also note Hesmondhalgh et al.'s characterisation of the CIC as the 2010 Conservative-Liberal Democrat coalition government's version of Labour's Creative Industries Task Force, 'stacked with figures from the corporate industries, and a few associated with the IT sectors' (2015, p. 195), and the fact that earlier in 2013 the Council also emphasised the 'importance of data as an aid to promoting the Creative Industries both at home and abroad' (2013b, p. 1).

This process eventually results in a new nine sector model of the creative industries, containing essentially the same activities as the 13 sector model previously in operation in the following configuration:

1. Advertising and marketing
2. Architecture
3. Crafts
4. Design and designer fashion
5. Film, TV, video, radio and photography
6. IT, software and computer services
7. Publishing
8. Museums, galleries and libraries
9. Music, performing and visual arts. (DCMS 2018a, p. 12)

Stage Three: The Persistent Economic Success of Creativity (2014–?)

Redefinition of creativity, then, results in a set of official statistics that return to mirror their previous form; the Economic Estimates of 2014 use the ABS and Annual Population Survey (APS) as sources—the APS combines variables from the LFS with a boost sample (UKDS 2012)— and so again data sources are broadly comparable in this period. The 2014 figures based on the newly adopted definition reveal that the creative industries, with a wider category of software returned to the fold, now constitute 5% of total UK GVA, with software returning to its place as the largest individual subsector, accounting for 43% of total creative industries GVA. Total creative employment is at this point set at 2.5 million, or 8.5% of total employment (DCMS 2014a). Given that we thus see a significant repair of the narrative of economic success regarding the creative industries, we can review the figures from the final CIEE report using this model, from 2016, to see what time series data regarding the performance of creative industries over a period of almost two decades reveals. Figure 5.9 includes the data from the 2009

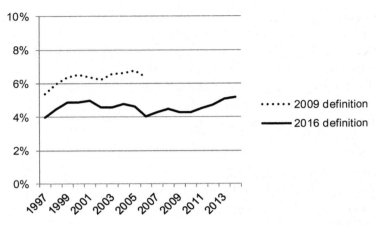

Fig. 5.9 Proportion of total UK GVA attributable to creative industries (2009/2016 definition) (*Source* DCMS [2009, 2016a])

estimates shown in Fig. 5.1, in comparison with the GVA figures provided by this new model in 2016.

The average proportion of total UK GVA attributable to creative industries over this period is 4.6%, and there is broadly a year-on-year rise in this period to a 2014 high of 5.2%. The dominant claims of 8% of GVA from earlier periods thus seem even more optimistic by this stage, and Fig. 5.9 effectively ends at the level where Fig. 5.1 began. Although relative GVA figures are lower, growth patterns are very similar between the 2009 and 2016 definitions, and the outperformance of the creative industries grouping remains, as shown in Fig. 5.10. Software's dominance of the GVA figures also persists, as Fig. 5.11 shows.

Data which could enable a similarly long comparison of employment patterns is not provided in the 2016 CIEE report, but in the period 2011–2015 total creative economy employment rises from 8 to 9% of total UK employment by this model, and mirroring the patterns in Fig. 5.6, software accounts for 31% of creative economy employment in this period. IDBR data for the period 2012–2016 also shows the proportion of creative industry enterprises falling into the 'IT, Software and Computer Services' category rising consistently year-on-year from 45 to 49% (ONS 2017).

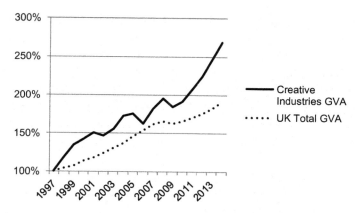

Fig. 5.10   Creative industries vs. total UK GVA growth—proportion of 1997 levels (2016 definition) (*Source* DCMS [2016a])

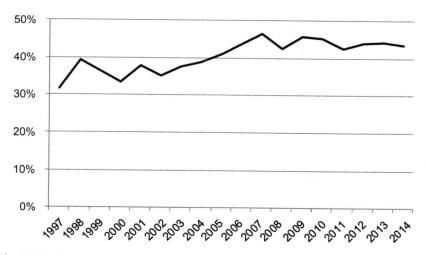

Fig. 5.11   Proportion of creative industries GVA attributable to software (2016 definition) (*Source* DCMS [2016a])

Does Software Become More Prominent in Discussions of Creativity?

Given that there is quite a period of turmoil after which software returns to the creative industries fold, and also given that this period sees earlier arguments around the centrality of cultural, expressive industrial activities give way to the centrality of a more widely defined set of creative occupations, we may expect the importance of software to the overall grouping to be clearer by this later period, and for discussion of the creative industries to no longer be as clearly aligned with artistic, cultural practices. When the headline figures above are released in this period, however, we continue to see the explicit alignment of total economic output with specifically cultural industries. For instance:

> Official statistics published today reveal that the UK's creative industries, which includes the film, television and music industries, are now worth £71.4 billion per year to the UK economy. (DCMS 2014b)

Indeed, in some press releases, almost every sector *except* software is mentioned:

> The UK's booming creative industries made a record contribution to the economy in 2016, new statistics show. Industries including advertising and marketing, arts and film, TV and radio, and museums and galleries are all part of this thriving economic sector, which is now worth almost £92bn. (DCMS 2017a)

Again, it is not that these industries are not worthy of discussion, but it tells us something about the Creativity Agenda that the largest subsector is almost never mentioned. In making the case for culture, then, this period also sees the persistence of the idea that art is at the 'core' of wider economic activity. The Chair of Arts Council England, Sir Nicholas Serota, for instance claims:

> To me the most interesting thing about the role of art and culture is the impact they make across the rest of the creative industries [...] the sector is now bigger than automotive, life sciences, oil and gas and aerospace combined in the UK. (2017)

Given the continued importance of 'evidence' in this era, Serota points to an Arts Council report to substantiate this claim further. This report provides evidence of the role for the arts in the wider creative economy largely from five short case studies of a thousand words or so, gathered in early 2017 (SDG Economic Development 2017). Following the patterns identified in Chapter 4, here we can once again highlight the continuing issues with a reliance on anecdotal data in the arts sector. This report also does little to discourage the drawing of questionable links between sectors. In a box entitled 'Basic information about the Games sector', the number of games companies in the UK is reported along with levels of consumer spending, and a note that 'IT, software and digital games account for around 50% of the creative industries' contribution to UK GVA' (SDG Economic Development 2017, p. 18), but it is not clarified that DCMS figures produced in this period estimate that computer games specifically account for around 1% of this total (DCMS 2016a). Prominent media reporting also continues to link economic statistics predominantly with cultural practice in this period, with total GVA figures being referred to as a 'creative arts windfall' (Partington 2018), aligned with 'industries like design and entertainment' (Boren 2014), and headlines produced such as 'Arts "as important to future economic success as traditional industries"' (Belfast Telegraph 2017).

The arts and culture are nevertheless a major part of these statistics. Indeed, regardless of calculations of creative intensity, as the nine creative industries sectors specified by DCMS in this new period cover essentially the same activities as in prior periods, the positions set out above regarding the essential difference of software remain pertinent. If software is once again separated out on this basis, however, we can see that there is definitely a case to be made for software as an unusually high-growth sector over the period in which the Creativity Agenda has risen, but that the figures available do not show such a pattern for the remaining creative industries when compared to overall UK GVA growth, as demonstrated in Fig. 5.12.

The other creative industries are obviously of economic importance and, perhaps more crucially, extremely valuable in many other ways, but to continually align the economic performance of the creative industries as a whole with every industry except software does not seem appropriate in light of this pattern.

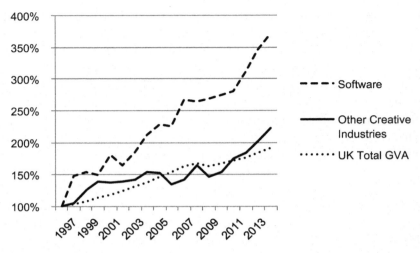

Fig. 5.12 Software vs. other creative industries GVA growth—proportion of 1997 levels (*Source* DCMS [2016a])

The Separation Out of Culture?

Alongside the adoption of a broader definition of creativity in line with some of the positions considered in Chapter 3, in which the centrality of culture becomes somewhat fuzzier, what we also see in this period of data gathering are moves towards the separating out of culture from the specifically creative, and again DCMS statistics here seem to be responding to positions first clearly outlined by Nesta. 2016 sees the last CIEE report published. It also sees a Nesta 'provocation' echo the position above regarding the specifically important role of less cultural areas such as software:

> Cultural interests have benefited from their blurring with the creative industries, insofar as it has allowed them to take credit – directly or indirectly – for the £87 billion in GVA generated by the creative industries, when in fact as much as 43.5 per cent of it is accounted for by 'IT, software and computer services' alone. [...] the conflation between creative industries and cultural policy has, we argue, been detrimental to the UK's interests. It has meant that insufficient attention has been paid

in economic policy to the biggest drivers of creative industries growth which, notwithstanding important economic spillovers from the arts, are largely in service sectors like software, advertising and design, and it has meant that inadequate attention has been given to the cultural reasons for promoting the cultural wellbeing of the nation. (Bakhshi and Cunningham 2016, p. 6)

Where once cultural and expressive activity was positioned as being central to the creative industries, here there are moves to argue that more attention needs to be paid to the biggest economic drivers in the field—a worrying sign for those not in these sectors that those who live by the economic output statistics may die by them also. Following the above method, it is thus argued that the cultural sector should be separated out from creative industries, and that evidence for the role of culture in fields beyond the economic needs to be 'marshalled' (2016, p. 7). Given the discussion in Chapter 4, we may be cautious as to the likely success of such attempts. In any case, by this point on, we seem to have once again looped back to the start of the discourse on creative industries, trying to effectively define what is 'cultural', and how this may differ from what is 'creative'.

Reflecting this, DCMS shifts their statistical reporting to producing separate economic estimates by 'sector', with creative industries being one sector and the cultural sector being an overlapping but smaller sector: 20 SIC codes are used to generate data on the 'cultural sector', 16 of which are also included in the list of 31 codes used to generate data on the 'creative industries' (the 4 activities which are 'cultural' but not 'creative' are 'reproduction of recorded media', 'manufacture of musical instruments', 'retail sale of music and video recordings in specialised stores' and 'operation of historical sites and buildings and similar visitor attractions'). This separation does not stop the figures relating to creative industries being linked to specifically cultural activities (and responses to consultation on this process continue to question the appropriateness of including the category of software [DCMS 2017b, p. 8]), but Fig. 5.13 shows the difference in magnitude of statistics for these newly demarcated sectors.

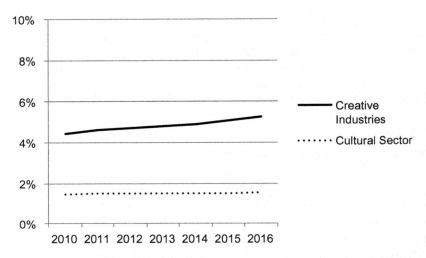

Fig. 5.13 Proportion of total UK GVA attributable to cultural sector and creative industries (*Source* DCMS [2017c])

A similar picture can be seen with respect to employment in Fig. 5.14 (figures for 'creative economy' are also shown in this figure to enable comparison with Fig. 5.2).

In this same period, Arts Council England engages in a parallel evidence production process, commissioning a number of reports from the Centre for Economics and Business Research (CEBR) on the 'contribution of the arts and culture to the national economy'. This also results in a diminution of the headline figures on economic activity attributable specifically to culture. The definition utilised in the first report results in the 'arts and culture industry' being responsible for '0.48 per cent of all employment in England' and 'approximately 0.4 per cent of GVA in England' (CEBR 2013, pp. 2–3). A 2015 update reported a 'buoyant' rise of 36% to GVA between 2010 and 2013, resulting in a 'respectable £7.7billion' (CEBR 2015, p. 6), or 0.56% of GVA in England (p. 31) being attributable to arts and culture. Whilst growth of 36% was merely 'buoyant' between 2010 and 2013, however, a subsequent update reports further growth of 12% as 'staggering' (CEBR 2017, p. 4), resulting in these industries representing 0.66% of GVA in England (p. 23), with employment remaining close to previous figures at 0.46% of total employment in England (p. 24).

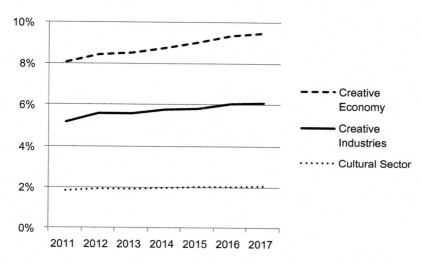

Fig. 5.14 Proportion of total UK employment attributable to cultural sector, creative industries and creative economy (*Source* DCMS [2018b])

Similarly, in this period, yet another definition employed in the DCMS Culture White Paper puts the 'value of culture' as somewhere between £3.5 and £5.5 billion, or around 0.3% of total GVA (2016b, p. 16).

One may question whether a cultural sector that consistently makes the case in this later period that it is worth less than 1% of GVA and total employment is playing its strongest hand. Whilst the value of the arts is still discursively aligned with a narrative of high-growth, economically successful creative industries, this gradual breaking away of culture in statistical production risks the emergence of a less celebratory narrative than the one that held sway in earlier years. If a linkage between arts and software under the banner of 'creativity' was, as we have seen Garnham argue,

> a shorthand reference to the information society [...and] an attempt by the cultural sector and the cultural policy community to share in its relations with the government, and in policy presentation in the media, the unquestioned prestige that now attaches to the information society and to any policy that supposedly favours its development... (2005, p. 20)

...we are left to ponder what happens if this prestige is taken away. Certainly, a statement by the UK Arts and Humanities Research Council's 'first Creative Economy Champion' Andrew Chitty offers an indication of the direction of travel:

> The idea of the Creative Industries is about 20 years old now. But some people still think of it as 'culture' and somehow not as proper as making things like jet engines or cars. (AHRC 2017)

Perhaps as more time passes, the Creativity Agenda will remain malleable enough to drift further from a focus on culture, towards a concern with the 'proper' quality of the industries labelled as creative. Nevertheless, in terms of arguing for economic success we seem to end the second decade of data gathering on creative industries with statements almost identical to those found when such data gathering began:

> The UK's creative industries keep growing at breakneck pace. According to the latest statistics from the Department for Digital, Culture, Media and Sport (DCMS), the number of jobs in the sector grew 4.5 per cent times faster than in the economy overall between 2011 and 2016, while their contribution to value added growth grew twice as fast between 2010 and 2015. (Mateos Garcia et al. 2018, p. 9)

Conclusion

Given the changes traced above, we may ask how much has changed since the early DCMS Creative Industries Mapping Documents. The 2001 Creative Industries Mapping Document argued that the creative industries accounted for 5% of GDP (DCMS 2001, p. 10) and employment of 1.3 million (p. 11), which at that point in time would represent around 5% of total employment. The sector estimates published in 2017 show creative industries accounting for 5% of total UK GVA and 6% of total national employment (DCMS 2017c, d). Whilst the methods of data gathering have undergone many changes, the overall picture presented is almost exactly the same. Yet, although they are from one perspective standing still, the creative industries also still manage to maintain a narrative that they are speeding ahead, and so the narrative of special importance established in the late 1990s persists. This chapter has sought to demonstrate the means by which this has occurred and therefore to establish another series of persistent patterns underlying the Creativity Agenda.

Whilst early data gathering has been presented as somewhat ad hoc, the economic statistics it produced helped the UK model of creative industries to proliferate globally, and to make the case for creativity nationally and regionally. Although over the majority of this period the case for the centrality of cultural and expressive activity was made, when this case eventually resulted in the outputs of the subsector of software being removed from output statistics, a period of reflection ensued and a new model emerged with a broader definition of creativity at its heart which allowed data relating to software to return to the fold. Software thus returned to its role as the largest subsector of statistics in the UK, a role it plays elsewhere (e.g. Heinze and Hoose 2013). We can thus once again usefully consider Law and Urry's theories on the role of methods in 'enacting the social' (2004). The form the creative industries take is not fixed and clear, but in part constituted by the methods used to define them. The categories used to query data sources, the data sources available and the evidence gathered from these sources all have a role to play in constructing an object in a certain form. We have also seen how the Creativity Agenda is flexible enough to allow the object of creativity to be reconstructed in new forms by new methodological approaches at any crisis point in its constitution. When one definition is undermined, a differing one emerges, yet the overall agenda remains largely the same. It is thus also useful in this context to consider Prince's work on the role of consultants in forming the 'global assemblage of culture and creativity' in which,

> evidence is sought to support policy decisions that have effectively been made in advance. But this is not just a reversal of causation. Neutral, seemingly pre-theoretical quantitative evidence, gives policy concepts objective status. (2014, p. 98)

This returns us to a consideration of the status of quantitative data first noted in Chapter 2 (see Rose 1991, p. 674). Contingent data categories can quickly become resilient and lead to objective-seeming, 'neutral' information, substantiating and entrenching certain positions (e.g. Beer 2016). Certainly, the role of such quantitative information seems to continue its importance for the Creativity Agenda.

In more recent periods, however, there are indications that some seek to empty out earlier notions of culture from creativity. Hewison argues that the 1997 renaming of the Department of National Heritage to the Department for Culture, Media and Sport was 'profoundly ideological' (2014, p. 27). We may in this context consider the 2017 renaming of this department to the Department for *Digital*, Culture, Media and Sport ('digital' being used here as a noun), and the ensuing creation of the role of 'Minister for Digital and the Creative Industries'. Bakhshi notes that the department's focus has a constraining impact on how statistics regarding creativity are collated (2016, p. 5), and a shift in focus raises the possibility that the cultural sector will increasingly have to argue its case as a digital innovator in order to continue its alignment with the economic success stories traced above. In this context, DCMS' publication of a report in 2018 entitled 'Culture is Digital' (2018c), which positions technology and culture as 'the ultimate power couple' (p. 5), may be instructive. There is certainly a role for digital innovation in the cultural sector, as in many others, but if such innovation is the quality most valued, cultural policy risks collapsing into technical development. For the time being, however, software continues to be the 'elephant in the room' when it comes to the value associated with the creative industries—domineering to a great degree yet strangely unacknowledged.

From the analysis above, it is thus reasonable to agree with Garnham's assessment that whatever levels of growth there have been due to the emergence of a 'new' economy 'stem *not* from what we normally think of as media and culture [...] but from business information services' (2005, p. 22, emphasis added). Whilst Garnham was writing in Stage 1 outlined above, and noting a sound of caution about the alignment of such cultural and non-cultural activities, by Stage 3, influential voices would argue that this alignment is entirely appropriate as all are 'creative' in a more nebulous sense of carrying out tasks without clear direction, creating outputs with an element of novelty, and so forth. Indeed, such voices also begin to suggest that if we are interested in the benefits of creativity, we should turn our attention *more* towards business information systems. The unexceptional economic performance of the majority of the creative industries thus begins to raise real questions for their assumed role as economic regenerators. From the picture presented in this chapter, therefore, we must be extremely cautious about policies which purport to bring about such regeneration via the operation of creative industries which intervene solely in terms of culture and the arts. Whilst there is a massive overlap between the two in terms of the activities they encompass, as revealed above there is also a crucial disjuncture to contend with. Despite this disjuncture, though, the alignment provided by the overarching Creativity Agenda persists.

References

AHRC. (2017). *Interview: Professor Andrew Chitty.* Retrieved from https://ahrc.ukri.org/research/readwatchlisten/features/interview-professor-andrew-chitty/.

Arts Council England, Association of Independent Museums, Cultural Learning Alliance, English Heritage, The Heritage Alliance, Heritage Lottery Fund, … Visit England. (2010). *Cultural capital—A manifesto for the future.* Retrieved from http://webarchive.nationalarchives.gov.uk/20160204122224/ http://www.artscouncil.org.uk/advice-and-guidance/browse-advice-and-guidance/cultural-capital-manifesto-future.

Babani, D., & Gerrard, N. (2011, April 3). Will funding cuts be good for the arts? *The Observer.* Retrieved from https://www.theguardian.com/culture/2011/apr/03/arts-funding-cuts-debate.

Bakhshi, H. (2013). *Measuring the creative industries in the UK.* Retrieved from https://www.arts.gov/art-works/2013/measuring-creative-industries-uk.

Bakhshi, H. (2016). *Putting creativity on the map—Classification, measurement and legitimation of the creative economy.* Retrieved from https://www.nesta.org.uk/sites/default/files/putting_creativity_on_the_map.pdf.

Bakhshi, H., & Cunningham, S. (2016). *Cultural policy in the time of the creative industries.* London: Nesta.

Bakhshi, H., & Freeman, A. (2012). *How big are the UK's creative industries?* Retrieved from http://www.nesta.org.uk/home1/assets/blog_entries/how_big_are_the_uks_creative_industries.

Bakhshi, H., Freeman, A., & Higgs, P. (2013). *A dynamic mapping of the UK's creative industries.* London: Nesta.

Bakhshi, H., Davies, J., Freeman, A., & Higgs, P. (2015). *The geography of the UK's creative and high-tech economies.* London: Nesta.

Banks, M., & O'Connor, J. (2009). After the creative industries. *International Journal of Cultural Policy, 15*(4), 365–373.

Banks, M., & O'Connor, J. (2017). Inside the whale (and how to get out of there): Moving on from two decades of creative industries research. *European Journal of Cultural Studies, 20*(6), 637–654.

Bazalgette, P. (2017). *Independent review of the creative industries.* Retrieved from https://www.gov.uk/government/publications/independent-review-of-the-creative-industries.

Becker, H. S. (2017). Creativity is not a scarce commodity. *American Behavioral Scientist, 61*(12), 1579–1588.

Beer, D. (2016). *Metric power.* London: Palgrave Macmillan.

Belfast Telegraph. (2017, April 15). *Arts 'as important to future economic success as traditional industries'.* Retrieved from https://www.belfasttelegraph.co.uk/business/news/arts-as-important-to-future-economic-success-as-traditional-industries-35624848.html.

Bilton, C., & Leary, R. (2002). What can managers do for creativity? Brokering creativity in the creative industries. *International Journal of Cultural Policy, 8*(1), 49–64.

Boren, Z. (2014, January 12). *Chancellor should invest in Britain's thriving creative industries, says think tank.* Retrieved from https://www.independent.co.uk/news/uk/politics/chancellor-should-invest-in-britain-s-thriving-creative-industries-says-think-tank-9053756.html.

CEBR. (2013). *The contribution of the arts and culture to the national economy.* London: Centre for Economics and Business Research Ltd.

CEBR. (2015). *The contribution of the arts and culture to the national economy—An update of our analysis of the macroeconomic contribution of the arts and culture industry to the national economy.* London: Centre for Economics and Business Research Ltd.

CEBR. (2017). *The contribution of the arts and culture to the national economy—An updated assessment of the macroeconomic contributions of the arts and culture industry to the national and regional economies of the UK.* London: Centre for Economics and Business Research Ltd.

CIC. (2013a). *Creative Industries Council (CIC) meeting 2.00 pm to 3.30 pm, Wednesday 27 November 2013*. Retrieved from https://assets.publishing. service.gov.uk/government/uploads/system/uploads/attachment_data/ file/265414/CIC_minutes_27_Nov.pdf.

CIC. (2013b). *Creative Industries Council—Minutes of the meeting held January 31st 2013 3.00 pm–4.30 pm at DCMS*. Retrieved from https://www.gov. uk/government/uploads/system/uploads/attachment_data/file/136338/31_ Jan_2013_Creative_Industries_Council_Minutes.docx.

Comedia. (2004). *Culture and regeneration: An evaluation of the evidence.* Nottingham: Comedia.

Davis, R. (2011, October 30). Are Britain's art schools in crisis, as fees stifle a creative generation? *The Observer.* Retrieved from https://www.theguardian. com/education/2011/oct/30/art-and-design-students-college-fees.

DCMS. (2001). *Creative industries mapping documents 2001.* Retrieved from https://www.gov.uk/government/publications/creative-industries-mapping-documents-2001.

DCMS. (2004). *DCMS evidence toolkit—Technical report.* London: DCMS.

DCMS. (2007). *The creative economy programme: A summary of projects commissioned in 2006/7.* London: DCMS.

DCMS. (2009). *Creative industries economic estimates statistical bulletin.* London: DCMS.

DCMS. (2010). *Creative industries economic estimates (experimental statistics)—Full statistical release.* London: DCMS.

DCMS. (2011). *Creative industries economic estimates—Full statistical release.* London: DCMS.

DCMS. (2013a). *Summary explanation of our proposals to change how we classify and measure the creative industries.* London: DCMS.

DCMS. (2013b). *Classifying and measuring the creative industries—Consultation on proposed changes.* London: DCMS.

DCMS. (2014a). *Creative industries economic estimates.* London: DCMS.

DCMS. (2014b). *Creative industries worth £8million an hour to UK economy.* Retrieved from https://www.gov.uk/government/news/creative-industries-worth-8million-an-hour-to-uk-economy.

DCMS. (2016a). *Creative industries economic estimates.* London: DCMS.

DCMS. (2016b). *The culture white paper.* London: DCMS.

DCMS. (2017a). *Creative industries' record contribution to UK economy.* Retrieved from https://www.gov.uk/government/news/creative-industries-record-contribution-to-uk-economy.

DCMS. (2017b). *Economic estimates: Consultation response summary*. London: DCMS.

DCMS. (2017c). *DCMS sectors economic estimates 2016: Gross value added*. London: DCMS.

DCMS. (2017d). *DCMS sectors economic estimates 2017: Employment and trade*. London: DCMS.

DCMS. (2018a). *DCMS sector economic estimates methodology*. London: DCMS.

DCMS. (2018b). *DCMS sectors economic estimates 2017: Employment*. London: DCMS.

DCMS. (2018c). *Culture is digital*. London: DCMS.

DCMS, BERR, & DIUS. (2008). *Creative Britain: New talents for the new economy*. London: DCMS.

Evans, G. (2001). *Cultural planning*. London: Routledge.

Fleming, T., & Erskine, A. (2011). *Supporting growth in the arts economy*. London: Arts Council England.

Flew, T., & Cunningham, S. (2010). Creative industries after the first decade of debate. *The Information Society, 26*(2), 113–123.

Foord, J. (2008). Strategies for creative industries: An international review. *Creative Industries Journal, 1*(2), 91–113.

Economics, Frontier. (2007). *Creative industry performance—A statistical analysis for the DCMS*. London: Frontier Economics Ltd.

Garnham, N. (2005). From culture to creative industries. *International Journal of Cultural Policy, 11*(1), 15–29.

GLA Economics. (2004). *London's creative sector: 2004 update*. London: Greater London Authority.

Government Statisticians Collective. (1979). How official statistics are produced: Views from the inside. In J. Irvine, I. Miles, & J. Evans (Eds.), *Demystifying social statistics* (pp. 130–151). London: Pluto Press.

Heartfield, J. (2006). A business solution for creativity, not a creativity solution for business. In M. Mirza (Ed.), *Culture vultures: Is UK arts policy damaging the arts?* (pp. 71–92). London: Policy Exchange.

Heinze, R. G., & Hoose, F. (2013). The creative economy: Vision or illusion in the structural change? *European Planning Studies, 21*(4), 516–535.

Hesmondhalgh, D. (2007). *The cultural industries*. London: Sage.

Hesmondhalgh, D., & Meier, L. M. (2018). What the digitalisation of music tells us about capitalism, culture and the power of the information technology sector. *Information, Communication & Society, 21*(11), 1555–1570.

Hesmondhalgh, D., & Pratt, A. C. (2005). Cultural industries and cultural policy. *International Journal of Cultural Policy, 11*(1), 1–13.

Hesmondhalgh, D., Oakley, K., Lee, D., & Nisbett, M. (2015). *Culture, economy and politics—The case of New Labour.* Basingstoke: Palgrave Macmillan.

Hewison, R. (2014). *Cultural capital: The rise and fall of creative Britain.* London: Verso.

Higgs, P., Cunningham, S., & Bakhshi, H. (2008). *Beyond the creative industries: Mapping the creative economy in the United Kingdom.* London: Nesta.

HMSO. (2002). *UK standard industrial classification of economic activities 2003.* London: Her Majesty's Stationery Office.

Holden, J. (2007). *Publicly-funded culture and the creative industries.* London: Arts Council England.

Jäger, S., & Maier, F. (2009). Theoretical and methodological aspects of Foucauldian critical discourse analysis and dispositive analysis. In R. Wodak & M. Meyer (Eds.), *Methods of critical discourse analysis* (2nd ed., pp. 34–61). London: Sage.

Jones, S., & Wright, S. (2007). *Making good work: Realising the values of young people's creative production.* London: Demos.

KEA European Affairs. (2006). *The economy of culture in Europe.* Retrieved from http://www.keanet.eu/ecoculture/studynew.pdf.

KEA European Affairs. (2009). *The impact of culture on creativity.* Retrieved from http://www.keanet.eu/docs/impactculturecreativityfull.pdf.

Last, B. (2016). *Connecting creativity, value and money.* Retrieved from https://zenodo.org/record/55754/files/CREATe-Working-Paper-2016-10.pdf.

Law, J., & Urry, J. (2004). Enacting the social. *Economy and Society, 33*(3), 390–410.

Mandelson, P. (2009, August 29). Taking something for nothing is wrong… That's why we must stop illegal file sharing and give the creative industries a breathing space. *The Times.* Retrieved from http://www.timesonline.co.uk/tol/comment/columnists/guest_contributors/article6814187.ece.

Mateos Garcia, J., Klinger, J., & Stathoulopoulos, K. (2018). *Creative nation—How the creative industries are powering the UK's nations and regions.* London: Nesta.

Miller, M. (2013, June 20). I argued for the arts—And won. We will keep the philistines from the gates. *The Guardian.* Retrieved from https://www.theguardian.com/commentisfree/2013/jun/20/argued-for-arts-and-won-philistines-economic-case.

Montgomery, J. (2005). Beware 'the creative class'. Creativity and wealth creation revisited. *Local Economy, 20(4)*, 337–343.

Mould, O. (2017). *Urban subversion and the creative city*. London: Routledge.

Nesta. (2006). *Creating growth—How the UK can develop world class creative businesses*. London: Nesta.

Oakley, K. (2004). Not so cool Britannia: The role of the creative industries in economic development. *International Journal of Cultural Studies, 7*(1), 67–77.

Oakley, K. (2008). Any answer as long as it's right: Evidence-based cultural policymaking. In L. Andersen & K. Oakley (Eds.), *Making meaning, making money* (pp. 18–41). Newcastle upon Tyne: Cambridge Scholars.

Oakley, K., Hesmondhalgh, D., Bell, D., & Nisbett, M. (2014). The national trust for talent? NESTA and New Labour's cultural policy. *British Politics, 9*(3), 297–317.

OECD. (2006). *OECD workshop on the international measurement of culture—Discussion summary and recommendations*. Retrieved from http://www.oecd.org/dataoecd/38/59/38228150.pdf.

OECD. (2007). *National accounts and financial statistics: International measurement of the economic and social importance of culture*. Retrieved from http://www.oecd.org/dataoecd/56/54/38348526.pdf.

ONS. (2006). *Economic trends no. 627*. London: Her Majesty's Stationery Office.

ONS. (2009). *UK standard industrial classification of economic activities 2007 (SIC 2007)—Structure and explanatory notes*. Basingstoke: Palgrave Macmillan.

ONS. (2010a). *A profile of business*. Retrieved from http://www.ons.gov.uk/ons/rel/regional-trends/painting-pictures-of-place-series—topic-profiles/business-topic-profile/business-topic-profile—2010.pdf.

ONS. (2010b). *Annual business inquiry*. Durham: Nomis.

ONS. (2017). *UK SIC 2007 classes in the creative industries 2012 to 2016*. Retrieved from https://www.ons.gov.uk/businessindustryandtrade/business/activitysizeandlocation/adhocs/007075analysisofenterprisesindistrictsoftheukforuksic2007classesinthecreativeindustries2012to2016.

Partington, R. (2018, February 24). *Creative industries fear tuition fees will kill supply of talent*. Retrieved from https://www.theguardian.com/business/2018/feb/24/creative-industries-compelling-case-investing-arts-education.

Prince, R. (2014). Consultants and the global assemblage of culture and creativity. *Transactions of the Institute of British Geographers, 39*(1), 90–101.

Rhodes, C. (2017). *Business statistics—House of Commons library briefing paper 06152*. London: House of Commons Library.

Rindzevičiūtė, E., Svensson, J., & Tomson, K. (2016). The international transfer of creative industries as a policy idea. *International Journal of Cultural Policy, 22*(4), 594–610.

Rose, N. (1991). Governing by numbers: Figuring out democracy. *Accounting, Organizations and Society, 16*(7), 673–692.

Schlesinger, P. (2009). Creativity and the experts: New Labour, think tanks, and the policy process. *The International Journal of Press/Politics, 14*(3), 3–20.

SDG Economic Development. (2017). *Exploring the role of arts and culture in the creative industries*. Leeds: SDG Economic Development.

Serota, N. (2017, November 4). Sir Nicholas Serota: Creative sector is taking a leading role in boosting the UK economy. *The Times*. Retrieved from https://www.thetimes.co.uk/article/sir-nicholas-serota-creative-sector-is-taking-a-leading-role-in-boosting-the-uk-economy-vktdcnll0.

Silver, J. (2012). *DCMS downgrades value of creative industries?* Retrieved from https://jeremy1.wordpress.com/2012/01/14/dcms-downgrades-value-of-creative-industries/.

Smith, C. (1998). *Creative Britain*. London: Faber and Faber.

Stoneman, P. (2009). *Soft innovation: Towards a more complete picture of innovative change*. London: Nesta.

Taylor, C. (2006). Beyond advocacy: Developing an evidence base for regional creative industry strategies. *Cultural Trends, 15*(1), 3–18.

Technology Strategy Board. (2009). *Creative industries technology strategy 2009–2012*. Swindon: The Technology Strategy Board.

The Work Foundation. (2007). *Staying ahead: The economic performance of the UK's creative industries*. London: The Work Foundation.

Throsby, D. (2008). Modelling the cultural industries. *International Journal of Cultural Policy, 14*(3), 217–232.

Throsby, D. (2015). The cultural industries as a sector of the economy. In K. Oakley & J. O'Connor (Eds.), *The Routledge companion to the cultural industries* (pp. 56–69). London: Routledge.

UKDS. (2012). *Using the Labour Force Survey and Annual Population Survey to explore the labour market*. Retrieved from https://www.ukdataservice.ac.uk/use-data/data-in-use/case-study/?id=139.

Volkerling, M. (2001). From cool Britannia to hot nation: 'Creative industries' policies in Europe, Canada and New Zealand. *International Journal of Cultural Policy, 7*(3), 437–455.

White, A. (2009). A grey literature review of the UK Department for Culture, Media and Sport's creative industries economic estimates and creative economy research programme. *Cultural Trends, 18*(4), 337–343.

Wills, A. (2013). *The arts, the creative economy and the truth!* Retrieved from http://4creativentrepreneurs.wordpress.com/2013/04/27/the-arts-the-creative-economy-and-the-truth/.

6

Liverpool: A Case Study in Persistent Creativity

This chapter considers how the Creativity Agenda is taken up in practice by examining activity around the award of the annual European Capital of Culture (ECoC) title to the city of Liverpool in the UK for the year of 2008. Both the justifications made in bidding for this event and earlier cultural policy in the city can be seen to mirror the patterns established thus far, and a rapidly established narrative regarding the programme's success helped to further buttress the Creativity Agenda from 2009 onwards. This chapter will examine how the ECoC competition as a whole becomes linked to goals of economic regeneration, and how in making the case for the 'impact' of the year, Liverpool can also be seen to further develop attempts to build an appropriate evidence base regarding the role of culture. It will be seen that this evidence base plays a part in making the case for the establishment in the UK of a national 'city of culture' programme, first hosted in 2013, and is used to make claims of successful economic outcomes which are taken up by a range of stakeholders. This economic case is aligned to the operation of creative industries, which are positioned as a key concern for both national and international city of culture programmes. Whilst there is an alignment with dominant narratives, however, this chapter will also

© The Author(s) 2019
P. Campbell, *Persistent Creativity*, Sociology of the Arts,
https://doi.org/10.1007/978-3-030-03119-0_6

consider the challenges that this case raises for these narratives, suggesting, although it promises much, that the Creativity Agenda is limited in its influence and increasingly conventional in its application.

Liverpool Before Capital of Culture

Whilst this chapter cannot give a comprehensive account of Liverpool's lively cultural, social and political history, in establishing how the Creativity Agenda is promoted in this specific location, it is important to consider some key markers from Liverpool's history which lay the groundwork for its tenure as ECoC. Looking back to the nineteenth century, O'Brien gives a succinct account of the city's historic wealth and its deployment in the establishment of cultural institutions:

> The wealth generated by Liverpool's former role as a crucial spoke in the British Imperial system left a lasting legacy in the city that was ploughed into culture. […] Liverpool became one of the leading Victorian cities for founding cultural institutions, including the Liverpool Academy of Arts in 1810; the Royal Liverpool Philharmonic Society, one of the oldest classical concert organisations in the world, in 1840; William Brown Library and Museum in 1853; and the Walker Art gallery in 1877. (2014, p. 96)

The city would not continue to be characterised by its wealth, however. As Wilks-Heeg notes, in the twentieth century Liverpool descended from being an internationally significant 'world city' to a 'pariah city' (2003, p. 36). Whilst in the early twentieth century, Liverpool played a key role in the development of *local* cultural policy, with the Liverpool Corporation (the precursor to the current City Council) making grants from local rates to enable the Walker Gallery to purchase art (Minihan 1977, p. 177; O'Brien 2014, p. 96), by the late twentieth century, following decades of decline (Wilks-Heeg 2003), the city played a key role as a testing-ground for policies seeking to achieve urban regeneration of the kind first considered in Chapter 2.

Whilst no longer a centre of global commerce in the twentieth century, given the focus in previous chapters on the emergence of mass cultural commodities, we may note that Liverpool has an unusually strong, global, cultural reputation, in no small part due to it being home to the single most successful group in the era of popular recorded music, the Beatles. Their success from the 1960s, however, is not one that is dependent on industries based in Liverpool, nor one that has been consistently well capitalised upon in the city itself. As such, this cultural flourishing, and the resultant international reputation, did little to stem the wider challenges the city faced. Throughout the later twentieth century, levels of employment amongst Liverpool's population, and the level of the population itself, showed significant decline and through the 1970s, cultural activities remained low on the local political agenda, as was the case in many local authorities in the UK (O'Brien 2010, p. 119). In the 1980s, however, Liverpool hosted one of the earliest national events posited as offering a form of cultural regeneration— the first UK Garden Festival of 1984. A model adopted by the national Conservative government, based on the biennial *Bundesgartenschauen* which have operated in Germany since the 1950s, these festivals were 'intended to both stimulate development and steer design on a site that would otherwise remain derelict' (Theokas 2004, pp. 2, 5). Whilst the focus here on renovating derelict land to accommodate and attract new housing and employment is somewhat different to the cultural festivals considered later in this chapter, there are similarities here in the use of a festival to stimulate urban development, image change, and to attract tourists to a site otherwise characterised by decline. Indeed, in the 1980s the Liverpool Garden Festival became the most visited tourist attraction in Britain (Theokas 2004, p. 153). Without political support at local level, however, this success was a temporary one, and the festival site was closed in 1987. (After five biennial iterations, the entire UK scheme itself ceased with the final festival hosted by Ebbw Vale in 1992.)

As discussed in Chapter 2, attempts to use the arts and culture in urban regeneration became more prominent and direct as the 1980s progressed, and in this period, Liverpool became an early exemplar of trends that came to characterise the Creativity Agenda later taken up more widely. For instance, when the Tate Gallery, founded in the late nineteenth century, set up its first 'outpost' in 1988, this was housed in disused dock buildings in Liverpool (Evans 2011, p. 9). Gray argues that this was 'largely discussed in terms of urban regeneration and social cohesion and it took some time before more traditional concerns of the museum system, such as curatorship, began to be considered' (2007, p. 210). In addition to the installation of a high-profile gallery in space left disused as a result of some of the economic transformations traced in Chapter 2, in this period the city was also 'one of the first to identify the role of the arts and cultural industries' (Evans 2011, p. 9). Nevertheless, this can only be concretely traced back to the mid-to-late 1980s; prior to this, others have claimed that the city was 'in the dark ages' regarding the role that 'arts and cultural industries' may play (Evans 1996, p. 13).

From this period, the role of cultural policy in economic regeneration is discussed directly in City Council strategy documents (Parkinson and Bianchini 1993, p. 162), and it should be noted that the city's wider cultural reputation remained strong in this period. To once again briefly consider popular musicians from Liverpool, Frankie Goes to Hollywood's 'Relax', released in 1983, remains one of the ten best-selling singles since the emergence of music charts in the UK, alongside the Beatles' 'She Loves You' released two decades previously (everyHit, n.d.). Of this later act, however, an early 'Arts and Cultural Industries Strategy' for the city notes that being home to such prominent cultural figures does not necessarily mean that a city will reap any related economic benefits, and argues that 'none of the £250m earnings from Frankie Goes To Hollywood's first album benefited the local music industry in Liverpool' (Liverpool City Council 1987, p. 7). Despite an identification of such issues, and developments such as the establishment of Britain's first local government Film Liaison Office (Parkinson and Bianchini 1993, p. 166) in an attempt to promote the cultural industries in the city, in reflecting on this period, O'Brien refers to a 'brief flourish of creative industry policy' which had 'little or no effect on raising the profile of cultural policy' within the City Council more broadly (2010, p. 120). Later attempts to develop creative industries also saw mixed success: the proposed establishment of a 'creative industries quarter' in the early 1990s, presented as 'crucial to the council's cultural policy-led regeneration strategy' (Parkinson and Bianchini 1993, p. 172), involved the sale of the freehold of city centre land to a

London-based developer 'Charterhouse', and projections of investment of £100m and the creation of 2500 jobs. This proposal faced many challenges, however, as outlined by Evans:

> Stagnating land and property values in the area, failure to secure the massive resources needed to refurbish many of its buildings, contraction of public subsidies for small arts and media enterprises, the limited appeal and to some, seedy character of clubland, and insufficient critical mass in the arts and cultural industries given the considerable physical extent of the area all slowed progress and later in 1992 Charterhouse went into liquidation. (1996, p. 16)

Although its early successes may therefore be subject to question, we can see that in the staging of cultural festivals promoting redevelopment and tourism, the establishment of major arts interventions in disused spaces, the attempts to develop cultural and creative industries quarters, and consideration of the economic outcomes of cultural policies, Liverpool adopts many aspects of the Creativity Agenda *avant la lettre*. Whilst development of cultural industries seems vexed in this period, the successful tourism effect of the Garden Festival seems to be replicated by Tate Liverpool: although no breakdown of origin is offered, and many visits will be by local residents, by the mid-1990s Tate's director reported 600,000 visits to the gallery per year (Biggs 1996, p. 63).

Nevertheless, Liverpool's major urban challenges continued into the 1990s. In terms of population, Liverpool is the largest of five boroughs which make up the area of Merseyside, to which the European Union's 'Objective One' funds (distributed to areas where GDP is below 75% of the EU average, with the aim of supporting economic development) were first allocated between 1994 and 2000. Notably for the discussion here, as part of this designation in the early 1990s, one of five key 'drivers' identified to transform the region was to develop the 'culture, media and leisure industries' (Couch 2003, p. 177). To this end, European funding resulted in the establishment in 1997 of 'Merseyside ACME', an organisation based in Liverpool which continued to exist in the post-Objective One period (and which was eventually subsumed in 2009 into the first Urban Regeneration Company established in the UK, 'Liverpool Vision') with the stated aim of 'developing creative industries' in the sub-region (Merseyside ACME 2005). Wider regeneration funding in the city at this time also saw organisations set up to, for instance, provide 'arts-based training for young people not in employment, education or training' (Burghes and Thornton 2017, p. 9).

Curiously, although being in many ways early to the Creativity Agenda, after a decade of activity in this field, and by the time the agenda was becoming prominent at the level of national government, there are signs that Liverpool had not developed the capacity to take a lead on this agenda, but instead also became an early exemplar of the pattern of imitative intervention that comes to characterise the field. Whilst by the late 1990s Liverpool had long housed Tate Liverpool, which is a key reference point in the field of cultural regeneration, perhaps the most emblematic building in the history of the concept is the Guggenheim Bilbao. Opened in 1997, the Guggenheim Bilbao accelerates the global tendency to adopt a form of building Evans refers to as 'Karaoke architecture' (2003, p. 417), which becomes a key aspect of the broader, and by this point fast-proliferating, Creativity Agenda. Referring to Helsinki's tenure as ECoC in 2000, for instance, Evans notes the adoption of an emerging 'standard' form of intervention:

> The city has embraced the cultural industries and arts flagship strategy, which includes developing a cultural production zone [...] music conservatoire, and cultural consumption quarter [...with the] obligatory contemporary art museum, *Kiasma* ('a crossing or exchange'), designed by American architect Steven Holl and like Guggenheim-Bilbao, hosting a private, imported collection. (2003, p. 426)

Despite, or perhaps because of, a continuing weakness in local cultural policy (O'Brien 2010, p. 119), as the 1990s end, Liverpool also moves in this direction, with suggestions that the city will not just build the 'obligatory contemporary art museum', but that this will actually also be an outpost of the Guggenheim itself, and that the city will also seek to host the ECoC award. Contemporaneous news reports note the link here with the Objective One funding mentioned above...:

> Inspired by the fame and riches the new Guggenheim museum has brought to Bilbao in Spain, councillors and officials want to put together a £60m package for a building to house more of the priceless art collection of the late Solomon R Guggenheim. [...] By forming a partnership with a variety of regional and national funding bodies, including the lottery, [Liverpool] hopes to unlock some of the aid due to it as one of the poorer regions of the EU. (Ward 1999)

...and the link with the ECoC:

> The scheme to bring the [Guggenheim] museum to King's Dock is one of the high-profile projects that Liverpool is planning to support its aim of becoming the European City of Culture in 2008. (Bennattar 1999)

Indeed, by seeking to further its regeneration by hosting the ECoC, Liverpool is also adopting a specific tactic that by this point is well established.

The European Capital of Culture

As with the history of Liverpool, it is not possible here to give a thorough history of the ECoC project but, briefly put, in the early 1980s this was seen as a potential route by which to counterbalance a European Community overly focussed on economic matters and to give the European project a 'human face' (Bullen 2013, p. 19). Early host cities, beginning with Athens in 1985, all had long-standing global reputations as exceptional cultural centres, and so the award sought to act as a 'celebration' of the fruits of European culture, with the aim of fostering harmony amongst European nations (Connolly 2013, p. 168). Initially arriving at a different European country each year, on its first visit to the UK in 1990 the award took a different turn, aligning more closely with the broader structural precursors to the Creativity Agenda traced in Chapter 2:

> The 1990 award marked a shift in emphasis away from the original model, rooted in a liberal humanist approach to culture, to one where culture was seen as a tool for urban marketing and economic regeneration [...] in line with the urban entrepreneurial drive associated with the then ruling Conservative Party, the UK government initiated an inter-urban competition for the 1990 accolade, which was won by the city of Glasgow. [...] its strategy was not the result of some visionary policy making, but a series of marketing exercises born out of the perceived need to reposition the city in the service economy due to the collapse of its traditional industrial base. (Connolly 2013, p. 168)

Indeed, Griffiths argues that Glasgow—like Liverpool, also previously the host of one of the five UK Garden Festivals—ultimately gains the support of national government following this competition 'largely because of the city's plans to use the year as cultural capital as a means of promoting economic regeneration and image transformation' (2006, p. 418). The award itself is very quickly taken up as evidence of the success of this regeneration strategy. In contemporaneous assessments, for instance, we can find claims such as this:

> Glasgow is undoubtedly the city in Great Britain which is best known for its development of an arts directed urban regeneration strategy. This strategy has been so successful that, in 1987, it applied, and was awarded the title, European City of Culture, for the Year, 1990. (Wynne 1992, p. 91)

Whilst the 1980s saw cities which already had international profiles and, amongst other strengths, strong cultural-tourist economies such as Amsterdam and Paris holding the title, the 1990s saw less high-profile cities such as Glasgow and Thessaloniki designated ECoC, and this divergent trend continued into the early 2000s with sites as diverse as Cork, Patras and Sibiu holding the title. Whilst neither Glasgow nor these other sites are in any way bereft of culture to celebrate, this shift in emphasis positions the ECoC as having a role in transforming fortunes more broadly, and as playing a significant role in achieving the culture-led regeneration considered previously (García 2004a, p. 319). This shift also serves as a spur to further the prominence of the 'creative city' notion previously encountered (Scott 2014, p. 567).

As the 1990s continued and the Creativity Agenda came to further prominence, host cities, or potential host cities, became much more likely to articulate the value of the ECoC not as a way of celebrating European culture, or of making links between nations, but in explicitly economic terms, highlighting the role for the award in processes of urban development (McGuigan 2005; Palmer/Rae Associates 2004, p. 47). Indeed, later reflections on the award note that the programme had become transformed, becoming 'closely intertwined with the sphere of economics, with its emphasis on tourism, place promotion and the fostering of creative industries' (Lähdesmäki 2012, p. 69). Given its role in this transformation, Glasgow thus becomes a recurrent reference point. Evaluations of subsequent ECoCs refer to the success of Glasgow's approach (Deffner and Labrianidis 2005; Richards and Wilson 2004), and the notion of the 'Glasgow model' is one which gains resonance for urban policymakers (García 2004a, 2005). This is perhaps not surprising in the broader context seen in previous chapters in which funding of arts organisations increasingly becomes justified in economic terms, within the context of a trend towards the encroachment of quasi-market principles more broadly across the public sector (Keat 2000, p. 1).

Before considering how this potential regenerative effect was articulated in the Liverpool case, however, it should be noted that the actual substance of any link between the ECoC programme and creative industries development, or any wider economic regeneration, is subject to question in the Glasgow case, despite a largely celebratory uptake of the notion of the 'Glasgow model'. For instance, in the direct aftermath of 1990, Glasgow had still to contend with major problems of deprivation, and Booth and Boyle concluded of local industrial development that,

> there is little evidence to support the argument that Year of Culture 1990 made a clear contribution to local economic development. There was extensive rhetorical reference to the economic and social benefits of developing cultural industries [...] but there were few tangible policies and

fewer projects that linked job creation or training to the very successful program of events. (1993, p. 45)

In 2004, Mooney would characterise the by then entrenched 'Glasgow Model' as a 'myth' (2004, p. 328), and in later analysis, Miller argues that there was no sustained growth resulting from the 1990 programme in Glasgow (2007, p. 45). Similarly, García finds that entrepreneurs in the creative sector in Glasgow 'doubt that the ECOC has been a catalyst for the city's cultural industries and do not feel that the event has had a direct impact on their work' (2005, p. 859), adding:

> Creative entrepreneurs maintain that, if an event as generously funded and publicly acclaimed as Glasgow's ECOC has not resulted in clearly sustainable cultural schemes, there is little hope for any other such initiative to change the trend. (p. 860)

Indeed, on examining the relationship between the ECoC programme and purported economic regeneration across a wide range of host cities in 2004, Palmer/Rae Associates found that 'very few cities' engage on this topic 'in any meaningful way', and that 'economic objectives were stated in reports and in interviews, but there appeared to be much rhetoric but few independent analyses of actions and outcomes' (2004, p. 103). As such, it seems in the case of the ECoC, we once again have an example of a persistent narrative of success founded on comparatively little evidence. Indeed, García concludes that the ECoC programme should not be seen as a robust method of achieving urban regeneration due to 'the poor standards of event monitoring and evaluation, particularly in the long term' (2005, p. 863), and Green similarly notes that although the Capital of Culture model continues to proliferate worldwide beyond Europe, evaluation remains underdeveloped (2017, p. 23). Despite this underdevelopment, however, García emphasises the points above:

> Discourses of success have led to a practically unquestioned mythology developing about Glasgow's ability to tackle its many social and economic problems through arts programming. (2004b, p. 105)

Liverpool's Successful Bid to Become European Capital of Culture

Although there are question marks around the precise role that the ECoC can play, by the late 1990s there was at least a strong belief that the 'Glasgow model' could be deployed in multiple locations. What was also clear as Liverpool prepared to submit its ECoC bid documents in the early 2000s was that the city remained in need of 'regeneration' in many forms, EU Objective One status having been allocated to Merseyside for a second time in 2000, as GDP remained below the European average. Jones and Wilks-Heeg noted in this period that,

> the city-region is eclipsed only by Glasgow [...] as the biggest concentration of low wage households in the country. (2004, p. 347)

The ECoC is positioned in the bidding period as being vital to the process of reversing Liverpool's historically ailing fortunes via the 'Glasgow Model' discussed above (Liverpool Culture Company 2003a, p. 3), and Jones and Wilks-Heeg argue that a central reason for Liverpool being awarded the role of UK host city was that it was 'widely considered the candidate city most likely to replicate the 'Glasgow effect' of using the ECoC award as a central plank of a wider project of urban renaissance' (2004, p. 342). That said, the fact that a decade after its award Glasgow also remained a rival to Liverpool in the poverty stakes should perhaps sound a note of warning. Nevertheless, the goal of regeneration is key to Liverpool's bid: the ECoC bidding process was overseen by Liverpool City Council's regeneration department, and Connolly cites then leader of the council Baron Storey stating of the 2008 ECoC that, '08 is not about culture but about regeneration' (2013, p. 163). In 2003, following an internal competition akin to the selection process resulting in Glasgow's nomination, the UK's second, and likely final, ECoC was selected. O'Brien and Miles suggest that Liverpool was 'an unlikely choice':

> Liverpool, despite the wealth of its cultural infrastructure, seemed an unlikely choice for ECoC 2008, given the city's previous lack of

competence and interest in cultural policy and the difficulties surrounding its relationship with the local cultural sector. (2010, p. 4)

Liverpool's earlier plans to host a Guggenheim Museum were not
progressed, and plans for another 'iconic' building containing a
museum posited by the leader of Liverpool City Council as 'key to
the Capital of Culture bid' (Storey cited in Ward 2004) were also subsequently abandoned (Jones 2011). Nevertheless, despite some local
signals that the culture-led regeneration model may be limited in its
benefits, in that the site of the Liverpool Garden Festival remained
in an 'unresolved state' twenty years after the festival (Theokas 2004,
p. 140), Liverpool proceeded with bidding, and was ultimately chosen as the UK's second ECoC. In the successful bid for the ECoC,
we can see a tangible deployment of the Creativity Agenda encountered previously. The five long-term goals for the ECoC, as stated in
Liverpool's bid, are:

- Contributing to the economic, social and physical regeneration of
  Liverpool.
- Increasing access to education and learning which develops creativity
  and skills relevant to the knowledge economy and cultural businesses.
- Sustaining a strong infrastructure of cultural organisations, activities,
  facilities and services.
- Creating an attractive environment for cultural businesses and creative
  people.
- Contributing to a vibrant city centre and revitalised neighbourhoods
  across the city. (Liverpool City Council 2003)

From this, it is clear to see that the ECoC was represented at the level
of local government as being able to contribute strongly to a virtuous, regenerative triad of social, economic and cultural redevelopment
within the city, with a particular emphasis on business operations,
exemplifying the notion of culture-led regeneration. We can also see
a more detailed evocation of some of the ideas encountered in earlier
chapters deployed in such documents. The Liverpool Culture Company
(the body responsible for bidding for and subsequently staging
Liverpool's ECoC), for example, claim that as a city Liverpool is,

moving completely away from old-style city governance to a new model where creativity is at the core of innovative regeneration [...] Ours is a creative city agenda; a liberating agenda which empowers its citizens and stakeholders and helps unleash their creative potential. Planning and delivering the Capital of Culture programme is itself a challenge to creativity. (2005, p. 6)

The ECoC and the 'creative potential' of citizens are thus seen as playing important parts within a 'creative city', references to which abound in the documentation produced by the Liverpool Culture Company (e.g. 2002, p. 104; 2003b, p. 3; 2003c, p. 3; 2003d, p. 102) and which can be used to deal with a wide range of challenges:

There is also a need to use creativity to tackle and address issues such as social exclusion, the reconfiguration of neighbourhoods, environment, heritage and health. (Liverpool Culture Company 2005, p. 21)

As well as leveraging the wider 'creative city' concept, one of a number of key documents produced by the Culture Company around the bidding process for the ECoC aligns the social outcomes listed above with more directly economic concerns stating that, 'with its potential to drive both tourism and inward investment, as well as contribute to the enormous challenges of regenerating communities, culture is the chosen key tool in dealing with facing and embracing change' (2003a, p. 3). The particular role that the ECoC is seen as being able to play in serving these ends is also to some degree aligned to the operation of creative industries. In his analysis of the range of documents produced by all cities which bid to secure the UK nomination for the 2008 ECoC title, Griffiths notes that,

perhaps the most notable feature of the bids [...] is the emphasis they all place on the relationship between culture and social cohesion. Each of them draws attention to the economic benefits that culture can bring to a city. Significantly, it is the economic importance of the cultural and creative industries that is played up, rather than that of tourism and visitors. (2006, p. 427)

This is not particular to the UK case; in their comprehensive review of the ECoC's history, Palmer/Rae Associates find that 'an expansion of creative industries' (2004, p. 103) is commonly stated as an economic goal for host cities. Whilst this focus on the creative industries may be true for the majority of bids, it would be wrong to imply that Liverpool's bid is therefore reticent about the tourism benefits it expects should it be awarded the ECoC title (e.g. Liverpool Culture Company 2002, pp. 601, 606). Liverpool's bid argues, for example, that the award will make the city a 'key destination' for 'cultural, creative and tourism businesses' (Liverpool Culture Company 2002, p. 1004), creating 'an attractive environment for cultural businesses and creative people' (p. 301), and also stimulating 'new products, innovations and businesses' (p. 302) via a broader climate of creativity that will emerge from the year's events, which will result in 'a sustainable culture of innovation, excellence and achievement in arts, sports, tourism and creative industries' (p. 303). Creativity is discussed throughout all related literature as a natural bedfellow of the cultural programme of the ECoC, and the tourism agenda is never seen as taking precedence over a creative industries one; rather, culture, tourism and creativity are positioned as all forming the interlocking parts of a larger whole in relation to the assumed benefits of the ECoC award. The way in which evidence is deployed relating to these sectors, however, takes us back to the issue of definition considered in detail in Chapter 5.

A key claim made regarding the potential for Liverpool's ECoC prior to 2008 is a continued reference both at local and at national level to the expected emergence of '14,000 jobs' in the city's 'culture sector' (e.g. Liverpool Culture Company 2003c, p. 7; DCMS 2004, p. 13). Indeed, Jones and Wilks-Heeg argue that 'the rationale for Liverpool's bid is best captured' in the production of this narrative of an increase in employment in 'the cultural and creative industries' (2004, p. 350). Here, we already see an example of the slippage in language to which this area is prone—are we talking about 14,000 expected jobs solely in the 'culture sector', or in the wider category of 'creative industries'? And what is the base which this figure of 14,000 will add to? This projection comes from a report produced by the ERM Economics Group commissioned by Liverpool City Council. One may assume that it is the smaller subset of specifically cultural industries that is under consideration given the manner in which Liverpool's focus is discussed in this report:

> Liverpool has adopted a regeneration strategy that places the cultural industries, the development of its cultural infrastructure and the delivery of the culture strategy at the centre. Therefore, the growth of the cultural industries sector is a key indicator of the success of its regeneration programme. (ERM Economics 2003, p. 3)

The report specifies that in 2001 'the broad cultural industries in Liverpool employed 29,000 people' (p. 17). Why '*broad*'? The unusual definition utilised here introduces significant breadth:

> We estimate that employment in the 'cultural sector' (defined as tourism, sports, heritage and the creative industries) could grow by some 13 200 direct jobs in Liverpool by 2012 based on trend growth, new cultural investments and a successful Capital of Culture bid. (ERM Economics 2003, p. 54)

Once again, we see here the effect that definition has on measurement and data. Firstly, it should be noted that the cultural sector is defined here as containing jobs in tourism, and it is the tourism subsector that dominates these figures. Of the total 29,000 jobs in the 'broad cultural industries' in Liverpool in 2001, 62% are in tourism (ERM Economics 2003, p. 17). As was the case in Chapter 5, therefore, the issue of definition is once again fundamental:

> This is not a matter of semantics: it has huge implications, since one of the main generators of employment within Liverpool's economy, tourism, is now cast within the 'creative' sector. This leads the report to claim that 'the broad cultural industries accounting for 14% of the total workforce in 2001'. (Connolly 2013, p. 172)

Of the 29,000 employed in the 'broad cultural sector', only 17% are specifically in the creative industries (ERM Economics 2003, p. 17). Rather than ignoring tourism in favour of creative industries, then, this report helps to argue that the ECoC will augment the creative sector by including tourism *within* this sector. These numbers are then, however, taken up by other sources as representing 'the cultural sector' or 'the cultural and creative industries'. Looking specifically at the figures given for creative industries, these suggest that in the city 2% of workers were employed in creative industries in 1991, rising to 3% in 2001, with a projection of 3150 additional jobs by 2012 as a result of the ECoC award (p. 35). Whilst part of the case made for the ECoC then seems to frame this as an 'investment' resulting in 14,000 extra jobs in the creative sector in 2008, even at this level of speculative projection, the more specific reality is a forecast of an extra 3150 jobs in creative industries over the period to 2012—a quite different prospect.

That said, as noted above, Liverpool at this time was also host to Merseyside ACME, a body whose explicit goal is stated as 'developing creative industries' (Merseyside ACME 2005) in the local area, and which had been operating since the 1990s. Not only is the work of ACME referenced within the ECoC bid, ACME were partly responsible for the form of that bid and their operations leading up to, and during, 2008 were positioned as having the potential to secure a 'legacy' for the ECoC. Initially, a considerable part of ACME's operations lay in providing financial resources for start-up companies within the creative sector. What is perhaps peculiar in the case of the operations of ACME, but also emblematic of the issues at hand, is that a body working to support the creative industries sector was also intimately involved in the support of community arts projects and initiatives such as the 'Creative Communities' programme which was a key plank of Liverpool's ECoC programme. Rather than specific creative industries development programmes, it is this community arts activity which was largely responsible for ACME's place within the narrative constructed around the benefits of the ECoC, but the flexibility of the concept of creativity allows the promotion of new business ventures to be coherently posited as a potential outcome of the ECoC process due to ACME's involvement on these multiple fronts. These two processes are aligned in the ECoC bid document which states that as a key organisation involved in delivering the year's programme, there is an important place for:

Merseyside ACME whose purpose is to support the successful development of creative businesses on Merseyside, and the regeneration of local neighbourhoods through arts-based activities. (Liverpool Culture Company 2002, p. 403)

The bid document also provides some quantitative data on this front, noting that 'ACME has directly funded over 120 arts projects, planned and managed by 517 local people, involving 9389 participants and welcoming 23,000 adults and children as audience members' (2002, p. 402). Given the broad range of this remit, it should be noted that ACME was not an organisation with, for example, an arts team, a strategic team and a business support team, but historically had consistently fewer than five employees, yet as part of the ECoC process was also charged with 'implementation of a 5 year plan' for the creative sector, 'spearhead[ing] strategic investment and growth', and developing 'international markets' for the creative industries (Liverpool Culture Company 2003d, p. 45), in addition to being responsible locally for the level of 'arts-based' activity referenced above. The idea that these activities would naturally sit together within one organisation and influence one another is both the result of the discourse of a unified, overlapping nature of a holistic form of creativity, and of a tendency, both in all policy documents relating to the ECoC and in cultural policy more generally, towards faith in the wider regenerative power of this creativity to do good, and to promote 'social cohesion' (Griffiths 2006)—the Creativity Agenda in action. Upon such a basis, cultural policy may continue its traditional concerns of promoting 'engagement' with culture and/or creative practice, with this expected to eventually translate into the existence of successful creative industries via a gradual rippling out of influence. ECoC bidding documents, for instance, note that ACME's 'support for local creative businesses' is 'balanced' by work which demonstrates 'the power and effectiveness of creativity within community based regeneration activity' (2003d, p. 45). Again, we see the positioning of creativity as operating in multiple, divergent, but interlinked ways.

What is also reflective of the wider agenda, despite this especially broad-ranging utilisation of the notion of creativity, is the ultimate centrality of the arts and culture. In terms of actual interventions, the main focus for the Liverpool bid, and for the programme of the eventual year itself, is not predominantly the broader creative sector discussed or alluded to in bidding documents, but rather the arts organisations within the city, with the city's sporting strengths present as something of a 'cultural' (in the broader sense) adjunct; the programme for the year is framed as having its basis in the 'strengths of the current Liverpool cultural infrastructure which in terms of music, sports and the visual arts is, we believe, matchless' (Liverpool Culture Company 2002, p. 305). The list of organisations involved is very heavily weighted towards arts venues (Liverpool Culture Company 2002, pp. 404–410), with a lesser number of sporting and educational organisations listed. Regardless of broad-church statements such as those given at the opening of the Liverpool bid to the effect that this event is positioned as a 'celebration of culture in all its aspects – not just of 'the arts'' (2002, p. 101), as was found when discussing other manifestations of the Creativity Agenda, it is clear that in practice there *is*, in fact, an emphasis on the arts and artistic expression in the ECoC programme and particularly on the traditionally funded organisations which are usually the objects of cultural policy, rather than any broader category. Of course, this is in no way inappropriate for such a cultural festival. It must be noted, however, that this cultural activity is narrated as entailing an eventual rise in employment and an increase in the productive capacities of the city of Liverpool, both in directly cultural industries and in the wider creative sector. Whilst the role of arts organisations in drawing in the tourism framed as part of the 'broader cultural sector' is reasonably clear, the power of such endeavour to bolster local industrial capacity is more open to question.

At a practical level, then, the level to which the Liverpool ECoC is actually concerned with the specific operation of creative industries is also questionable. Rather, the notion of culture as discussed in ECoC-related literature is most often something external which the citizens of Liverpool can experience and incorporate into their lives; it is not necessarily something which comes *from* the population, but rather comes *to* them. A large part of the ECoC bidding process is, therefore, essentially a push towards the traditional 'engagement' strand of

cultural policy. Even a report on the 'Creative Communities' programme aimed at increasing *active* participation amongst 'ordinary people' (Liverpool City Council and DTZ Pieda Consulting 2005, p. 32)
uses language demonstrating this consumption-led approach: the programme can eventually be considered successful, 'by virtue of increased
'cultural consumption' by larger and more broad ranging local audience'
(2005, p. v). This is not to say, however, that the people of the city
are positioned wholly as occupying the role of passive spectators to a
year-long show put on by arts institutions consisting of celebrations of
work from outside the city, nor that there is no place whatsoever for
production within the ECoC. Bidding documents state, for instance,
an intention that 'we will not be repeating the experience of Glasgow
and elsewhere of buying in the huge preponderance of 'cultural product'
from beyond the city' (Liverpool Culture Company 2002, p. 305), but
rather that the aim is to 'show off' 'indigenous capacity' and enable its
development, partly by making increased funding levels available. There
is, therefore, a sense in which at least some of the creative industries
subsectors are assumed to have direct involvement in the operations of
the ECoC, essentially as clients of the Liverpool Culture Company, providing the arts for the populace, and for audiences from beyond the city
boundaries. This may be a fairly narrow way of utilising 'creativity as a
key driver for the future', but it is at least a step in this direction, and
the development of the ECoC programme from 2003 onwards certainly
involved direct employment of some creative practitioners within the
city.

Although the main focus of Liverpool's ECoC bid is clearly on what
could be seen as a fairly traditional, albeit greatly expanded, cultural
policy model based heavily around the maintained arts sector, then, it
is nevertheless clear that the broader Creativity Agenda is in operation.
The stated goal of 'increasing access to education and learning which
develops creativity and skills relevant to the knowledge economy and
cultural businesses', for instance, clearly links the ECoC intervention to
the 'new economy', and that of 'creating an attractive environment for
cultural businesses and creative people' (Liverpool Culture Company
2002, p. 301) fits with the notion of entrepreneurship and business
creation being linked to more cultural creativity. In both of these aims,

there is a clear affinity with the logic of the 'creative class' thesis discussed in Chapter 3 whereby those who are most likely to create new businesses, and have the levels of skill and resources to do so, are drawn to areas with a strong cultural infrastructure. This concept presents one pathway by which the ECoC could be seen to have a positive influence upon the level of creative industries within the city. Liverpool's tenure as ECoC, for example, is framed as being able to facilitate regeneration in the city by 'exploiting its creativity and developing its talent for innovation' (Liverpool Culture Company 2002, p. 1101), thereby positioning the city as a key destination for creative businesses (Liverpool Culture Company 2002, p. 1004).

Evidence of Success

As with the history of Liverpool, and the ECoC itself, it is not possible to give a detailed account of the actual operation of the Liverpool ECoC here, and this is partly due to its impressive scope. Whilst small in relation to wider regeneration programmes, in comparison with other ECoCs, Liverpool's total budget of £130m is large (Green 2017, p. 32). There are questions around how much of this budget was attributable solely to the ECoC and would not have been spent elsewhere, or been part of regular budgets absent the ECoC (Cox and O'Brien 2012, p. 97), but Liverpool certainly puts significant resources behind its stated goals. García summarises Palmer/Rae Associates' research on funding sources by indicating that the major source of funds for ECoCs on average is national government (2005, p. 844), but in the Liverpool case, the biggest source of funds is Liverpool City Council itself, responsible for £75m of the £130m total (García et al. 2010, p. 17).

Given that the source of funds may come from within the city itself, rather than from without, we may question positions which present such high expenditure levels as evidence that the ECoC is 'one of the most financially rewarding competitions for any city' (Doyle 2018, p. 51), but the 'rewards' of Liverpool's ECoC are subsequently demonstrated in a range of other ways. Following the patterns discussed in

Chapter 4, it will be little surprise that the evidence base regarding the longitudinal impacts of the ECoC programme remained under-developed by the point of Liverpool's appointment as ECoC. In 2005, however, the Strategic Business Plan of the Liverpool Culture Company—which notably describes the 2008 award as 'the rocket fuel for Liverpool's economy' (Storey in Liverpool Culture Company 2005, p. 5)—outlined that:

> A research team will be appointed in summer 2005 to undertake a major programme of research, monitoring and evaluation of the Capital of Culture programme; this programme will be known as the Liverpool Model. (2005, p. 33)

The 'Impacts 08' research programme, a collaboration between Liverpool John Moores University and the University of Liverpool, ran from 2005 to 2010[1] and aimed to provide a model for capturing the impacts of a range of urban cultural strategies (Campbell and O'Brien 2017, p. 149). Whilst, like the ECoC programme itself, the entire five-year programme of research is too broad-ranging to be captured here, a suite of research was conducted to offer insight regarding the themes of 'cultural access and participation', 'economy and tourism', 'cultural vibrancy and sustainability', 'image and perceptions' and 'governance and delivery process' (García et al. 2010).

Given the patterns identified in previous chapters, it is no surprise that in some quarters, it is the headline figures of economic impact which are most enthusiastically taken up. The final Impacts 08 report, for instance, contains these figures regarding the success of the ECoC in attracting tourists:

> In total, 9.7m visits to Liverpool were motivated by the Liverpool ECoC in 2008. This generated an economic impact of £753.8m (based on esti-mated direct spend) attributable directly to the Liverpool ECoC title and events programme. The majority of this spend occurred within the city and city region, and the remainder within the North West region. (García et al. 2010, p. 25)

This information comes from a report by 'England's Northwest Research Service for Economic Development and Tourism' commissioned by Impacts 08. This report emphasises that delineating economic impact was not the primary concern of the overall research project (2010, p. 2), and the Impacts 08 research team have placed a greater emphasis on issues of cultural governance, image change and altered perceptions of culture within Liverpool (Campbell and O'Brien 2017, p. 151). Nevertheless, simple economic headlines such as this come to the fore in key locations. The generation of the £753.8m figure follows a fairly standard impact calculation method. The originating report gives a more detailed account of methodology and challenges, but to give a brief account: 2017 on-street interviews were conducted in Liverpool throughout 2008 (2010, p. 10), and 48% of respondents stated that the ECoC was somewhat or very important in motivating their visit to the city (p. 20). Tourism monitoring data was used to suggest a total of 27.7m visits to the city in 2008, and a conclusion was drawn that 35% of these would not have occurred without the ECoC, leading to the 9.7m figure above. Based on survey responses regarding spending during the visit on accommodation, eating out, shopping, travel and attractions (which suggest, for example, that those influenced to visit by the ECoC on a day visit from home spent on average £52 during their visit, and those on a trip staying in Liverpool spent on average £176 within these categories), these visits are calculated to result in direct spending of £521.6m within the city, and £232.2m elsewhere, leading to the £753.8m figure above (p. 40).

O'Brien notes how such figures of economic impact are taken up more broadly 'with no sense of specificity, particularity or nuance' (2014, p. 111). Such uptake is also perhaps unsurprising at this stage. Although other information is presented, when in May 2009, the story of Liverpool's ECoC is taken up in a central government report focussed on the role of culture 'at the heart of the new economy', the data deployed concentrates on patterns of tourism and economic impact (DCMS 2009, pp. 19–20). Just as the case for Liverpool's ECoC draws on the Creativity Agenda, then, so pieces of evidence such as this help to maintain the continuing story of the economic success that can be drawn from culture, and we can point to the repeated deployment of this data long after 2008 to make this case. For instance:

- 'Culture is an asset: music contributes nearly £5 billion to the UK economy, with £1.3 billion of that coming as export earnings. The economic impact of theatre is £2.6 billion a year. Liverpool's year as European Capital of Culture generated £800 million for the local economy and attracted 27% more visitors to the city' (Arts Council England et al. 2010, p. 7).
- 'The evaluation report, Creating an impact: Liverpool's experience as European Capital of Culture, calculated that 9.7 million visits to Liverpool were motivated by the European Capital of Culture programme (ECoC). This generated an additional economic impact of £753.8 million' (Arts Council England 2014, p. 20).
- 'In 2004, Liverpool was selected to be the 2008 European Capital of Culture (ECoC), which created significant economic and social benefits for the city. The ECoC attracted 9.7 million additional visits to Liverpool during 2008 (35% of all visits that year) as well as an additional 1.14 million visitor nights in Liverpool hotels' (Bazalgette 2017, p. 66).
- 'Cultural and creative investment can drive economic growth by making them attractive locations to live and work. Margate's Turner Contemporary gallery and Belfast's Titanic Studios - home to Game of Thrones - highlight the impact that creative anchor institutes can have on pride and economic performance in an area. During Liverpool's Capital of Culture year, the local economy generated almost £754m of additional income' (HM Government 2018, p. 22).

What is problematic here, albeit not novel, is that these final two extracts are from reports a decade after Liverpool's ECoC specifically aiming to explain the importance of creative industries. As shown in Chapter 5, by this stage these industries are being defined as those which exploit the variously defined creativity of their workforce and not united around cultural practice. Whilst Liverpool's bid certainly leveraged this wider sense of creativity, these figures are expressly derived from a piece of research into spending by visitors on items including food and shopping as part of their visit to a cultural festival, not to the direct economic output of productive creative industries which apparently continue to be valued for their own rates of employment and growth, rather than for their ability to induce spending on accommodation by tourists. Many years on, then, it seems that a version of the 'broader' cultural sector conceived of above which posits tourism as part of the creative sector is being deployed without any explicit acknowledgement of this. Again, though, the flexibility of the Creativity Agenda allows each of these elements to be glossed with the unifying sheen of creativity, defined in one manner for the deployment of one set of statistics, defined in another fashion elsewhere.

That said, it is also the case that in addition to the quick, and persistent, uptake of these headline figures on economic impact after 2008, so there are also rapid assertions of its specific impact on the creative industries themselves. Not only was Liverpool's tenure as ECoC swiftly argued by then Culture Minister Lady Hodge to have proven the case for such events in broad terms, demonstrating that 'culture changes people's lives, and has the power to transform cities and economies' (BBC 2009), so in 2009 did the then Secretary of State for Culture, Media and Sport, Andy Burnham, argue for the specifics of the role of Liverpool's ECoC for developing a creative economy. Liverpool's tenure as ECoC had shown how 'culture and creativity are part of the answer to tough economic times', how 'creative skills will be more important – not less – in the economy of the future' and also how we must consider 'the links between a vibrant cultural base, culture and creativity in schools and the digital economy' (Burnham 2009). As noted previously, the Creativity Agenda also transcends party politics; this is not merely the position of representatives of a Labour administration, concerned with augmenting the case for its Creative Economy Programme. After a change in national government in mid-2010, UK Prime Minister David Cameron held firm with the view that the ECoC provided interlinked benefits for tourism and creative industries:

> Look at how Liverpool benefited from being the European Cultural Capital in 2008. Jobs in the city's hotels and bars rose by over a quarter,

jobs in the creative industries increased by half and one million hotel beds were sold in the city. (Cameron 2010)

What can also be seen to persist in this period is the influence of key figures in the Creativity Agenda. Under the heading 'The Government's New Guru', a 2010 *Economist* article identified how Richard Florida and his theories on creativity were proving influential upon Cameron's UK government, with a note that 'his adoption as the government's philosopher means that people will carry on talking about Mr Florida' (*The Economist* 2010).

Continuing Creativity in Liverpool and Beyond

The influence of Florida and the broader Creativity Agenda is maintained in the 'Liverpool Cultural Strategy' (LCS), devised during 2008 to ensure the ECoC continued to provide an ongoing 'legacy'. In this document, we find statements regarding the role of culture in the city's future success such as: 'our prospects as a city will rely upon creative responses to present and future challenges and our cultural assets and values must play a central role' (Liverpool First 2008, p. 4). Once again we can consider Böhm and Land's argument concerning UK policy more broadly that, 'the assumption seems to be that 'creativity' is a transferable skill, and that developing the population's artistic creativity will deliver creativity and innovation in other sectors' (2009, p. 80). Such an assumption would explain the linkages posited in the LCS whereby, for example, Liverpool's 'creativity' results in 'competitive advantage' through the 'research and innovation of our universities', and this strength can be developed by 'leadership [...] and vision from the city council *and the cultural sector*' (Liverpool First 2008, p. 13, emphasis added).

This sense of a unified form of creativity tracing a single orbit around the nucleus of the arts is by this point familiar, as is the flexibility of definition in play. The 'links between the city's *creative core* and economic growth' (Liverpool First 2008, p. 17, emphasis added) are asserted, but from the context in which it is used this 'creative core' seems to consist mainly of employees of the creative industries, rather than a wider group akin to those within Florida's 'super-creative core', again showing how susceptible the language of creativity is to the production of perennially unstable referents. Similarly, there is a clear evocation of the logic of Florida's thesis in the assertion that, 'the range and diversi[t]y of Liverpool's cultural offer [...] enhances quality of life, provides a powerful magnet to attract skilled, entrepreneurial people and drives a visitor economy which makes an increasing contribution to the local economy' (Liverpool First 2008, p. 7).

Long-standing ideas thus continue to be leveraged, but positioned as newly successful in this context. For instance, as a result of the 2008 ECoC, over twenty years after the city's first strategy to promote cultural industries, the pro-vice chancellor of one of the city's universities stated that 'people *now* see the creative industries as having a role to play in the economy rather than just being about lifestyle' (NWDA 2009, p. 15, emphasis added). What also occurs after 2008, however, is the attempt to leverage Liverpool's success elsewhere in the UK. Given the patterns cited by Cameron above, this does not seem entirely unreasonable. From these, it seems the Creativity Agenda has been demonstrated to be successful, and swiftly so. A story emerges of the nature of Liverpool's ECoC that emphasises that the city was right to push the Creativity Agenda, and thus Liverpool's experience is especially prominent in the continuation of this agenda at local, national and international level. Sacco explains that Liverpool has joined Glasgow and Lille in the "trinity' of cases of indisputable successful editions of the ECoC' (2017, p. 251), and Bullen notes that,

> amongst decision makers in Liverpool, but also at the UK government level and in EU policy circles there is what has been called a 'myth of success' surrounding the event. For example, the British government decided to develop a national Capital of Culture programme in the wake of the 'extraordinary success' of Liverpool. (2013, p. 156)

In discussing the legacy of the ECoC and the launch of the UK City of Culture (UKCoC) programme, Burnham (2009) provides a clear echo of now long-standing ideas about novelty: 'the world in January 2009 is a fundamentally different place to what it was in January 2008'. As a result, immediately at the end of Liverpool's ECOC year, a national 'City of Culture' competition is established to 'unlock the cultural and creative power in the whole of the UK' based on the notion that, in an echo of Florida, 'all British cities are full of talent' (Burnham 2009). This national programme is also itself not a novel idea—Green notes a range of national capital of culture programmes mirroring international programmes such as the ECoC, dating back to 2003 (2017, p. 9). In explaining the reason to establish the UK competition, Bullen cites Burnham's statement that 'regeneration led by culture and cultural projects can be the most successful and durable, stimulating a new creative economy' (2013, p. 156), and it is argued that the UKCoC will bring about the same 'impressive economic benefits' to any host city as it did to Liverpool (DCMS 2009, p. 4). Here, then, Liverpool is positioned as having demonstrated the benefits of the Creativity Agenda and the need for its continuation. Indeed, Vickery notes that in the 2009 process of planning for the UKCoC a goal of 'urban regeneration' moves from a *possible* framework' for cities to deploy to 'an *imperative*' at the point bids are solicited (2012, p. 32, emphasis added), and as with Liverpool in the run-up to 2008, a case can certainly be made for the initial UKCoC hosts of Derry-Londonderry in 2013 and Hull in 2017 being in need of 'regeneration' in some form: the 2010 Northern Ireland Multiple Deprivation Measure shows 'the majority of the most deprived areas in Northern Ireland are in Belfast and Derry' (NISRA 2010, p. 25), and in the 2015 English Index of Multiple Deprivation, Hull was the third most deprived local authority in the country (Culture, Policy and Place Institute 2018, p. 25).

As discussed in Chapter 5, in the period in which the UKCoC was being established the centrality of arts and culture to the definition of creativity used to generate statistics regarding the economic performance of creative industries was being reconsidered, yet we nevertheless see UKCoC bidding documents in part predicated on the expected impact on these industries. The local administration of a city such as Norwich, for instance, put forth the argument that the award would 'provide a model for the future for medium sized UK cities who want to drive social and economic change through culture and creativity', and would serve to 'make Norwich a national leader in the UK Knowledge Economy and make us a recognised national and international centre of excellence in the Creative Industries' (Norwich City of Culture 2010). The bid of eventual award winner Derry-Londonderry discussed the familiar notion of 'culture at the heart of regeneration', the necessity of 'making culture accessible' to its population and the 'opportunities for our creative industries' (Derry-Londonderry City of Culture 2013, 2010). Indeed, the bidding process required potential hosts to offer an assessment of the 'current nature and strength of the cultural and creative sectors' in their area, as well as an assessment of how the UKCoC programme would 'help to boost these sectors' (DCMS 2013, p. 19). Later, the bid of 2017 UKCoC host Hull specified a target to 'grow the current 1400 creative industry jobs by 10%' (Hull City Council 2014), indicating that the size of the creative industries sector continues to be seen as a key indicator of the impact of cultural programmes such as this, despite any wider reconsideration of the links between the two.

The extent to which any success on Liverpool's part can be replicated, however, has been questioned. Despite the comparatively high budgets for the UKCoC as a national title (Green 2017, p. 19), so far these are closer to £30m than the £130m spent across Liverpool's 2008 programme. Outside of budget, the extent to which successes associated with the ECoC are actually derived from the programme or come about from events which may have occurred in any case is also questioned (e.g. Lähdesmäki 2014, p. 482). Cox and O'Brien also point to the very specific circumstances in Liverpool referred to above including the city's historic cultural institutions, global cultural reputation, receipt of Objective One funding in addition to massive private sector investment and a planning period which occurred immediately prior to a global economic downturn (2012, p. 97). Indeed, the variability of success across different ECoC hosts can perhaps be emphasised by the fact that participants in a 2011 research network from cities shortlisted to host the 2013 UKCoC, 'could not name the current (2011) European Capital of Culture, despite the relative significance and impact of Liverpool 08' (Wilson and O'Brien 2012, p. 15). Whilst the extent to which Liverpool's success can be replicated is questionable, what can also be asked at a longer remove than the immediate aftermath of the event in which the UKCoC award was instituted is what the nature of this success actually consists of. Cameron's claim of creative employment in the city increasing by 50% as a result of the 2008 award was considered above, and this association between the ECoC and increased creative employment continues both at a national and international level:

> Cultural and creative industries also contribute to the competitiveness and social cohesion of our cities and regions. European Capitals of Culture such as Lille, Liverpool and others show that investing in this sector creates jobs. (European Commission 2010)

The patterns cited by Cameron, however, are not accurate. The source of his claim is not clear, but it is possible the cited increase of 50% in employment in creative industries may be drawing on the *projections* of potential impacts made by ERM Economics in 2003 discussed above:

> Our cautious assessment is that employment in the creative industries could grow by 5950 to 2012, of which 3150 additional jobs are above what would be expected based on trend growth. (2003, p. 35)

Whilst a narrative of the successful impact of Liverpool's ECoC on the creative economy is quickly established, with the benefit of hindsight, we can consider figures from research commissioned by Arts Council England published in 2013 which are more likely to be accurate:

> During 2008, Liverpool's year as European Capital of Culture, the number of creative businesses there increased by eight per cent. (CEBR 2013, p. 6)

Clearly, this is quite a different picture to a rise of 50%. Despite a rhetorical concern with evidence, it takes years for figures such as this to emerge. An optimistic narrative of success, however, is available immediately. Despite its broad-ranging research, even the pioneering Impacts 08 programme, with its rare longitudinal scope, remained limited in its ability to draw conclusions regarding impact by the time period in which it operated. The figures referred to above, for instance, on likely spend by tourists were based in part on overall tourism-level figures for 2008 which were not fully available until 2010 (England's Northwest Research Service & Impacts 08 2010, p. 41). Other forms of administrative data experience a similar time lag. So, whilst the longer-term Impacts 08 research was, as noted in Chapter 4, seen by some as being able to provide evidence which had previously been 'lacking' (O'Brien 2014, p. 95) and whilst robust baselines were established in many areas by this research programme, its final report focusses on findings 'up until early 2009' (García et al. 2010, p. 13). To celebrate the success of 2008 as soon as the year is over, therefore, can only be based on partial information—Cox and O'Brien note that this absence of later evidence 'is fundamentally problematic to understanding what has happened in Liverpool, as well as what could usefully be applied or eschewed elsewhere' (2012, p. 95), and so in a certain sense the optimism of the Creativity Agenda serves to fill these gaps. In addition to its other achievements, then, considering the case of Liverpool helps to reveal a compulsion to continue the Creativity Agenda, regardless of evidence. For instance, the caution in findings such as…

> *some* creative industries enterprises reported a growth in their client base which they viewed [as] *partly* attributable to the Liverpool ECoC, but this was by no means a universal picture. (Impacts 08 2009, p. 3, emphasis added)

….seemed not to temper the enthusiasm of ex-Culture Minister Lady Hodge who interpreted them thus: 'That makes me hugely optimistic about what UK City of Culture can do for strengthening the profile of cities and encouraging the creative sector' (Hodge 2010). A story of cultural regeneration resulting in successful creative industries and the successful performance of these industries thus persists. Evidence of a successful *story* around such linkages, however, is not evidence for their *reality*, although the acceptance of this story will have real effects. The sense that Liverpool's ECoC programme did not eventually focus on creative industries and thus did not have a special impact upon them is supported by findings from a survey of creative industries conducted by the Impacts 08 research programme. This found that the main impact (or expected impact) on business that respondents believed would result from 2008 was a general 'improved external image of Liverpool' (2009, pp. 66, 69), with a majority of respondents agreeing that the ECoC may have affected their business indirectly by 'generating a higher profile for Liverpool' (2009, p. 70). Findings such as these, though, are notably different to those from an earlier survey carried out *before* the ECoC where an expectation for 'more commercial/business opportunities' was the main theme in responses regarding the potential impact of the ECoC (2009, pp. 58, 61). This may have resulted from the discussion in policy documents around the ECoC at the bidding stage noted above to the effect that: 'we will not be repeating the experience of Glasgow and elsewhere of buying in the huge preponderance of 'cultural product' from beyond the city' (Liverpool Culture Company 2002, p. 305). Later, however, there was dispute as to whether the programme of the ECoC appropriately drew on local creative expertise. This same Impacts 08 report references more qualitative work with creative industries, concluding that, 'across all consultations there were respondents who had a sense of not being directly involved [...] there was a great sense of a lack of involvement and engagement with ECoC 2008' (2009, p. 40). This study, for example, refers to 'a general sense of disappointment that there had not been any specific ECoC initiatives whereby procurement from local creative businesses was encouraged, or any explicit policy to encourage local procurement' (2009, p. 44), and narratives from local creative industries entrepreneurs mirror this (Campbell 2011). This disconnect was also seen above in a consideration of the view of creative practitioners in Glasgow and can also be seen in other ECoC hosts (e.g. Bergsgard and Vassenden 2011). As we have also seen, though, it is not these relevant research findings on creative industries that are presented in the 2018 UK Industrial Strategy specifically relating to these industries, but rather the economic headline relating to spend from tourism. In terms of the difference between a strategy to develop local creative industries, and one to promote image change and tourism, it is useful to return to Bianchini's take from the earliest stages of the Creativity Agenda:

It can be risky in the long term for cities to rely on consumption-oriented models of cultural policy-led economic development, even if they may be profitable in the short term, by creating visibility and political returns. The success of strategies that use cultural policy to boost retailing and consumer services industries, expand tourism and attract external investment increasingly depend on factors over which cities have very limited control, ranging from airfare prices to changes in the level of the residents' and visitors' disposable incomes [...] the employment generated by the 'customer effect' of cultural policies – which is particularly strong in sectors such as retailing and hotel and catering – is frequently low-paid, part-time, and characterised by deskilling and poor levels of job satisfaction, legal rights and working conditions. (Bianchini 1993, p. 203)

In the UK case, it seems these are warnings still worth heeding. Looking further afield, the role allocated to creative industries continues to become more prominent in cities bidding for and hosting the ECoC programme (Comunian et al. 2010, p. 7; García and Cox 2013, pp. 59–61); however, similar caution is noted in these locations on the likely actual impact on creative industries themselves of these events (e.g. Heinze and Hoose 2013, p. 530).

A Sustainable Narrative?

More recently, the extent to which any such programme can ever be truly 'evidence-based' seems to be being faced more directly in at least some quarters. The 2018 report assessing the impact of Hull's 2017 UKCoC programme, for instance, is framed explicitly as a consideration of '*preliminary* outcomes' and is rightly cautious on this issue:

Many of the most important outcomes will only be fully assessable one, two, five or even ten years after the end of 2017, at which points any sustained changes in outcomes for the city and surrounding areas can be better understood. At a more practical level, the timing means that a number of important datasets that would typically be used to assess the 2017 outcomes are not yet available, and will not be available until much later in 2018 or in early 2019. (Culture, Place and Policy Institute 2018, p. 19)

On this basis, goals such as those stated above regarding the growth of creative industries during the UKCoC cannot be reasonably assessed at such a short remove. This, however, has not stopped the rapid emergence from central government of yet more questionable linkages between such programmes and wider outcomes:

> Government funding for Hull of £15 million unlocked £3.3 billion worth of investment in the City since winning the [UKCoC] nomination in 2013. Analysis shows that changes in the perception of the City is attributed as a key factor in securing that investment. Hull's culture led regeneration plan has created 7000 + jobs. (DCMS 2018a, p. 26)

There are, though, also signs of more cautious assessments in this period:

> In Hull nearly 800 jobs have been created and almost £220 million invested in Hull's tourism and cultural sectors since the city was named UK City of Culture 2017. (DCMS et al. 2018)

Whilst assessment of the scale of the impact of such events can be made in very different ways, then, it seems that emphasising economic headline figures still seems to be the go-to choice for policymakers, and the fact that ministers drew conclusions about the city of Hull having changed 'for good' less than a fortnight after the end of 2017 (DCMS and Hancock 2018) indicates that the Creativity Agenda still has a significant hold after twenty years in force.

Regardless of magnitude, we must also ask how likely any effects are to last beyond the specific interventions which prompted them. Evaluation of the ECoC programme as a whole, for instance, shows much variability (García and Cox 2013), and to return to the early interventions in culture-led regeneration considered at the outset of this chapter, if we consider visitor levels at Tate Liverpool, as shown in Fig. 6.1, we may have pause regarding the extent to which an event like the ECoC provides a lasting effect even in the 'broader' cultural sector.

Excluding 2008, the average number of visits per year in this period was 600,000, the same level as cited above from the mid-1990s. It

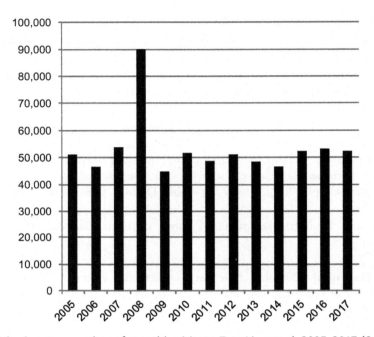

Fig. 6.1 Average number of monthly visits to Tate Liverpool, 2005–2017 (*Source* DCMS [2018b])

seems reasonable to conclude, therefore, that over its history visit levels to Tate Liverpool have been fairly stable, apart from in the single year of 2008. In addition, whilst extra visitor numbers may not be sustained, research into other ECoCs shows that these extra visits may not even occur in the first place (Liu 2014, p. 502). Whilst there has certainly been an increase in prominent media coverage of the ECoC between the 1990 and 2008 ECoCs in the UK (García 2017, p. 3188), Liu also notes that changes here may also have only short-term benefits:

> Image generation in itself does not ensure tourism inflow. In many cases, in fact, if the event is not sustained or followed-up by strategic marketing initiatives or valid investments, no significant medium- to long-term changes to local place image will stem even from a well-executed event. (2014, p. 505)

Although those taking the Creativity Agenda forward frame cultural festivals as 'proving' the case for the creative economy, the extent to which these festivals actively seek to develop the creative economy is questionable. Whilst tourists may indeed be attracted by a prominent cultural festival, it is problematic to frame this as being part of the creative economy on the terms considered in previous chapters. Nevertheless, we have seen how Liverpool does this in the run-up to 2008 by considering the 'broader' cultural sector, and this continues in some form in Hull's reporting on the 2017 UKCoC which considers the level of new jobs made in the 'creative and visitor economy' (Culture, Policy and Place Institute 2018, p. 10). Indeed, the need to provide research evidence for culture-led regeneration, and the framing of such projects in terms of 'regeneration' once again shows the patterns of persistence in this field. Nevertheless, the more recent experience of the cities considered here raises deepening challenges. In 2009, Secretary of State for Culture Andy Burnham argued,

> In times past, when the economy dipped, these sectors were regarded as the first to be cut, wrongly seen as luxuries for better days. In the recessions of the 1980s and 1990s, budgets were slashed at national and local level. That mistake will not be repeated. (DCMS 2009, p. 4)

Mistake or not, with the change in UK government in 2010, this is yet another area in which we see repetition of earlier patterns, with local authorities (the biggest source of arts funding in the country since the late 1980s (Belfiore 2002, p. 96)), subject to significant budget reductions. Analysis of Hull's UKCoC, for instance, points out that in the run-up to 2017,

> there was over a four-fold increase in funding available for cultural events and activities in the city from 2013 - perhaps all the more impressive given the national picture of austerity, particularly within the sphere of local authority cut-backs in service provision, not least within the cultural sector, from local to national level. (Culture, Policy and Place Institute 2018, p. 103)

Whilst definition remains a challenge for statistics here too, it has been suggested that investment in arts and culture by English councils has fallen by 17% since 2010 (Crewe 2016). In this context, City Council cuts to cultural funding of 'only' 10% in Liverpool are positioned as a sign of success and of the city's exceptional commitment to this area (McColgan cited in Wilson and O'Brien 2012, p. 11), and perhaps appropriately so. Nevertheless, this raises problems for the Creativity Agenda. Whilst earlier chapters have considered the 'neoliberal' context for the rise of this agenda, this context arguably had a greater impact in framing the benefits of the arts and culture in economic terms and in placing an increased emphasis on performance indicators, rather than in prompting cuts in public spending— however measured, resources for the arts increased significantly during Labour's tenure in power until 2010 (Hesmondhalgh et al. 2015). Since this point, though, the funding landscape is characterised by cuts, and not just at the local level, with predictions that 'the arts and culture industry' will be particularly harmed by reductions in government spend (CEBR 2013, p. 33). Such reductions are hard to square with prevailing narratives. If 'investing' £120m in Liverpool's ECoC is posited to give a 'return' of £750m in tourism spend, or if cultural activity can spur 'sustainable' regeneration in a 'new creative economy', will cuts in this area not have a doubly negative effect, reducing the level of cultural activity itself, but also reducing its multiplied outcomes in tourism revenue and high-growth employment fields? Although this kind of advocacy has been easy to suggest in the context in which the Creativity Agenda rose, it is harder to sustain such positions when faced with dramatic cuts to local authority budgets which raise ever more pressing questions of how to balance these reductions across the wide range of services these budgets must maintain, from culture and heritage to education, highway maintenance, support for social care services, public health and so on. Or, rather, if the same positions continue to be held, they risk becoming ever more detached from reality.

Whilst experience in Liverpool is positioned as a clear demonstration of the power of culture, achieving such success that the national UKCoC award was established, and continuing to be 'widely perceived' as demonstrating the success of culture-led regeneration and the ability of the ECoC to achieve image transformation (García 2017, p. 3178), when faced with a political climate such as this, the limitations of the kinds of activities traced in this chapter become clear. Whilst such clarity only emerges over time, the Creativity Agenda proceeds without heeding this. Despite the long persistence of a narrative of success around Glasgow's tenure as ECoC (e.g. European Commission 2009), reflections back on this tenure after many years raise important issues about the relative limitations of such an award. Just as we saw above that 'many years after the rhetoric, there has been no sustained growth' in Glasgow (Miller 2009, p. 96), we may point to a success that is often at the level of rhetoric in Liverpool also: in local government, the 2008 ECoC is framed as 'the most successful ever European Capital of Culture' (Liverpool City Council 2014, p. 7), and, as was the case in 2005, culture is still being posited as the 'rocket fuel' for the city's 'continuing regeneration' (p. 2), with references in Liverpool's future planning to 'creative cities' (p. 16), and the creative industries as 'a potential source of new jobs and growth at a time of economic difficulty' (p. 19) all present and correct as the Creativity Agenda remains in force. Nevertheless, this narrative of success has to contend with an increasingly challenging political climate. Boland referred to a £90million 'black hole' in the finances of Liverpool City Council in 2009 immediately following the ECoC (2010, p. 630), and in 2012 Liverpool's mayor wrote of the impact of central government cuts since 2010 thus:

> Over the last two years, Liverpool has had to make savings of £141m. Over the next four years we estimate we have got to cut the budget by another £143m, from a total spend of £480m. In total, it means we will have lost more than 52% of our controllable government grant income since 2010. (Anderson 2012)

In 2016, media reports emphasised that the city, like other locations in the UK facing the same constraints, could soon 'run out of money' (Murphy 2016), with reports in 2018 stating that the city is 'staring over a financial cliff edge' (Thorp 2018a). It seems likely, then, that Liverpool's need for economic regeneration will remain pressing in the near future. In this context, it is instructive to consider Mooney's take on Glasgow 1990 over a decade after the ECoC award:

> The developments in Glasgow since the 1990s did not occur in an economic or political vacuum but in the context of a wide-ranging attack on living standards of the less well off. [...] Therefore, it is less an issue of the success or failure of the ECOC and similar strategies, more a realisation that it could be little other than a form of city 'spin'. Glasgow ECOC 1990, together with the other events and awards that the City has received in the past 14 years are not about tackling Glasgow's structural problems, the social divisions, the inequalities and the poverty. (2004, p. 337)

In Liverpool too, therefore, given the picture traced above, to ask about the success or failure of the ECoC, or of the nature of the evidence for this, may also be to ask the wrong question. In light of the seemingly entrenched challenges the city faces, what is it that an award such as this is reasonably expected to do? If the Creativity Agenda continues to trade on myths, though, these may do little to help cities such as Liverpool address these persistent challenges.

In the meantime, the persistence found thus far to be characteristic of the Creativity Agenda seems to be much in evidence in Liverpool. After being 'mooted for years as a creative quarter' (Houghton 2009), post-2008, there has been an influx of creative industries businesses into an area of the city designated the 'Baltic Triangle', with development partly funded by the European Regional Development Fund. However, just as Liverpool's earliest plans for a creative quarter were affected by the financial situation of property developers, so recent media reports note similar challenges:

> On Norfolk Street, in Liverpool's trendy Baltic Quarter, stands the six-storey concrete carcass of what was supposed to be Baltic House, launched in 2015 as a "groundbreaking" development of student flats and creative live-work units. It was the first phase of the Gallery + project, an "elegant, cool, urban and edgy" mixed-use scheme, centred around a gallery of Banksy murals that had been ripped from nearby walls. It was one of many such glamorous projects devised by property company

North Point Global [...] Three years on, the company has pulled out of its planned £360m suite of projects across the city and stopped picking up the phone, leaving buyers to believe they are the victims of a ruthless scam, fiercely denied by the developers in question. [...] The Banksy murals, including the 12-metre high Liverpool Rat and Love Plane, which were promised to return to public display, have been sold for £3.2m to an anonymous buyer in Qatar. (Wainwright 2018)

The continuing redevelopment of industrial space in the area is currently mooted to bring about further 'regeneration' by housing 'creative and artisan manufacturing [...] alongside digital businesses' (Place North West 2018) and, perhaps reflecting the more recent trends in the creative industries narrative noted in Chapter 5, this area of the city is posited by local voices in the specifically *cultural* sector as having developed in a direction 'more suited to tech and digital businesses' rather than cultural production per se (Torpey 2017). However, where property development schemes in the area are successful, these may serve to replace existing cultural venues (Guy 2018), leading the Community Interest Company established to develop creative and digital businesses in this area to conclude that 'our culture is still for sale', and that without clear plans to protect cultural spaces, local cultural policy 'seems disconnected from reality' (Kelly 2018).

The 'regeneratingliverpool.com' site set up by Liverpool City Council to provide information on 'investment opportunities' in the city also lists the chance to invest in two *further* creative districts at the time of writing, 'Ten Streets' and the 'Fabric District' (Regenerating Liverpool 2018a), the summary of the latter offering a case of creative *déjà vu*:

Ten Streets is set to become a new "creativity district" for start-up creative businesses, including artists, independent creatives, makers and digital and technology sectors. The scheme will see circa 125 acres of former dockland between the northern edge of the city centre to Bramley Moore Dock, transformed with up to 1 million square feet of development, delivering around 2,500 new jobs. (Regenerating Liverpool 2018b)

Time will tell, but there are currently positive signs for the city in terms of creative production in film and television with plans for a £50m project to build an outpost of London-based Twickenham Studios (Ritman 2018). Other recent developments, however, indicate a sense of 'business as usual' for the Creativity Agenda. Echoing the patterns seen in Chapter 4, the city has for instance recently seen fit to calculate the economic impact of the Beatles Heritage industry ('£39m turnover and 690 jobs in 2014' (Institute of Popular Music et al. 2015, p. 2)), leading to the proposal of a 'regeneration area' to improve tourist facilities (BBC 2018), and echoing the 1990s bid for Channel 5 (Evans 1996, p. 16), the city bid in 2018 to host a new national headquarters for Channel 4, with chair of the UKCoC selection panel Phil Redmond supporting the bid with the justification that 'outside London – Liverpool is the premier creative city' (Parry 2018). This bid was rejected, though, apparently as a result of consideration of the city's transport infrastructure (Anderson 2018). Claims continue to be made that 'for every pound spent on culture the city gets a £12 return' (Thorp 2018b), and the Liverpool City Region has established a 'borough of culture' award, with the title held on a rotating annual basis by each of the six boroughs in the region (St Helens Council 2018), with the importance of celebrating culture in this way being justified in part by the £91.8bn in Gross Value Added attributable to the 'creative industry sector' in the UK (Liverpool City Region Combined Authority 2018, p. 6). The Creativity Agenda persists here, as elsewhere.

Conclusion

Thirty years after plans were first made to establish a creative industries quarter in Liverpool, the three areas currently so designated, with their stated goals of achieving a form of regeneration, may well succeed in transforming the city's fortunes. There is, however, reason to be cautious. Although posited as a means to build new sustainable creative economies, there was little sense that Liverpool's year as ECoC actually sought to intervene in a sustained way with local creative businesses and, despite early celebratory statements, later reflection suggests the rise in the numbers of such businesses was not substantial. Despite a purported reliance on evidence, therefore, we see from this case that the

Creativity Agenda will not wait for evidence. The effect of an intervention must be known almost before it is completed, success celebrated, and the game continued. But how is this game won? Although the idea of high-growth creative jobs being vital to economic success is always in the air, eventual success often seems to ultimately be cast in terms of attracting spending from outside. Bullen characterises her discussions with Liverpool City Council officials in 2012 regarding local cultural policy as resting on an idea of,

> the new 'business friendly' city which needs a 'great' cultural programme to 'sell the city to a global audience'. Cultural policy now seems to have fallen back on turning the city into a 'destination' for agents of inward investment (tourists or businesses). (Bullen 2013, p. 161)

It should be noted that these patterns are in no way exclusive to Liverpool, but having been an early adopter, Liverpool perhaps shows us the increasingly tight circles in which the Creativity Agenda is now spinning—a regional borough of culture award, another national city of culture award, another creative quarter, another economic impact report, more 'regeneration', up to and including the regeneration *of* regeneration: after 'numerous regeneration attempts', recent reports suggested that the site of the 1984 Liverpool Garden Festival could be transformed by becoming a 'world class cultural destination' (Murphy 2015). Perhaps in the future the Creativity Agenda will only be able to persist by autocannibalism. There is, however, the irony that it is continually associated with newness. As Gibson and Klocker note, 'creativity remains interesting to academics and policy-makers precisely because it implies a departure from norms, being genuinely (even radically) new – an antidote to discipline and restriction' (2005, p. 100). As time passes, however, we find the contradiction of uncreative 'creativity', of established techniques leveraged *as though* new and creative, and thus expected to bring about the new state of affairs they are assumed to be part and parcel of. Liverpool, after all, instigated attempts at culture-led regeneration many years after the 'Glasgow model' of utilising the ECoC award to affect processes of regeneration had gained traction, yet an assumption persists that engaging with creativity in any sense automatically involves 'innovation'. When discussing his creative city theory, for instance, Landry makes the case for the necessity of intervening in creative ways as, 'the idea that the future will resemble the past is long gone' (2000, p. 50). Even if one is in agreement with this claim, in the case of the persistent Creativity Agenda, it seems that the future currently bears many similarities to the past, including a similar set of challenging circumstances: after the many successes of its ECoC year, and multiple wider regeneration programmes, 'Liverpool is the local authority with the largest number of neighbourhoods in the most deprived one per cent of all neighbourhoods nationally' (DCLG 2015, p. 11), and many of these areas have been consistently in the most deprived 1% over the course of a decade of data gathering (Smith et al. 2015, p. 61). It would not be reasonable to expect the ECoC award to change all this, but as Chapter 7 will argue, it seems necessary at this stage to try to establish a more useful understanding of 'creativity' and of what it may, and may not, achieve.

Note

1. For the record, I was employed as assistant to the programme from April 2006 to January 2008.

References

Anderson, J. (2012, November 12). *Cuts are hitting deprived cities hardest. That's no surprise in Liverpool.* Retrieved from https://www.theguardian.com/commentisfree/2012/nov/15/cut-deprived-cities-liverpool.

Anderson, J. (2018, July 23). [Tweet]. Retrieved from https://twitter.com/mayor_anderson/status/1021355533503262721.

Arts Council England. (2014). *The value of arts and culture to people and society: An evidence review.* Manchester: Arts Council England.

Arts Council England, Association of Independent Museums, Cultural Learning Alliance, English Heritage, The Heritage Alliance, Heritage Lottery Fund, … Visit England. (2010). *Cultural capital—A manifesto for the future.* Retrieved from http://webarchive.nationalarchives.gov.

uk/20160204122224/http://www.artscouncil.org.uk/advice-and-guidance/ browse-advice-and-guidance/cultural-capital-manifesto-future.

Bazalgette, P. (2017). *Independent review of the creative industries*. Retrieved from https://www.gov.uk/government/publications/independent-review-of-the-creative-industries.

BBC. (2009). *UK cities bid for culture title*. Retrieved from http://news.bbc.co.uk/1/hi/entertainment/arts_and_culture/8414596.stm.

BBC. (2018). 'Beatles Quarter masterplan' proposed by Liverpool City Council. Retrieved from http://www.bbc.co.uk/news/uk-england-merseyside-43752376.

Belfiore, E. (2002). Art as a means of alleviating social exclusion: Does it really work? A critique of instrumental cultural policies and social impact studies in the UK. *International Journal of Cultural Policy, 8*(1), 91–106.

Bennattar, M. (1999, July 8). Liverpool hopes for Guggenheim Museum. *The Independent*. Retrieved from https://www.independent.co.uk/news/liverpool-hopes-for-guggenheim-museum-1105146.html.

Bergsgard, N. A., & Vassenden, A. (2011). The legacy of Stavanger as Capital of Culture in Europe 2008: Watershed or puff of wind? *International Journal of Cultural Policy, 17*(3), 301–320.

Bianchini, F. (1993). Culture, conflict and cities: Issues and prospects for the 1990s. In F. Bianchini & M. Parkinson (Eds.), *Cultural policy and urban regeneration* (pp. 199–213). Manchester: Manchester University Press.

Biggs, L. (1996). Museums and welfare: Shared space. In P. Lorente (Ed.), *The role of museums and the arts in the urban regeneration of Liverpool* (pp. 60–68). Leicester: Centre for Urban History.

Böhm, S., & Land, C. (2009). No measure for culture? Value in the new economy. *Capital & Class, 33*(1), 75–98.

Boland, P. (2010). 'Capital of Culture—You must be having a laugh!' Challenging the official rhetoric of Liverpool as the 2008 European Cultural Capital. *Social and Cultural Geography, 11*(7), 627–645.

Booth, P., & Boyle, R. (1993). See Glasgow, see culture. In F. Bianchini & M. Parkinson (Eds.), *Cultural policy and urban regeneration* (pp. 21–47). Manchester: Manchester University Press.

Bullen, C. (2013). *European Capitals of Culture and everyday cultural diversity: A comparison of Liverpool (UK) and Marseille (France)*. Amsterdam: European Cultural Foundation.

Burghes, A., & Thornton, S. (2017). *The social impact of the arts in Liverpool 2015/16—A review of the Culture Liverpool Investment Programme*. Liverpool: Collective Encounters.

Burnham, A. (2009). *Five lessons from Liverpool's year as Capital of Culture.* Retrieved from http://webarchive.nationalarchives.gov.uk/20100512152919/http://www.culture.gov.uk/reference_library/minister_speeches/6182.aspx.

Cameron, D., (2010). *Speech on tourism.* Retrieved from http://webarchive.nationalarchives.gov.uk/20130103015528/http://www.number10.gov.uk/news/pms-speech-on-tourism/.

Campbell, P. (2011). Creative industries in a European Capital of Culture. *International Journal of Cultural Policy, 17*(5), 510–522.

Campbell, P., & O'Brien, D. (2017). Whatever happened to the Liverpool model? Urban cultural policy in the era after urban regeneration. In M. Bevir, K. McKee, & P. Matthews (Eds.), *Decentring urban governance: Narratives, resistance and contestation* (pp. 139–157). London: Routledge.

CEBR. (2013). *The contribution of the arts and culture to the national economy.* London: Centre for Economics and Business Research Ltd.

Comunian, R., Chapain, C., & Clifton, N. (2010). Location, location, location: Exploring the complex relationship between creative industries and place. *Creative Industries Journal, 3*(1), 5–10.

Connolly, M. G. (2013). The 'Liverpool model(s)': Cultural planning, Liverpool and Capital of Culture 2008. *International Journal of Cultural Policy, 19*(2), 162–181.

Couch, C. (2003). *City of change and challenge.* Aldershot: Ashgate.

Cox, T., & O'Brien, D. (2012). The "Scouse Wedding" and other myths and legends: Reflections on the evolution of a "Liverpool model" for culture-led regeneration. *Cultural Trends, 21*(2), 93–101.

Crewe, T. (2016). *The strange death of municipal England.* Retrieved from https://www.lrb.co.uk/v38/n24/tom-crewe/the-strange-death-of-municipal-england.

Culture, Policy and Place Institute. (2018). *Cultural transformations: The impacts of Hull UK City of Culture 2017—Preliminary outcomes evaluation.* Hull: University of Hull.

DCLG. (2015). *The English indices of deprivation 2015.* London: Department for Communities and Local Government.

DCMS. (2004). *Culture at the heart of regeneration.* London: DCMS.

DCMS. (2009). *Lifting people, lifting places.* London: DCMS.

DCMS. (2013). *UK City of Culture 2017. Guidance for bidding cities.* Retrieved from https://www.gov.uk/government/uploads/system/uploads/attachment_data/file/89369/UK_City_of_Culture_2017_Guidance_and_Criteria.pdf.

DCMS. (2018a). *Culture is digital.* London: DCMS.

DCMS. (2018b). *Monthly museums and galleries visits.* Retrieved from https://www.gov.uk/government/uploads/system/uploads/attachment_data/file/697242/Monthly_museums_and_galleries_February_2018.xlsx.

DCMS, & Hancock, M. (2018). *Celebrating the Creative Industries Federation's 3rd anniversary.* Retrieved from https://www.gov.uk/government/speeches/celebrating-the-creative-industries-federations-3rd-anniversary.

DCMS, BEIS, Clark, G., & Hancock, M. (2018). *Creative industries sector deal launched.* Retrieved from https://www.gov.uk/government/news/creative-industries-sector-deal-launched.

Deffner, A., & Labrianidis, L. (2005). Planning culture and time in a mega-event: Thessaloniki as the European City of Culture in 1997. *International Planning Studies, 10*(3), 241–264.

Derry-Londonderry City of Culture 2013. (2010). *Summary of our bid.* Retrieved from http://www.cityofculture2013.com/Images/Download/Executive-Summary-low-res.aspx.

Doyle, J. E. (2018). The economic (and other) benefits of losing. In B. Mickov & J. E. Doyle (Eds.), *Culture, innovation and the economy* (pp. 51–61). London: Routledge.

The Economist. (2010). Bring me sunshine. Retrieved from https://www.economist.com/node/17468554.

ERM Economics. (2003). *European Capital of Culture 2008: Socio-economic impact assessment of Liverpool's bid.* Manchester: ERM Economics.

England's Northwest Research Service & Impacts 08. (2010). *The economic impact of visits influenced by the Liverpool European Capital of Culture in 2008.* Retrieved from https://www.liverpool.ac.uk/media/livacuk/impacts08/pdf/pdf/Economic_Impact_of_Visits.pdf.

European Commission. (2009). *European Capitals of Culture: The road to success. From 1985 to 2010.* Luxembourg: Office for Official Publications of the European Communities.

European Commission. (2010). *Commission launches public consultation on future of cultural and creative industries.* Retrieved from http://europa.eu/rapid/pressReleasesAction.do?reference=IP/10/466&format=HTML&aged=0&language=EN&guiLanguage=en.

Evans, G. (2003). Hard-branding the cultural city—From Prado to Prada. *International Journal of Urban and Regional Research, 27*(2), 417–440.

Evans, G. (2011). Cities of culture and the regeneration game. *London Journal of Tourism, Sport and Creative Industries, 5*(6), 5–18.

Evans, R. (1996). Liverpool's urban renewal initiatives and the arts: A review of policy development and strategic issues. In P. Lorente (Ed.), *The role of museums and the arts in the urban regeneration of Liverpool* (pp. 11–26). Leicester: Centre for Urban History.

everyHit. (n.d.). *The best selling singles of all time.* Retrieved from http://www.everyhit.com/bestsellingsingles.html.

García, B. (2004a). Cultural policy and urban regeneration in Western European cities: Lessons from experience, prospects for the future. *Local Economy, 19*(4), 312–326.

García, B. (2004b). Urban regeneration, arts programming and major events. *International Journal of Cultural Policy, 10*(1), 103–118.

García, B. (2005). Deconstructing the City of Culture: The long-term cultural legacies of Glasgow 1990. *Urban Studies, 42*(5–6), 841–868.

García, B. (2017). 'If everyone says so…' Press narratives and image change in major event host cities. *Urban Studies, 54*(14), 3178–3198.

García, B., & Cox, T. (2013). *European Capitals of Culture: Success strategies and long-term effects.* Retrieved from http://www.europarl.europa.eu/RegData/etudes/etudes/join/2013/513985/IPOL-CULT_ET%282013%29513985_EN.pdf.

García, B., Cox, T., & Melville, R. (2010). *Creating an impact: Liverpool's experience as European Capital of Culture.* Retrieved from https://www.liverpool.ac.uk/media/livacuk/impacts08/pdf/pdf/Creating_an_Impact_-_web.pdf.

Gibson, C., & Klocker, N. (2005). The 'cultural turn' in Australian regional economic development discourse: Neoliberalising creativity? *Geographical Research, 43*(1), 93–102.

Gray, C. (2007). Commodification and instrumentality in cultural policy. *International Journal of Cultural Policy, 13*(2), 203–215.

Green, S. (2017). *Capitals of Culture—An introductory survey of a worldwide activity.* Retrieved from http://prasino.eu/wp-content/uploads/2017/10/Capitals-of-Culture-An-introductory-survey-Steve-Green-October-2017.pdf.

Griffiths, R. (2006). City/culture discourses: Evidence from the competition to select the European Capital of Culture 2008. *European Planning Studies, 14*(4), 415–430.

Guy, P. (2018). *Constellations to close in 2019 for 'residential development' as Liverpool suffers new venue blow.* Retrieved from http://www.getintothis.co.uk/2018/07/constellations-close-2019-residential-development-liverpool-suffers-new-venue-blow/.

Heinze, R. G., & Hoose, F. (2013). The creative economy: Vision or illusion in the structural change? *European Planning Studies, 21*(4), 516–535.

Hesmondhalgh, D., Nisbett, M., Oakley, K., & Lee, D. (2015). Were New Labour's cultural policies neo-liberal? *International Journal of Cultural Policy, 21*(1), 97–114.

HM Government. (2018). *Industrial strategy: Creative industries sector deal.* Retrieved from https://www.gov.uk/government/uploads/system/uploads/attachment_data/file/695097/creative-industries-sector-deal-print.pdf.

Hodge, M. (2010). *UK City of Culture festival will showcase creative industries.* Retrieved from https://web.archive.org/web/20110210171032/http://www.cabinetforum.org/blog/uk_city_of_culture_festival_will_showcase_creative_industries.

Houghton, A. (2009, October 22). £5m for new Liverpool creative quarter. *Liverpool Daily Post.*

Hull City Council. (2014). *The countdown has begun.* Retrieved from http://2017-hull.co.uk/uploads/files/Hull_Countdown_to_2017_web.pdf.

Impacts 08. (2009). *Liverpool's creative industries: Understanding the impacts of the Liverpool European Capital of Culture on the city region's creative industries.* Retrieved from https://www.liverpool.ac.uk/media/livacuk/impacts08/publications/liverpools-creative-industries.pdf.

Institute of Popular Music, Institute of Cultural Capital, & European Institute of Urban Affairs. (2015). *Beatles heritage in Liverpool and its economic and cultural sector impact: A report for Liverpool City Council.* Retrieved from https://iccliverpool.ac.uk/wp-content/uploads/2016/02/Beatles-Heritage-in-Liverpool-48pp-210x210mm-aw.pdf.

Jones, P. (2011). *The sociology of architecture—Constructing identities.* Liverpool: Liverpool University Press.

Jones, P., & Wilks-Heeg, S. (2004). Capitalising culture: Liverpool 2008. *Local Economy, 19*(4), 341–360.

Keat, R. (2000). *Cultural goods and the limits of the market.* Basingstoke: Macmillan Press.

Kelly, L. (2018). *Culture for sale: A heartbreaking open letter from the Baltic Triangle.* Retrieved from http://www.thedoublenegative.co.uk/2018/07/culture-for-sale-a-heartbreaking-open-letter-from-the-baltic-triangle/.

Lähdesmäki, T. (2012). Rhetoric of unity and cultural diversity in the making of European cultural identity. *International Journal of Cultural Policy, 18*(1), 59–75.

Lähdesmäki, T. (2014). European Capital of Culture designation as an initiator of urban transformation in the post-socialist countries. *European Planning Studies, 22*(3), 481–497.

Landry, C. (2000). *The creative city*. London: Comedia.

Liu, Y.-D. (2014). Cultural events and cultural tourism development: Lessons from the European Capitals of Culture. *European Planning Studies, 22*(3), 498–514.

Liverpool City Council. (1987). *An arts and cultural industries strategy for Liverpool*. Liverpool: Liverpool City Council.

Liverpool City Council. (2003). *Executive summary for European Capital of Culture bid*. Liverpool: Liverpool City Council.

Liverpool City Council. (2014). *Liverpool culture action plan 2014–18*. Liverpool: Liverpool City Council.

Liverpool City Council & DTZ Pieda Consulting. (2005). *Building the case for creative communities*. Liverpool City Council.

Liverpool City Region Combined Authority. (2018). *Culture and creativity framework—Draft for consultation*. Retrieved from http://liverpoolcityregion-ca.gov.uk/uploadedfiles/documents/DRAFT_LCR_Culture_Creativity_Strategy.pdf.

Liverpool Culture Company. (2002). *Liverpool—The world in one city: Liverpool 2008 Capital of Culture bid*. Liverpool: Liverpool Culture Company.

Liverpool Culture Company. (2003a). *Liverpool—The UK nomination for European Capital of Culture 2008*. Liverpool: Liverpool Culture Company.

Liverpool Culture Company. (2003b). *Liverpool Culture Company business plan*. Liverpool: Liverpool Culture Company.

Liverpool Culture Company. (2003c). *Liverpool—The world in one city: The story unfolds*. Liverpool: Liverpool Culture Company.

Liverpool Culture Company. (2003d). *Liverpool European Capital of Culture 2008 bid—Responses to DCMS questions*. Liverpool: Liverpool Culture Company.

Liverpool Culture Company. (2005). *Strategic business plan 2005–2009*. Liverpool: Liverpool Culture Company.

Liverpool First. (2008). *Liverpool cultural strategy*. Liverpool: Liverpool First.

McGuigan, J. (2005). Neo-liberalism, culture and policy. *International Journal of Cultural Policy, 11*(3), 229–241.

Merseyside ACME. (2005). *Supporting the creative industries on Merseyside*. (n.p.). Liverpool: Merseyside ACME.

Miller, T. (2007). Can natural luddites make things explode or travel faster? In G. Lovink & N. Rossiter (Eds.), *MyCreativity reader: A critique of creative industries* (pp. 41–49). Amsterdam: Institute of Network Cultures.

Miller, T. (2009). From creative to cultural industries. *Cultural Studies, 23*(1), 88–99.

Minihan, J. (1977). *The nationalization of culture*. London: Hamish Hamilton.

Mooney, G. (2004). Cultural policy as urban transformation? Critical reflections on Glasgow, European City of Culture 1990. *Local Economy, 19*(4), 327–340.

Murphy, L. (2015, June 2). Liverpool council agrees deal to buy Garden Festival site. *Liverpool Echo*. Retrieved from https://www.liverpoolecho.co.uk/news/liverpool-news/liverpool-council-agrees-deal-buy-9377210/.

Murphy, L. (2016, November 6). Mayor warns Liverpool faces running out of money. *Liverpool Echo*. Retrieved from https://www.liverpoolecho.co.uk/news/liverpool-news/mayor-warns-liverpool-faces-running-12181646/.

NISRA. (2010). *Northern Ireland multiple deprivation measure 2010*. Belfast: Northern Ireland Statistics and Research Agency.

Norwich City of Culture. (2010). *About the bid*. Retrieved from https://norwichcityofculture.co.uk/about-the-bid/.

NWDA. (2009). *315° the RDA magazine*. Retrieved from https://issuu.com/nwda/docs/315-mag-issue-18/.

O'Brien, D. (2010). 'No cultural policy to speak of'—Liverpool 2008. *Journal of Policy Research in Tourism, Leisure and Events, 2*(2), 113–128.

O'Brien, D. (2014). *Cultural policy: Management, value and modernity in the creative industries*. London: Routledge.

O'Brien, D., & Miles, S. (2010). Cultural policy as rhetoric and reality: A comparative analysis of policy making in the peripheral north of England. *Cultural Trends, 19*(1), 3–13.

Palmer/Rae Associates. (2004). *European Cities and Capitals of Culture—Study prepared for the European Commission*. Retrieved from https://ec.europa.eu/programmes/creative-europe/sites/creative-europe/files/library/palmer-report-capitals-culture-1995-2004-i_en.pdf.

Parkinson, M., & Bianchini, F. (1993). Liverpool: A tale of missed opportunities? In F. Bianchini & M. Parkinson (Eds.), *Cultural policy and urban regeneration* (pp. 155–177). Manchester: Manchester University Press.

Parry, J. (2018, April 23). Liverpool officially launches bid to become home to Channel 4's HQ. *Liverpool Echo*. Retrieved from https://www.liverpoolecho.co.uk/news/liverpool-news/liverpool-officially-launch-bid-become-14562616.

Place North West. (2018). *MgMaStudio wins Baltic Triangle consent*. Retrieved from https://www.placenorthwest.co.uk/news/mgmastudio-wins-baltic-triangle-consent/.

Regenerating Liverpool. (2018a). *Tailor-made plan for Fabric District*. Retrieved from http://regeneratingliverpool.com/news/tailor-made-plan-fabric-district/.

Regenerating Liverpool. (2018b). *Major project: Ten Streets*. Retrieved from http://regeneratingliverpool.com/project/ten-streets/.

Richards, G., & Wilson, J. (2004). The impact of cultural events on city image: Rotterdam, Cultural Capital of Europe 2001. *Urban Studies, 41*(10), 1931–1951.

Ritman, A. (2018). *London's Twickenham Studios to open major film, TV facility in Liverpool*. Retrieved from https://www.hollywoodreporter.com/news/londons-twickenham-studios-open-major-film-tv-facility-liverpool-1117958.

Sacco, P. L. (2017). Events as creative district generators? Beyond the conventional wisdom. In J. Hannigan & R. Richards (Eds.), *The Sage handbook of new urban studies* (pp. 250–265). London: Sage.

Scott, A. J. (2014). Beyond the creative city: Cognitive-cultural capitalism and the new urbanism. *Regional Studies, 48*(4), 565–578.

Smith, T., Noble, M., Noble, S., Wright, G., McLennan, D., & Plunkett, E. (2015). *The English indices of deprivation 2015: Research report*. London: Department for Communities and Local Government.

St Helens Council. (2018). *St Helens named as first Liverpool city region Borough of Culture*. Retrieved from https://www.sthelens.gov.uk/news/2018/march/20/st-helens-named-as-first-liverpool-city-region-borough-of-culture/.

Theokas, A. C. (2004). *Grounds for review: The Garden Festival in urban planning and design*. Liverpool: Liverpool University Press.

Thorp, L. (2018a, January 24). Council Tax set to rise by nearly 6% as local services face "financial cliff edge". *Liverpool Echo*. Retrieved from https://www.liverpoolecho.co.uk/news/liverpool-news/council-tax-set-rise-nearly-14193930.

Thorp, L. (2018b, June 20). Liverpool was the star of the small screen today—And Scousers absolutely loved it. *Liverpool Echo*. Retrieved from https://www.liverpoolecho.co.uk/news/liverpool-news/liverpool-star-small-screen-today-14805869.

Torpey, C. (2017). *Editorial. Bido Lito, 84,* 9.

Vickery, J. (2012). Reconsidering the cultural city. In K. Wilson & D. O'Brien (Eds.), *It's not the winning… Reconsidering the cultural city: A report on the Cultural Cities Research Network 2011–12* (pp. 32–34). Retrieved from https://iccliverpool.ac.uk/wp-content/uploads/2013/09/Cultural-Cities-FINAL-report-July-2012.pdf.

Wainwright, O. (2018, March 13). Edgy urban apartments, lavish promos—And a trail of angry investors. *The Guardian*. Retrieved from https://www.theguardian.com/cities/2018/mar/13/buyer-funded-development-scandal/.

Ward, D. (1999, July 9). Liverpool woos Guggenheim. *The Guardian*. Retrieved from https://www.theguardian.com/uk/1999/jul/09/davidward/.

Ward, D. (2004, July 20). Liverpool scraps plans for Cloud. *The Guardian*. Retrieved from https://www.theguardian.com/uk/2004/jul/20/europeancityofculture2008.arts/.

Wilks-Heeg, S. (2003). From world city to pariah city? Liverpool and the global economy, 1850–2000. In R. Munck (Ed.), *Reinventing the city? Liverpool in comparative perspective* (pp. 36–52). Liverpool: Liverpool University Press.

Wilson, K. and O'Brien, D. (2012). *It's not the winning… Reconsidering the cultural city: A report on the Cultural Cities Research Network 2011–12*. Retrieved from https://iccliverpool.ac.uk/wp-content/uploads/2013/09/Cultural-Cities-FINAL-report-July-2012.pdf.

Wynne, D. (1992). Urban regeneration and the arts. In D. Wynne (Ed.), *The culture industry: The arts in urban regeneration* (pp. 84–95). Aldershot: Avebury.

7

Clarifying the Creativity Agenda: More Persistent Challenges

Previous chapters have demonstrated the persistence of an agenda to promote creativity, and have considered what this agenda entails, how evidence for it may be gathered, and how it is deployed. This chapter will focus on another, related aspect of persistence: persistent challenges to this agenda that will need to be dealt with if the desired end state of 'cities powered by creativity' is ever to arrive. Whilst these challenges can sometimes be framed as temporary difficulties to be overcome, however, their very persistence (and, indeed, intensification) suggests the Creativity Agenda may continue to find itself up against an intransigent reality, which it will never be able to suitably acknowledge until the idea of creativity is deployed in a clearer and more nuanced manner. The flexibility in meaning which has assisted the rise of the Creativity Agenda thus also serves to limit its success beyond the level of rhetoric. As such, this chapter will suggest there is a good reason to think more cautiously about what the Creativity Agenda is, and what it can achieve. Current indications, however, are towards the continued deployment of 'traditional' understandings of creativity, and so we are likely to see the persistence of 'traditional' patterns.

© The Author(s) 2019
P. Campbell, *Persistent Creativity*, Sociology of the Arts,
https://doi.org/10.1007/978-3-030-03119-0_7

Persistence Through Opacity?

As we have seen so far, the Creativity Agenda has, both in theory and in practice, an inherent flexibility, allowing a range of diverse activities to be grouped under a common label (Grodach 2013, p. 1757). This common labelling is often presented as mirroring an underlying commonality in these activities. Whilst some argue for the productivity of this linkage, others see it as inviting opacity and contradiction, and at various points throughout the rise of the Creativity Agenda these contradictions have seemed to pose serious problems for its continuation. In 2009, for instance, after a period of flourishing, many questioned whether parts of this agenda could feasibly continue for much longer. Banks and O'Connor posed the question: 'are we entering a period 'after' the creative industries?' (2009, p. 367), querying the nature of the industries so-labelled, the lack of coherent policy support, and raising the need to challenge what was presented as the apparently 'contradiction-free marriage of culture and economics' (p. 366). As Chapter 5 demonstrated, shortly after this point, a transformation *did* occur in the nature of the statistical evidence base concerning the economic performance of the creative industries, which also seemed to pose challenges for the continuation of a predominantly economic case. As was also demonstrated, however, this statistical diminution was short-lived and the deployment of new methodological approaches allowed the economic case for creativity to be 'repaired', and so the flexibility inherent in the concept enabled a partially redefined creative industries to continue to be presented as a cultural and economic powerhouse.

Just as the arts and culture were no longer positioned as central to the rationale for the gathering of such statistics, but nevertheless remained prominent when such statistics were presented, so we saw in Chapter 6 how a cultural festival can be positioned as a major success in the development of creative industries, even if it does not primarily seek to intervene on these terms, and there is little evidence that such development has actually occurred. Assertion of such connections, however, chimes with the dominant agenda, and so as these assertions are prominently made, they serve to bolster the foundations for the Creativity

Agenda, strengthening the notion of creative commonality. We are, therefore, still awaiting a period 'after' the creative industries, but Banks and O'Connor were certainly correct a decade ago that creativity was entering a period in which it would become ever more chimerical, or, as Schlesinger has it, 'liquid'. At this time, Schlesinger noted that such ideas were not on the retreat, but rather 'being taken increasingly seriously', offering this explanation:

> The sheer pervasiveness of creativity discourse as a liquid synonym for dynamism, growth, talent formation and national renewal is quite remarkable. Herein lies its attractiveness. (2009, pp. 17–18)

What should be noted, then, is that the persistence of this agenda can be explained at least in part by its seemingly inexorable alignment with the dominant values of the age. If creativity is understood as being essentially a synonym for growth, renewal, innovation and so forth, then as the valuing of these persists, so will the promotion of this seemingly related agenda. There is a danger here, though, that in these close alignments we both lose a sense of what is actually being discussed, and continue the problematic notion that anything which can be called creative 'naturally' aligns with these values. What Oakley identified in 2009 as the 'collapse of culture into an innovation discourse' demonstrates the dangers of these blurred boundaries, but although Oakley raised the possibility at this point that as the then Labour government in the UK waned so may this configuration, rather the 'thin notion of cultural value, declining cultural sectors and [...] crude version of innovation' (2009, p. 412) she identified as permeating discourse at that point in time has proved to persist and to transcend party political boundaries. The terminal imprecision of the Creativity Agenda thus presents challenges. For instance, it raises the promise of meaningful, culturally rich work, yet develops in ways which undermine this possibility for most, as discussed below. This chapter thus concentrates on the need to persistently question what is really under consideration when 'creativity' comes to the table—in what manner is anything so labelled understood as deserving this label, and how is this creativity seen to operate? Only by emphasising these questions can a realistic assessment of the potential for this multifarious agenda be realised, but this is vital if creativity is not to be a free-floating, fuzzy signifier of goodness and positive outcomes which are often promised but seldom materialise. Without at least approaching such clarity, there can be no development of definitions or categories of inquiry, and so the constant demand for evidence to make the case for art, culture and creative industries will continue to lay its foundations on conceptual sand.

What Is Now Creative About Creativity?

In asking *what* creative activity we are talking about, and *in what way* it is creative, we can therefore again emphasise the point made at the end of Chapter 6 that, although *represented* as dynamic, innovative, new and so on, specific deployments of the concept of creativity are now made in ever more conservative ways, and apparently to ever more conservative ends. Osborne was early to the identification of this emerging paradox:

> Creativity is a value which, though we may believe we choose it ourselves, may in fact make us complicit with what today might be seen as the most conservative of norms: compulsory individualism, compulsory 'innovation', compulsory performativity and productiveness, the compulsory valorization of the putatively new. (2003, p. 507)

Perhaps just as importantly, Osborne also raises serious questions for the 'creativity' of artistic practice which, as seen in Chapter 5, is still seemingly posited as being fundamentally and inextricably creative for the purposes of data production. Conversely, Osborne argues for 'the complete irrelevance of the whole doctrine of creativity' to the actual practice of art, adding:

> Inventiveness in art is no doubt rather the repetition of attempt and the elimination of accomplishment. In that sense, it is desire not fulfilment, something which makes it more or less wholly at odds with most versions of the doctrine of creativity today. (2003, p. 521)

O'Connor adds to this sense that rather than being *by definition* creative, it is just as possible to argue that the Creativity Agenda is fundamentally antithetical to artistic achievement:

> The older traditions of the 'golden mean', the Chinese 'middle way', bal-
> ance and harmony; the idea of a life spent in the acquisition of a diffi-
> cult singular expertise, the artistic sacrifice of other routes, other skills,
> in order to master one; the gradual abandonment of self-expression in
> favour of other formal languages and meanings – all these appear archaic,
> irrelevant to the incessant innovation drive of creativity. (2007, p. 53)

Whilst creativity is perennially aligned with the new and the artistic, it
is just as possible to present it as both fundamentally conservative and
antithetical to cultural expression. Neither of these extremes is necessarily the 'correct' position, but this serves to demonstrate the imprecision of the Creativity Agenda. In addition to this problematic scope,
however, there is a double bind in operation. Whilst, like many words,
'creativity' can have multiple referents, and the Creativity Agenda can
problematically leverage this term without precision, this *in and of
itself* may be positioned as evidence of the 'creativity' of the processes
at hand. Hartley, for instance, notes that the creative industries are, 'so
varied in scale, organization and sector of economic activity that they
are barely recognizable as a coherent object of analysis' (2005, p. 23),
and that those working within the creative industries do not form any
alliances within their sector, or form any kind of identity related to their
inclusion in this grouping. Remarkably, this is not seen as problematic,
or a sign that an imposed definition has assumed a commonality that
is not manifest, but rather simply as a sign that this *new* sector must
be approached in a *new* way. If these industries are not found to have
any commonality in their practices this is because they are being looked
for in an *old* way, which is not sufficiently creative. No matter which
way one turns, then, the answer is creativity. When definition moves
to emphasise the importance of occupations rather than industries in
the creative economy, we are similarly told that 'uncertainty is a defining feature of emergent areas subject to persistent structural change like
the creative industries' (Bakhshi et al. 2013a, p. 3). But what kind of

uncertainty? We may be uncertain about the data available to measure these industries, or uncertain about how well it measures them, or how these industries may develop in the future, but we should surely not be uncertain about what kind of creativity we are interested in, or its defining characteristics. If we are uncertain about this, why would the creative industries be an object of interest in the first place?

The idea of creativity, inherently broad-ranging, therefore has a tendency to invite a lack of clarity, and as we have seen in previous chapters, this lack of clarity may actually assist in the persistence of the Creativity Agenda. When the object under discussion is so prone to mutation, however, it can easily take the form any particular interested party desires, and those utilising the concept may inadvertently talk past one another, assuming sympathy between contradictory positions. As this agenda spreads, so the situation seemingly worsens. Comunian et al. argue for the intensification of this issue over time:

> While there seems to be little disagreement on the fact that being 'creative' can be beneficial to individuals and society, the question of what 'creativity' entails and exactly what kind of benefits it brings is far from being solved. In fact, the term 'creative' has been applied in so many different contexts that, over time, it has become fuzzier rather than clearer. (2010, p. 389)

In light of the myriad problems which arise when the discourse of creativity moves away from a focus on explicitly cultural activity, Kong (2014, p. 603) and Oakley and O'Connor (2015, p. 10) have more recently, and appropriately, asserted that there are many reasons for a return to a focus on the concept of 'cultural industries'. As we saw in Chapter 5, however, a tighter focus on cultural activity does serious injury to the headline economic statistics most often leveraged to demonstrate the power of creativity, cultural and otherwise. As such, it is likely that for some time yet policy discourse will take advantage of the elbow room provided by the notion of creativity to sidestep these issues, whilst benefiting from the positive associations creativity maintains. Nevertheless, the increasing emphasis on versions of creativity that have, or are expected to have, direct economic benefits will continue to raise contradictions. As Vanolo puts it:

Only selective interpretations of 'innovation' and 'creativity' are deployed: creativity is only generally discussed where it is possible for it to be harnessed in productive ways for economic growth. Conceptualizations of creativity are therefore partial, fluid and even contradictory. (2013, p. 1788)

The Contradictions of Creativity

Given this potential for contradiction, it is posited here that, although ultimately necessary, clarifying the Creativity Agenda may serve to undermine some of its constituent parts, and so imprecision prevails. Given that significant resources are put into practical activities aligned with this agenda, though, as seen in Chapter 6, it is worthwhile to consider what the contradictions are that limit the success of such activities on the terms that the Creativity Agenda proposes. Often, these are related not to the novelty, or otherwise, of 'creative' practice, but to a pervasive sense that creativity is a particularly *open* field. This in part explains the reasons why creativity is leveraged particularly in locations seeking success in 'new' economic times—if creative success depends primarily on the human imagination (a contentious position, but a popular one), then there is potentially no location in which its power cannot be tapped. This idea of openness also suggests a field in which power relations can be disregarded or easily overcome.

Many, however, have argued that the use of culture to bring about some form of 'creative city', is a strategy that risks being of benefit primarily to an already privileged minority. Just as the earliest arguments by policymakers for the creative industries stressed 'individual talent' and a 'democracy of involvement' (Smith 1998, pp. 31, 144), so one of the most prominent early proselytisers of creative work, Charles Leadbeater, characterised the 'new' knowledge economy as inclined towards fairness, arguing for its 'powerful democratic impulse' and the importance that rewards 'flow to talent, creativity and intelligence', rather than being based on any inherited characteristics (1999, p. 224). When it comes to cultural 'talent' and creativity, however, it must be noted that despite a consistent rhetoric around the need to ensure, for instance, 'great art for everyone' (Arts Council England 2010), non-engagement with the cultural forms that cultural policy is mainly concerned with is the norm, with engagement mirroring lines of class and education (e.g. Caves 2000, p. 177; Miles and Sullivan 2009; Taylor 2016), and persistently so, with these patterns of cultural engagement demonstrating stability year-on-year, despite attempts at disruption (Hewison 2014, p. 87). Given the stability of cultural engagement, any activity based on the promotion of traditional cultural forms risks being predominantly of value to the minority engaged in such forms. This can in part explain the pattern identified by Scott, who argues that rather than being open to all,

> creative city policies help to turbo-charge gentrification processes thus exacerbating the exclusion of low-income families from central city areas and underwriting the takeover of those areas by the new bourgeoisie. (Scott 2014, p. 573)

The relationship is a complex one, however (Grodach et al. 2014), and Markusen advises that we should resist the temptation to point the finger predominantly at art and artists when considering the issue of gentrification, and should instead consider the broader social structures in which artists operate:

> Unequal wealth, a free market property rights system, and an active development industry in cities drive gentrification, not artists per se, even if some artists are caught in its fast-changing web. (2014, p. 570)

What is not in question, however, is that such gentrification does occur, and that cultural work and workers are often implicated or entangled in this process. Again, then, we see the obscuring power of creativity: what is presented as an open, 'democratic' field with potential economic returns for many can bring about the development of areas and activities valued by, and providing value for, a minority.

This takes us in some regards back to the 'creative class' theory considered previously. Early critiques demonstrated how the language of creativity being deployed in this theory implied a sense of openness that presented contradictions. If the theory asserts that 'everyone' is creative and so at least has the potential to enter the creative class, this leaves unanswered, as Peck puts it, 'the nagging question of who will launder the shirts in this creative paradise' (2005, p. 757). If everyone has the potential to be creative, who has to stay 'behind' in the 'working' and 'service' classes? What is perhaps more problematic here, though, is not so much the contradictions regarding how open the creativity posited by this theory is, but rather the contradictions presented when the theory's explanatory power is interrogated. By aligning with the values of the age and basing his theories on a range of numerical indices (although also claiming that these are essentially incidental to his fundamental position [Florida 2004, p. 327]), the statistical bases of Florida's various rankings are usefully open to scrutiny. Although such quick-to-digest rankings and tables contribute to the speed with which this theory is taken up, and its broad popularity (Mould 2017, p. 55), when these rankings are considered in detail, numerous difficulties emerge. For instance, soon after these indices get taken up in relation to the UK, questions are asked regarding whether data has been deployed in an appropriate fashion:

> Florida concludes that Leicester is the second most creative city in the UK. This simply cannot be true; one suspects that too much weighting has been allowed for the fact that Leicester has a large non-white population, and this has been assumed to be an indicator of creativity (Montgomery 2005, p. 339).

This result may be accounted for by data relating to 'Tolerance' which is one of the '3 T's' deemed by Florida as important to understanding the creative class ('Talent' and 'Technology' being the others), but such arguments must ultimately return to the question of specificity: of what kind of 'creativity' is tolerance an indicator of? As Comunian et al. conclude:

> The 'creative class' as defined by Florida, is too broad to enable a meaningful empirical analysis. It includes very different occupations (such as physicists and artists which can hardly be thought of as having similar

characteristics) and this unaccounted heterogeneity can lead to mislead-ing results. (2010, p. 392)

Comunian et al. also refer to a range of work which argues that the con-cept of 'creativity' being deployed in Florida's indices maps so closely to measures of educational attainment that the two are virtually indistin-guishable and, whilst levels of formal education do map strongly to eco-nomic growth, additionally taking the number of 'super-creative' workers into consideration does not make a significant contribution to this anal-ysis (2010, p. 393). This again helps to demonstrate the power of the 'creativity' label: a theory about the need for cities to ensure they have a suitable environment for the 'educated professional class' would probably not have travelled so far or been so successful in this era, but what the language of creativity adds, other than attractiveness, and a potentially misleading sense of openness, is certainly up for debate. We thus return to some of the questions around data, categorisation, labelling and evi-dence gathering that came up in Chapter 5. As Brouillette has it:

> Florida's definition of what constitutes a creative profession is itself so capacious that his statements about a vanguard creative-class takeover seem like the product of statistical maneuvering. (2014, p. 46)

Indeed, statistical analysis by other scholars suggests that rather than being drawn to creative environments and bringing their creative talents along with them, 'place attractiveness' alone is unlikely to result in sig-nificant economic migration, and that 'for most migrants the availabil-ity of appropriate economic opportunities is a prerequisite for mobility' (Houston et al. 2008, p. 133). Others conclude as a result of statistical analysis that there is essentially no additional explanatory power in the specifics of the creative class theory, with Hoyman and Faricy being par-ticularly strident in their conclusions:

> What evidence is there that the creative class theory generates growth in cities? The creative class failed consistently across multiple statisti-cal tests to explain either job growth, growth in wages, or absolute lev-els of wages. Additionally, the individual characteristics of the creative

class—talent, technology, and tolerance—were negatively correlated with all our economic measurements. The totality of results regarding the creative class model should halt policies that cities are adopting to spur job growth and innovation based on creative class strategies. (2009, p. 329)

Whilst problems such as these were identified relatively early on in the concept's rise (e.g. Nathan 2005; Peck 2005), we last encountered Florida during Chapter 6 being touted as the 'government's new guru' in the UK in 2010, and his influence persisted in this period outside the UK also (e.g. Heinze and Hoose 2013, p. 521). Indeed, research points to the limited influence of critiques such as those above on policy in this period (Borén and Young 2013).

In more recent years, however, enthusiasm for the concept of the creative class has somewhat tempered. Although the term remains in use, and indeed, Florida himself continues to employ his standard definition (e.g. 2017, p. 137), together with his fondness for generating rankings and indices (e.g. 2017, p. 18), his position on what the role of such a class is has shifted:

I realized I had been overly optimistic to believe that cities and the creative class could, by themselves, bring forth a better and more inclusive kind of urbanism. (Florida 2017, p. xxii)

Florida's earlier work, however, is also quite clear that areas which are deemed to be highly creative also demonstrate high levels of income inequality (2004, p. 354) and that the 'creative economy' itself generates 'all sorts of social and economic problems' (2007, p. 65). Whilst almost incidental to earlier theorising, though, and certainly not a noted part of the Creativity Agenda, these concerns come increasingly to the fore in later work. Although Florida maintains his optimism about the potential to ameliorate the situation, he identifies significant challenges with commercial creative industries and the 'new' economy more widely. One significant challenge is the fact that, although theoretically open and able to operate 'anywhere', the new economy has thus far taken root and successfully grown in a relatively small number of locations. Both within creative industries themselves, and in the locations they successfully operate from, research points to a 'winner takes all' pattern, with a small number of major successes accompanied by a far larger number of more modest achievements. As Florida puts it:

> As I pored over the data, I could see that only a limited number of cities and metro areas, maybe a couple of dozen, were really making it in the knowledge economy; many more were failing to keep pace or falling further behind. Many older industrial "Rustbelt" cities, like Detroit and Cleveland in the US, or Liverpool and Birmingham in the UK, are still grappling with the devastating combination of deindustrialization and urban decay. (2017, p. xxiii)

Replicable Exceptionality?

These patterns thus reveal challenges for the successful deployment of the Creativity Agenda. Literature arguing for the potential of creativity in urban locations during the rise of the agenda often alludes to locations such as Greenwich Village, Soho or la Rive Gauche (e.g. Wynne 1992, p. 19; Florida 2004, p. 15) with the implication that, whilst perhaps not directly replicable in influence, any location can reasonably aim to develop a 'creative quarter' of its own. Indeed, by 2004, Oakley argued in the UK that 'no region of the country [...] is safe from the need for a 'creative hub' or 'cultural quarter'' (p. 68). Whilst there is a range of language in use, with Hesmondhalgh and Pratt, for instance, arguing that the 'creative city' concept grows out of 'cultural quarter' policies, which produce the 'offshoot concept of "the cultural cluster"' (2005, p. 4), Schlesinger points to an underlying commonality in usage, referring to the work of the Department for Culture, Media and Sport (DCMS) 'Creative Economy Programme' in 2007:

> 'Creative hubs' have replaced 'clusters' as the 'in' phrase, but the fundamental idea is the same. Both underline the 'significance of place as the main driver of creativity in the UK'. (2007, p. 385)

If we consider the role of place revealed by the economic statistics first considered in Chapter 5, however, we see that after persistent attempts to create hubs, quarters or clusters in many locations, just one location dominates the creative field in the UK: London. London's exceptionality is common in many domains, as the UK is centralised in a number of regards, but, as Florida notes, 'London's dominance over the rest of the UK in the creative industries is especially pronounced [...] And London's dominance has been growing' (2017, p. 55). Analysis shows, for instance, that 'finance is far less London-centric than the creative industries' (Bernick et al. 2017, p. i). Indeed, the creative industries have been characterised not as being dispersed or having multiple strong locations, but rather as effectively having a single hub in the UK, in that 'there is only one location with significant activity' (2017, p. 11). Figure 7.1 gives figures for total Gross Value Added (GVA, see Chapter 5) to demonstrate London's dominance of the UK economy as a whole.

Despite this dominance, other regions do have a visible presence in this figure. In considering, the statistics discussed in the later stages of Chapter 5 on either the DCMS-defined Creative Industries, or the more tightly defined 'Cultural Sector', however, London's dominance is much starker, as shown in Figs. 7.2 and 7.3 respectively.

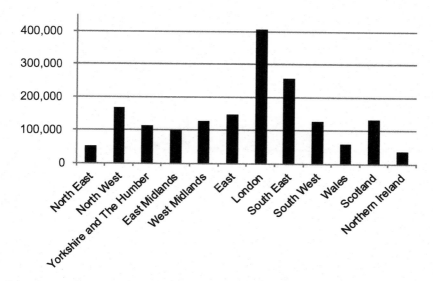

Fig. 7.1 Total GVA by UK region—2016 (£m) (*Source* DCMS [2018])

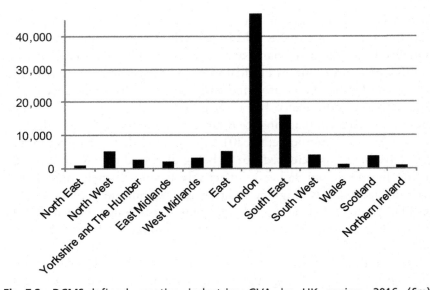

Fig. 7.2 DCMS-defined creative industries GVA by UK region—2016 (£m) (*Source* DCMS [2018])

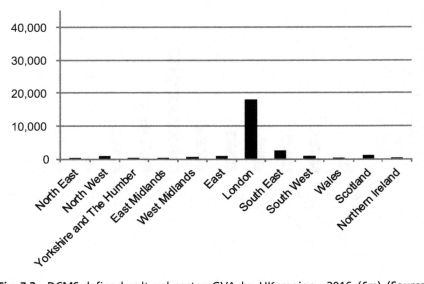

Fig. 7.3 DCMS-defined cultural sector GVA by UK region—2016 (£m) (*Source* DCMS [2018])

Despite the promotion of creative hubs and clusters being one of the key means of enacting the Creativity Agenda, the economic output from cultural and creative industries not only remains concentrated in London, but this concentration actually *increases* as the Creativity Agenda continues to exert its influence. Figure 7.4 shows GVA figures for London as a proportion of the UK total.

Whilst over this period the proportion of GVA across the whole economy generated in London has risen by 1.7 percentage points, the proportion of GVA in the DCMS-defined Creative Industries has risen by 4.8 points, with London now accounting for over half of UK GVA. Similarly, GVA in London in the DCMS-defined cultural sector has risen by 3.3 points in this period, with the London figure standing at 67% in 2016. Whilst the rhetoric of creativity suggests openness, the reality shows increased concentration. Stark et al.'s report considering London's dominance of the cultural sector provides a thorough consideration of the nature of this dominance; the following extract is merely illustrative of some aspects of this:

Higher Education is a major provider of and contributor to the cultural life of cities. Of 153 Higher Education degree-awarding institutions in

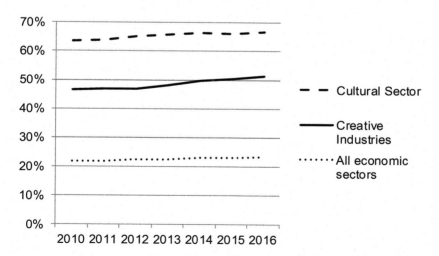

Fig. 7.4 London GVA as proportion of UK total, 2010–2016 (*Source* DCMS [2018])

England, 42 are in London, as are more than 90% of the specialist institutions for professional art, music, dance, film and drama training [...]
London, as the production base for arts journals and radio and television
programmes and the perceived location of interested readers, listeners and
viewers, also provides the home base and focus for the work of England's
specialist critics and commentators in the arts. It can at times appear that
the cultural life of the nation becomes synonymous in the national media
with what is happening in 'central' London. (2013, p. 27)

The concentration of education, media and professional bodies in a single city form a virtuous circle, and one difficult for other locations to
tap into. Scott's analysis of the 'cultural economy of cities' (2000) is also
instructive in understanding these patterns, noting that those geographical regions which pioneer successful development in cultural fields are
liable to 'lock out' contenders elsewhere (p. 22), with any replication
of existing successes being difficult as certain fields become 'irreversibly
dominated' (p. 27). In later work, Scott refers to 'high levels of path-de-
pendency' in the 'creative field' (2006, p. 16). Considering the emergence of new sectors, he writes:

When a new industry emerges, it will sometimes assume an agglomerated
geographic pattern at the outset, and will then rapidly begin to generate
localized increasing returns effects. In this manner, the agglomeration as a
whole benefits from so-called first-mover advantages, and it will tend sys-
tematically to outstrip all later competitor agglomeration by reason of its
advanced dynamic of specialized entrepreneurship, innovation, and economic development. (Scott 2006, p. 17)

The pattern identified in Florida's later work of a small number of
dominant 'superstar cities' (2017, p. 17) seems to attest to the continuation of these effects in the modern creative field. Whilst in earlier
periods the success and renown of standard reference locations such as
'1960s Rive Gauche and 1970s SoHo' could be argued to have 'struck
at the roots of their very success as alternative spaces of creativity'
(Mommaas 2004, p. 521), Florida argues that there is no sign yet of this
occurring in modern 'superstar' locations.

In considering attempts to promote creative clusters, Mommaas notes that not only were these standard reference locations not deliberately planned as such but, in detailed research of specific 'planned' clusters outside of these locations during the rise of the Creativity Agenda, that none demonstrated fruitful agglomeration effects (p. 515), adding:

> Most of them are rather consumption- instead of production-oriented and, where production is central, clusters have not (yet) developed to the point where intracluster transactions or a sharing of information and markets is of great significance. (p. 517)

Nevertheless, the literature shows that as the Creativity Agenda rises such attempts to 'cluster' creativity were influential not only nationally in the UK (O'Connor 2005, p. 48), but replicated internationally, although this process often occurred based on assumptions of how such clustering may succeed, 'with little confirmatory evidence' to back this up (Foord 2008, p. 99). Whilst such quarters or clusters may indeed be a precondition of the operation of successful creative industries (Scott 2000, p. ix), this may often take place in the absence of, rather than as a result of, any policy intervention (Foord 2008, p. 100). Indeed, policy approaches to clustering in this field have often been identified as poorly conceived and implemented (Jayne 2005, p. 554), which is likely to prove a further barrier to the replication of any possible success. We must therefore be cautious regarding how much direct influence can be exerted in this field. Johnson and Reed (2008, p. 26) cite data to suggest that, considered more generally, specific policies to induce entrepreneurship have 'at best, no effect' on employment levels and, more specifically, McDonald et al. find that interventions to create 'clusters' of successful businesses largely occur via a process of self-selection by firms and detect little evidence of strong positive relationships between the interventions of government policies and such activity (2006, p. 535). Evans argues that these issues are intensified in the creative field, and that it is the specific character of 'these so-called creative industries' which means they are not 'likely to be responsive to a generalised economic and interventionist approach by government, let alone 'planners"

(2001, p. 153). In terms of the effects of creative clusters that *are* developed, Evans argues that evidence of a link between these clusters and improved innovation and competitiveness has been 'elusive' (2009, p. 1016), but we must also question whether any promoted creative clusters even count as clusters in a meaningful sense. Hesmondhalgh et al. cite Bennett's forthright reflections of the realities of such cluster promotion during the rise of the Creativity Agenda:

> There's a lot of shit talked about clusters. Very few of the people who were promoting clusters as a means of organisation […] had done proper research. […] one of the things of the Labour policies is that they didn't bother to criticise and they didn't exercise, I don't think, enough economic rigour in determining the investment priorities as to where was really a cluster and where was just a nice sitting room with some rather interesting graphic designers. (Bennett cited in Hesmondhalgh et al. 2015, p. 133)

Once again here we may see the ability of the Creativity Agenda to veil specificity. Just as anything 'creative' may be associated with innovation and dynamism, so any gathering of creative individuals can be presented as a 'cluster' or 'hub'. The realities of economic output, however, are less amenable to such flexibility, despite any discursive alignment, and more than mere co-location is required for the economic benefits associated with clustering to arise (Flew 2010, p. 87).

Over time, the problems associated with attempts at building clusters thus become increasingly noted. Reflecting back on 'decades' of intervention, Mould and Comunian summarise prevailing patterns thus:

> We could argue that much has been learnt about the development of CQ [Cultural Quarters] in UK in the last decades. However, looking more closely, we see homogenously designed urban spaces, failed flagships projects and the boom of private consultancy firms offering CQ design services, and the uncritical and unreflexive take-up of CQ as a neoliberalized "model" of urban renewal across the UK. (2015, p. 2366)

This is thus another field in which certain patterns persist; indeed, the promotion of clusters continues to be prominent and presented as a potential route for driving the Creativity Agenda forward. In 2017, for instance, Sir Nicholas Serota, Chair of Arts Council England, offered the following thoughts on potential development routes for the UK's economy:

> Imagine if London's model could be replicated nationally. We need to build 'creative clusters', large and small, as generators for new talent and business, across the UK. (Serota 2017)

Similarly, the UK's Industrial Strategy Sector Deal for the Creative Industries takes up this theme, aiming to 'tackle' concentration in London 'via new public investment and industry backing for leading creative industries clusters with the potential to compete globally' (HM Government 2018, p. 10). Clearly, these developments will not be the first such attempts, and whether another iteration of cluster strategies will see other regions of the UK challenge or replicate London's increasing dominance remains to be seen. The discussion above suggests caution would be warranted. Despite the long-standing, and continuing, identification of the dominance of London, and the prevalence of a pattern of industrial concentration into a few key centres (e.g. Pratt 1997), the assumed openness of creativity seems to remain in play. Over a decade ago, Oakley noted the problem with the notion that these are 'sectors that can be replicated and developed pretty much anywhere, without regard for the specifics of place' (2004, p. 72), and Montgomery put this even more directly, arguing that 'not all cities can be centres of creative industries production beyond meeting the demands of very localized markets. Birmingham cannot compete with London' (2005, p. 341). The competitive imperative, however, will not easily be altered and so, even though it 'cannot', there is a sense in which Birmingham (and other cities) *must* compete. The broader factors that result in London's increased dominance, however, will also not be easily altered. Even at the most basic level, we can consider the importance of overall city size for sourcing audiences for a range of work (e.g. London Development Agency 2008, p. 64), and for the existence of the dense networks identified by Scott as important for production in this field (1999, p. 807). In terms of successful business operation in the bulk of the creative industries, therefore, density matters, audience matters, and so, although not merely a matter of size, size matters. What can be achieved in Florida's 'superstar cities' such as London or New York, with populations over eight million, is unlikely to be feasible even in the second largest city in England cited above, Birmingham, with a population of one million, or in the majority of other, smaller, UK cities hoping to leverage the power of creativity to improve their economic circumstances. In any case, it is feasible to conclude in more recent periods, as Oakley et al. do, that:

> As it stands, the interventions to make towns and cities "creative" in the United Kingdom has not challenged London's dominance of this section of the labor force. [...] If we are to see society fairly reflected in its cultural workforce, then creative city policy must interact with broader issues of the uneven geography of the nation. (2017, p. 1527)

That said, we may also expect no more than limited change on this particular issue given the levels of government support touted. The initial details provided in the 2018 UK Industrial Strategy sector deal for the Creative Industries concentrate on the existence of a £20m 'Cultural Development Fund' to 'develop world-class clusters' (HM Government 2018, p. 14) and a £39m fund to enable partnerships between universities and industry to 'cultivate existing clusters' (p. 15). Perhaps lessons have been learned which will enable these interventions to break away from the previously dominant trajectory of interventions which had a tendency to be 'high on ambition but low on deliverability' combined with 'a proliferation of copycat engagements' (Fleming and Erskine 2011, p. 43). Nevertheless, with Flew raising the prospect that attempts to develop significant creative industries outside of global cities such as London may be 'somewhat delusional in the face of powerful forces promoting agglomeration and sustained competitive advantage' (2010, p. 87), it is appropriate to question why in the present day clusters 'large *and small*', as argued by Serota, are seen as an appropriate response in multiple locations. Indeed, to consider scale, the £20m 'Cultural Development Fund' referred to above is presented as a response to Bazalgette's call for a £500m 'Creative Clusters Fund'

(HM Government 2018, p. 66). This suggested £500m fund was positioned as having the potential to support 'up to 30-35 Creative Clusters' (Bazalgette 2017, p. 26) and so on this basis, presumably a £20m fund has the potential to support up to two clusters; guidance suggests there will be fewer than five areas in receipt of funds, with no one area receiving more than £7m (Arts Council England 2018). Nevertheless, such awards are positioned as having the potential to 'regenerate communities, create jobs and boost tourism' and 'replicate the huge success' of Hull's tenure as UK City of Culture considered in Chapter 6 (DCMS et al. 2018). *Plus ça change, plus c'est la même chose.* Whilst additional clusters may provide some transformation in the geography of creativity, given the discussion above, we may question whether the clusters arising from such a scheme would deserve the label in any meaningful sense. Just as with 'creativity', however, we can also see a flexibility in the deployment of this label: rather than the 'single hub' pattern discussed above, the 2018 Industrial Strategy argues, based on research by Nesta, that there are currently already 47 clusters operating in the UK, with many of these being 'up and coming' locations 'not yet large enough' to qualify in terms of their concentration of creative business, but currently demonstrating high growth (Mateos Garcia and Bakhshi 2016, p. 5), and so travelling *towards* such a position.

If one's concern is mainly with economic output, growth is certainly important, but eventual size also matters. Due to its alignment with ideas of nimble entrepreneurship, however, the Creativity Agenda often gives a special role to the creative *individual* exercising their natural creative abilities and generating exceptional economic output as a result. We have seen above how creativity is presented as having a tendency towards fairness and meritocracy on this individualised basis, and we have also seen how the focus on 'individual creativity' has persisted throughout the era of the Creativity Agenda. As such the promotion of creativity often occurs at this micro-level, with policy discourse focussing on the encouragement of smaller enterprises (Flew and Cunningham 2010, p. 119). Related to this is a sense that rapid growth from this micro-level is a natural component of creative industries. If a lack of growth in these industries is acknowledged, it is often within the context of this sense of a 'naturally' high-growth sector, and so if any businesses are not currently outperforming the rest of the economy, some intervention to restore them to their 'natural' place is required. National policy documents refer, for instance, to,

> a commitment to the creative industries grounded in the belief that they can be scaled and industrialised in the same way as other successful high-technology, knowledge industries such as bio-sciences have been. (DCMS and BIS 2009, p. 105)

Many creative businesses, however, give reason to think that such a belief might not be well founded. Earlier reports produced by Nesta, for instance, pointed to the fact that,

> most UK creative businesses lack scale in terms of size and reach. Many creative businesses are under pressure from increased international competition, and the vast majority of these are unable to respond effectively because they are too small [...] The current support infrastructure for the creative industries in the UK is disproportionately focused on start-ups. This has had the effect of emphasising creativity without a stronger understanding of industrial structure. A greater emphasis needs to be placed on helping more businesses to grow based on the realities of these sectors, in order to strengthen the stability of the UK's creative industries. (2006, pp. 26, 45)

Similar conclusions, however, could still be drawn by Nesta reports in 2013 (Bakhshi et al. 2013b, p. 46), and yet again in 2018:

> Simply promoting creative entrepreneurialism (that is, increasing the number of micro- businesses) will not make a dent in the productivity crisis. The reason for this is that creative micro-businesses are not more productive than the regional average, and in some regions they represent a miniscule share of employment. By contrast, however, 'scale-up policies' that increase the number of businesses with more than ten employees would be more beneficial because these businesses are more productive than firms in other sectors. (Mateos Garcia et al. 2018, p. 30)

In getting a realistic picture of the economic successes of the creative sector, then, not only is it important to consider the major role played by software companies as noted in Chapter 5, but also to consider the important role of larger companies (DCMS 2007, p. 2). Around 95% of creative businesses, however, are currently micro-businesses (DCMS 2018) and data pertaining specifically to the arts and cultural sector suggests over 90% of firms have one or no employees (CEBR 2017, p. 30). Whilst much of the discussion of creative growth is focussed on 'individual creativity' and the generation of intellectual property (IP), then, it is not so much the generation as the eventual *exploitation* of this property that is important economically. On this issue, we may, for instance, consider the position of the UK computer games sector. Despite being,

> recognized for its ability to create original IP, most independent studios do not have access to adequate support in order to maintain ownership of this content, and have to relinquish often 100% of the IP rights to (mainly) non-UK publishers, in return for initial investment. (DCMS and BIS 2009, p. 128)

It is factors such as this which underlie the continued dominance of many creative fields by large multinational conglomerates which permeate all stages of the value chain (Scott 2006, p. 14), and whose operations have an increasing tendency towards consolidation and monopoly (Miller 2004, p. 59), again reinforcing the 'winner takes all' picture sketched above. On this issue, it is also perhaps worth noting that in a report for the DCMS Creative Economy Programme on 'why multinational firms locate in the UK' that 'most of the case study firms required prompting to mention culture as a potential driver of their investment decision in the UK' (Frontier Economics 2007, p. 38), in contrast with their unprompted mention of other factors such as the UK skills base and graduate education.

We can thus once again point here to how a flexible narrative of interlinked creativity fails to take account of more blunt economic realities. As O'Connor notes of the earlier approaches by government departments to mapping the creative industries:

> The DCMS definition simply did not describe the complex structure of the creative industries nor the employment and remuneration

arrangements of the majority of those within it. The definition thus encouraged a deeper delusion, that policies to support and encourage such creative entrepreneurialism would suffice as an industrial strategy. (2007, p. 44)

It seems dealing with this delusion continues to be important. Whilst size is important to economic growth, what must also be contended with is the persistent issue of whether those operating in these predominantly micro-businesses feel the 'need' for growth outlined in policy documents. Lambing and Kuehl argue that for the 'classic' entrepreneur, 'the skills the entrepreneur needs will change as the business grows. He or she should no longer be involved in daily tasks but instead should concentrate on management and motivation' (2007, p. 121). For those less concerned with pecuniary reward or motivated precisely by involvement in 'daily tasks' however, this may not be an attractive prospect. In their early study of entrepreneurship within the creative industries, for instance, Leadbeater and Oakley suggest 80% have 'no ambitions for growth' (Leadbeater and Oakley 1999, p. 29) and that 'many want their businesses to stay small' (1999, p. 11), and in a later study of creative industries beyond the urban environment, Bell and Jayne similarly find that over 80% of practitioners do not seek to expand their business in terms of number of employees (2010, p. 212). This is characterised as a 'problem' in need of solution in prominent policy documents:

> The attitude of owners to ownership is another problem. Creative businesses are often an expression of the highly personal creativity of their founders and owners. More so than many of their counterparts in other economic sectors, they may not wish to have their vision or style of business diluted by the extraneous demands of equity finance partners. (DCMS et al. 2008, p. 46)

For whom is this a 'problem', though, if those running these businesses want to 'stay small'? After all, the concept of utilising non-pecuniary modes of value is not specific to these industries. As Keat notes, 'there is plenty of evidence that income acquisition is not the only significant motive of those working in market enterprises' (2000, p. 119).

Nevertheless, it should be noted that a lack of growth may not always be chosen: creative businesses whose goals do include commercial growth still face issues with basic tasks such as accessing appropriate finance due to their differing structure to 'traditional' industries (CBI 2014, p. 13). What must also be considered is the issue of who has the freedom to work in such a way that 'salaries do not carry much weight' when making decisions around working patterns (Comunian et al. 2010, p. 406).

The Closure of Creativity

A significant body of research attests to the fact that many creative workers make little money (Gerber 2017; Hesmondhalgh 2007, p. 73; McRobbie 2015; Selwood 2001), often due to a greater emphasis being placed on non-economic values, such as the achievement of a form of self-realisation through creative work (Hesmondhalgh 2007, p. 199), or seeing the practice of work rather than its eventual financial rewards as being paramount, via the 'art for art's sake' principle which,

> calls for proceeding with creative effort even at adverse personal economic cost, and hence implies that the creative artist might wish to carry on even when an ideally efficient governance system instructs her to halt the project. (Caves 2000, p. 137)

In considering the workforce of the creative industries in light of these factors, we once again face the challenges raised by the idea of creativity as a field open to anyone with talent or imagination, and especially open to a broad range of perspectives. For instance, we see claims that diversity 'is critical to the continuing success of the creative industries. The more diversity, openness and contestability are encouraged, the more likely it is that creativity will be fostered and productivity increased' (The Work Foundation 2007, p. 22), or that the creative industries have a 'long history of embracing multiculturalism and diversity' (Technology Strategy Board 2009, p. 12), or that they 'preserve and promote diversity' (European Parliament 2016, p. 7). This narrative, however, exists alongside another persistent pattern: 'access to livelihoods in the creative and cultural industries, like most other sectors, remains easier if you are white, middle class and male' (Parker et al. 2006, p. 3). In the context of an emphasis on non-economic forms of value, Parker et al. identify the role of unpaid work in skewing the creative workforce:

> Creatives, particularly those from non-traditional backgrounds, need experience in the marketplace to get ahead, but their potential employers are seldom prepared to meet the costs. The gap is filled by unpaid work and periods of unemployment which can be far more easily borne by those with financial and social resources. (2006, p. 2)

The persistence of this pattern is identified by a continually growing body of research showing the *lack* of diversity in creative and cultural fields (O'Brien and Oakley 2015) which exists alongside the narrative of openness. As a result of this contradiction, Banks characterises the persistent 'blind faith' of 'governments, industry and employers' in the openness of a field that, in reality, often actively works against equality of opportunity as 'shocking' (Banks 2017, p. 115). Indeed, in considering a broad range of literature, Banks and O'Connor conclude that 'the creative economy remains deeply unequal and profoundly unjust' (2017, p. 647).

Whilst the first UK government White Paper on culture in 1965 identified that 'the life of the artist is too precarious' and identified a role for government in ameliorating this situation (Lee 1965, p. 18), the issue of precarious work seems to have become ever more pronounced in recent years, with those in cultural fields being seen to exemplify the patterns of insecurity increasingly prevalent in other sectors (Gill and Pratt 2008). The predominance of insecure work and low wages identified at the outset of the rise of the Creativity Agenda (e.g. Lorente 1996, p. 6) persists and intensifies. For instance, considering the patterning of salaries for those with degrees in arts subjects ('bohemian graduates') and others working in creative fields, Comunian et al. conclude that,

> the lower salary level and poor career prospects of both bohemian graduates in general and non-bohemian graduates with creative occupations

seem to contradict most of the literature on the creative economy and economic development, which sees these as an 'engine' for local growth. (2010, p. 406)

The myriad ways in which such work can be characterised by insecurity, and the ways in which this works in favour of the already privileged has been identified by a range of scholars (e.g. McRobbie 2002; Foord and Ginsburg 2004; Banks and Hesmondhalgh 2009; Vivant 2013). This is perhaps exacerbated by a very persistent idea that working in the arts, or any intrinsically rewarding role, is reward enough in itself and need not be remunerated (e.g. Stevenson 1892; Graeber 2018). The level of unpaid labour continually expected in creative roles is therefore a significant barrier to those in the population who find they cannot live on 'thin air' (Leadbeater 1999), especially given that a vertiginous rise in housing costs in the UK coincides precisely with the rise of the Creativity Agenda (HM Land Registry 2018). Given the dominance of London in the UK's creative industries, it is also worth noting that research points to its dominance here too, with Oakley et al. referring to London as 'the engine for the growth, but seemingly also the inequality' within the sector (2017, p. 1522), and pointing to the fact that although workers in creative and cultural fields from privileged backgrounds earn more throughout the country, this is particularly acute in London.

Nevertheless, although these issues are increasingly acknowledged, much as with the hope that London's performance can be replicated elsewhere, the expectation seems to be that the success of a dominant, privileged group can be replicated by others if they are sufficiently encouraged. Bazalgette's independent review of the creative industries notes that 'people from under-represented groups and from areas outside London in particular think the industry does not offer a viable career path for them' and that there is 'a perception amongst many that jobs are poorly paid, insecure or not open to those without existing links into industry' (2017, p. 43). On current performance, we might applaud the insight of those holding such views. In terms of rectifying the situation, we may question how much schemes intended to boost the 'confidence' of a broad range of young people (Bazalgette 2017,

p. 44) will assist in reversing these entrenched and apparently deepening inequalities. The idea that 'an attraction strategy is needed to inform and excite young people' (p. 6), and discussion of plans to institute 'a major advertising campaign' to build diversity suggests the problem in this area is at least partly due to a lack of sufficient interest from people with disabilities, or from minority ethnic groups, or from the working class, or women, or people in whom these characteristics intersect. The idea that such people are sidelined in the creative economy due to a lack of interest or confidence, rather than a lack of opportunity (see Shorthouse 2010) might in part be explained by the persistent belief in the 'democratic'—or, rather, 'meritocratic'—nature of these fields, and that those with talent will flourish regardless of background. Taylor and O'Brien draw realistic conclusions about the patterning of such beliefs:

> Structural factors are predominantly recognised by those in the sector in precarious positions, whereas those in stronger positions are more likely to generate a meritocratic narrative of how people end up in their positions. It is difficult to see where the impetus for the situation to change will come from. (2017, p. 44)

Nevertheless, 'a diverse workforce' continues to be posited as essential to innovation, creativity and competitive advantage (Bazalgette 2017, p. 42). To the extent that the UK has achieved any competitive advantage, however, it has not thus far relied heavily on such diversity to achieve it. Plans to generate 'interest' amongst a wide constituency seem to return us to the wider processes of individualization operating across society, such as the processes involved in reconfiguring broader ideas around 'social inclusion' identified by Levitas:

> There has been a slippage towards [...] treating cultural capital as something that intrinsically resides in individuals rather than in groups, and can be acquired by them through participation in or consumption of the cultural and heritage industries. (2004, p. 53)

To the extent that the concept has use, however, cultural capital is fundamentally a social phenomenon. Research continues to identify the patterns delineated by Bourdieu (1986) that 'legitimate' culture is embedded within social stratification processes, and closely linked to education and social origin. As Markusen states in the context of the US:

> Working class cultural participants, although often intersecting with racial and ethnic cultures, have distanced themselves from the fine arts tradition, refusing to participate in events that are often riddled with pretension and requirements for having had arts training. Often the cultural expressions chosen by white working class people involve formats that make educated people uncomfortable: country music, tattooing, NASCAR racing, mud bogs (in rural areas), and more. (2014, p. 573)

There is thus the prospect that diversity in terms of demography is valorised only when it does not entail diversity in cultural engagement. This issue returns us to the broader problem of who engages, with what culture, and how (Stevenson et al. 2015); to conceive of the sector in an individualised fashion negates any *social* factors at play in the operation of the creative industrial field. As is the case with the notion of entrepreneurship more broadly (e.g. Blanchflower and Oswald 1998), however, despite being focussed on the individual, without relevant skills and resources, personal qualities alone are unlikely to be sufficient for success. Similarly, generating *interest*, even only in 'legitimate' cultural activity, will not necessarily translate into productive practice within the creative industries without such wider resources, even without considering the important broader questions of how such legitimation processes operate and who is excluded by them.

How Far Can Creativity Reach?

As in Chapter 6, therefore, we see how the apparent hope offered by the Creativity Agenda can all too quickly be eclipsed by issues of structural inequality. Nevertheless, we can see that the issue of diversity is at least noted in recent policy, which may mark the emergence of some progress, and as noted above, prominent voices such as Florida have also moved on to a consideration of larger issues such as these. Reflecting on his past advice as he 'travelled the world' talking to 'mayors, economic developers, and city leaders', Florida recalls:

> I told them, enduring success in the new people-driven, place-based economy turned on doing the smaller things that made cities great places to live and work – things like making sure there were walkable, pedestrian-friendly streets, bike lanes, parks, exciting art and music scenes, and vibrant areas where people could gather in cafés and restaurants. (2017, p. xxi)

Given the levels of polarisation and inequality that predominate and persist, however, Florida now argues for wider interventions to bring about 'urbanism for all' (p. 11), including investment in transport infrastructure, affordable housing and the lifting of the minimum wage. Whilst it would be hard to disagree with assertions that, for instance, 'we need large numbers of better jobs with higher wages' (p. 215), it is perhaps understandable that intervening on the 'smaller things' like bike lanes and exciting music scenes may remain a more attractive option to urban policymakers who may lack the power to deal with the larger challenges of housing, transport or employment policy. Given the patterns identified above, though, it should be noted that it would be unwise for most to search for these 'better jobs with higher wages' in the cultural sector.

This factor thus further enables us to understand some of the persistence of the Creativity Agenda. Due to its flexibility, and presentation of interconnectedness, it allows the persistence of an idea that we can intervene in one 'creative' area, and others will be affected. We thus return to the idea of 'uncreative' creativity: building a new gallery, installing public art, competing to win an established cultural title such as the European Capital of Culture, or promoting activity based on traditional cultural policy justifications around the value of engagement with arts and so on occurs, but as these actions are glossed with the language of creativity, they can be aligned to the promotion of a 'creative city' or 'creative industries', regardless of the appropriateness of these linkages. As Landry states, 'incorporating creativity into city management is problematic as cities are run by public officials who are accountable to electorates' (2000, p. 45). Paradoxically, therefore, there may only be space for a 'standard' creativity. In light of the discussion above, and the recurrent theme of economic calculation, it is instructive to consider the interpretation of Peck on 'the creativity script' as to the nature of policy intervention:

> Investments in the 'soft infrastructure' of the arts and culture are easy to make, and need not be especially costly, so the creativity script easily translates into certain forms of municipal action. Whether or not this will stimulate creative economic growth, however, is quite another matter. (2005, p. 749)

When creativity is positioned as covering a range of areas, which all interlink, why not intervene in the simplest, most economical way? Tension between the aims articulated by cultural policy and the interventions made to reach these aims will likely continue until clarity comes to the Creativity Agenda, without which 'creativity' is liable to become manifest in a series of 'standard' forms. In any case, as the above discussion demonstrates, creativity alone will not be sufficient to address the challenges presented.

Conclusion

The patterns identified above may result in this chapter being seen as a counsel of despair. It has been argued that a small number of locations and a small minority of privileged people dominate creative fields, and that after a range of attempts to ameliorate this situation, these patterns have actually intensified. A reasonable conclusion, however, is not to throw one's hands up in resignation, but to return to the idea that what is required here is a more realistic assessment of the idea of creativity, and the need to look these facts in the face if they are to be dealt with. In addition to being clear about what phenomena we talk about when we talk about creativity, and the manner in which such phenomena are understood to be creative, what must be left behind is the idea that creativity is an unalloyed good, or that imprecision in understanding is also somehow productive. These are the conditions which have allowed the more mythical aspects of the Creativity Agenda to flourish, such as the idea that creative success is dependent on diversity and openness, and as such is a viable option for almost anyone, almost anywhere. Such openness does not characterise current practice. Without facing the realities of the situation, economic contradictions will likely get more acute, particularly in the era of austerity discussed in the previous chapter, and policy interventions are liable to continue to have questionable success. As Kong argues:

> It is critical to recognize that it is difficult for the same policy and instrument to be a cultural and arts policy, and a social and economic policy all at the same time. There is no magic bullet. Too often, urban policies group multiple goals together, resulting in unfocused objectives and unrealized goals. (2014, p. 604)

The challenge, therefore, is not inconsiderable. Creative activities are not an escape into an open realm, but are embedded in social structures, and so, as even one of the most prominent proselytisers for the Creativity Agenda acknowledges, it is only much deeper interventions that will enable any changes in these patterns to be brought about. After two decades of various implementations of this agenda, however, it seems that the persistence that this book has concentrated on continues in discussion of plans to promote creative clusters across the country in the hope that London's success will somehow be replicated, and attempts to prompt interest in under-represented groups. When those in positions of power are liable to further the myth of meritocracy and openness, and when interventions are comparatively tiny (and uncreative) in the face of the large challenges presented, it may take some time for further clarity to emerge.

References

Arts Council England. (2010). *Achieving great art for everyone—A strategic framework for the arts*. London: Arts Council England.

Arts Council England. (2018). *9 things you need to know about the Cultural Development Fund*. Retrieved from https://www.artscouncil.org.uk/cultural-development-fund/9-things-you-need-know-about-cultural-development-fund.

Bakhshi, H., Freeman, A., & Higgs, P. (2013a). *A dynamic mapping of the UK's creative industries*. London: Nesta.

Bakhshi, H., Hargreaves, I., & Mateos Garcia, J. (2013b). *A manifesto for the creative economy*. London: Nesta.

Banks, M. (2017). *Creative justice: Cultural industries, work and inequality*. London: Rowman & Littlefield.

Banks, M., & Hesmondhalgh, D. (2009). Looking for work in creative industries policy. *International Journal of Cultural Policy, 15*(4), 415–430.

Banks, M., & O'Connor, J. (2009). After the creative industries. *International Journal of Cultural Policy, 15*(4), 365–373.

Banks, M., & O'Connor, J. (2017). Inside the whale (and how to get out of there): Moving on from two decades of creative industries research. *European Journal of Cultural Studies, 20*(6), 637–654.

Bazalgette, P. (2017). *Independent review of the creative industries*. Retrieved from https://www.gov.uk/government/publications/independent-review-of-the-creative-industries.

Bell, D., & Jayne, M. (2010). The creative countryside: Policy and practice in the UK rural cultural economy. *Journal of Rural Studies, 26*(3), 209–218.

Bernick, S., Davies, R., & Valero, A. (2017). *Industry in Britain—An atlas*. Retrieved from http://cep.lse.ac.uk/pubs/download/special/cepsp34.pdf.

Blanchflower, D., & Oswald, A. (1998). What makes an entrepreneur? *Journal of Labour Economics, 16*(1), 26–60.

Borén, T., & Young, C. (2013). Getting creative with the 'creative city'? Towards new perspectives on creativity in urban policy. *International Journal of Urban and Regional Research, 37*(5), 1799–1815.

Bourdieu, P. (1986). *Distinction: A social critique of the judgement of taste*. London: Routledge.

Brouillette, S. (2014). *Literature and the creative economy*. Stanford: University Press.

Caves, R. E. (2000). *Creative industries—Contracts between art and commerce*. London: Harvard University Press.

CBI. (2014). *The creative nation: A growth strategy for the UK's creative industries*. Retrieved from http://www.cbi.org.uk/cbi-prod/assets/File/pdf/cbi_creative_industries_strategy__final_.pdf.

CEBR. (2017). *The contribution of the arts and culture to the national economy—An updated assessment of the macroeconomic contributions of the arts and culture industry to the national and regional economies of the UK*. London: Centre for Economics and Business Research Ltd.

Comunian, R., Faggian, A., & Li, Q. C. (2010). Unrewarded careers in the creative class: The strange case of bohemian graduates. *Papers in Regional Science, 89*(2), 389–410.

DCMS. (2007). *The creative economy programme: A summary of projects commissioned in 2006/7.* London: DCMS.

DCMS. (2018). *DCMS sector economic estimates 2016: Regional GVA sectors.* Retrieved from https://www.gov.uk/government/uploads/system/uploads/attachment_data/file/684141/Regional_GVA_2016_Sector_tables.xlsx.

DCMS & BIS. (2009). *Digital Britain.* Norwich: The Stationery Office.

DCMS, BERR, & DIUS. (2008). *Creative Britain: New talents for the new economy.* London: DCMS.

DCMS, ACE, BEIS, & Ellis, M. (2018). *£20 million government boost for culture and creative industries in England.* Retrieved from https://www.gov.uk/government/news/20-million-government-boost-for-culture-and-creative-industries-in-england.

Economics, F. (2007). *Multinationals in the UK creative industries: A report prepared for DCMS.* London: Frontier Economics Ltd.

European Parliament. (2016). *Report on a coherent EU policy for cultural and creative industries.* Retrieved from http://www.europarl.europa.eu/sides/getDoc.do?pubRef=-//EP//NONSGML+REPORT+A8-2016-0357+0+DOC+PDF+V0//EN.

Evans, G. (2001). *Cultural planning.* London: Routledge.

Evans, G. (2009). Creative cities, creative spaces and urban policy. *Urban Studies, 46*(5–6), 1003–1040.

Fleming, T., & Erskine, A. (2011). *Supporting growth in the arts economy.* London: Arts Council England.

Flew, T. (2010). Toward a cultural economic geography of creative industries and urban development: Introduction to the special issue on creative industries and urban development. *The Information Society, 26*(2), 85–91.

Flew, T., & Cunningham, S. (2010). Creative industries after the first decade of debate. *The Information Society, 26*(2), 113–123.

Florida, R. (2004). *The rise of the creative class.* New York: Basic Books.

Florida, R. (2007). *The flight of the creative class.* New York: Routledge.

Florida, R. (2017). *The new urban crisis—Gentrification, housing bubbles, growing inequality and what we can do about it.* London: Oneworld Publications.

Foord, J. (2008). Strategies for creative industries: An international review. *Creative Industries Journal, 1*(2), 91–113.

Foord, J., & Ginsburg, N. (2004). Whose hidden assets? Inner city potential for social cohesion and economic competitiveness. In M. Boddy & M. Parkinson (Eds.), *City matters* (pp. 287–305). Bristol: Polity Press.

Gerber, A. (2017). *The work of art*. Stanford: Stanford University Press.

Gill, R., & Pratt, A. (2008). In the social factory?: Immaterial labour, precariousness and cultural work. *Theory, Culture & Society, 25*(7–8), 1–30.

Graeber, D. (2018). *Bullshit jobs: A theory*. London: Allen Lane.

Grodach, C. (2013). Cultural economy planning in creative cities: Discourse and practice. *International Journal of Urban and Regional Research, 37*(5), 1747–1765.

Grodach, C., Foster, N., & Murdoch, J. (2014). Gentrification and the artistic dividend: The role of the arts in neighbourhood change. *Journal of the American Planning Association, 80*(1), 21–35.

Hartley, J. (Ed.). (2005). *Creative industries*. Oxford: Blackwell.

Heinze, R. G., & Hoose, F. (2013). The creative economy: Vision or illusion in the structural change? *European Planning Studies, 21*(4), 516–535.

Hesmondhalgh, D. (2007). *The cultural industries*. London: Sage.

Hesmondhalgh, D., & Pratt, A. C. (2005). Cultural industries and cultural policy. *International Journal of Cultural Policy, 11*(1), 1–13.

Hesmondhalgh, D., Oakley, K., Lee, D., & Nisbett, M. (2015). *Culture, economy and politics—The case of New Labour*. Basingstoke: Palgrave Macmillan.

Hewison, R. (2014). *Cultural capital: The rise and fall of creative Britain*. London: Verso.

HM Government. (2018). *Industrial strategy: Creative industries sector deal*. Retrieved from https://www.gov.uk/government/uploads/system/uploads/attachment_data/file/695097/creative-industries-sector-deal-print.pdf.

HM Land Registry. (2018). *UK house price index*. Retrieved from http://landregistry.data.gov.uk/app/ukhpi/.

Houston, D., Findlay, A., Harrison, R., & Mason, C. (2008). Will attracting the 'creative class' boost economic growth in old industrial regions? *Geografiska Annaler: Series B, Human Geography, 90*(2), 133–149.

Hoyman, M., & Faricy, C. (2009). It takes a village: A test of the creative class, social capital and human capital theories. *Urban Affairs Review, 44*(3), 311–333.

Jayne, M. (2005). Creative industries: The regional dimension? *Environment and Planning C: Government and Policy, 23*, 537–556.

Johnson, M., & Reed, H. (2008). *Entrepreneurship and innovation in the North*. Retrieved from https://www.ippr.org/files/images/media/files/publication/2011/05/entrepreneurship_and_innovation_1619.pdf.

Keat, R. (2000). *Cultural goods and the limits of the market*. Basingstoke: Macmillan Press.

Kong, L. (2014). From cultural industries to creative industries and back? Towards clarifying and rethinking. *Inter-Asia Cultural Studies, 15*(4), 593–607.

Lambing, P. A., & Kuehl, C. R. (2007). *Entrepreneurship*. Upper Saddle River, NJ: Pearson.

Landry, C. (2000). *The creative city*. London: Comedia.

Leadbeater, C. (1999). *Living on thin air—The new economy*. London: Penguin Books Ltd.

Leadbeater, C., & Oakley, K. (1999). *The independents*. London: Demos.

Lee, J. (1965). *A policy for the arts: The first steps*. London: Her Majesty's Stationery Office.

Levitas, R. (2004). Let's hear it for Humpty: Social exclusion, the third way and cultural capital. *Cultural Trends, 13*(2), 41–56.

London Development Agency. (2008). *London: A cultural audit*. London: LDA.

Lorente, P. (1996). *The role of museums and the arts in the urban regeneration of Liverpool*. Leicester: Centre for Urban History.

Markusen, A. (2014). Creative cities: A 10-year research agenda. *Journal of Urban Affairs, 36*(s2), 567–589.

Mateos Garcia, J., & Bakhshi, H. (2016). *The geography of creativity in the UK—Creative clusters, creative people and creative networks*. London: Nesta.

Mateos Garcia, J., Klinger, J., & Stathoulopoulos, K. (2018). *Creative nation—How the creative industries are powering the UK's nations and regions*. London: Nesta.

McDonald, F., Tsagdis, D., & Huang, Q. (2006). The development of industrial clusters and public policy. *Entrepreneurship and Regional Development, 18*(6), 525–542.

McRobbie, A. (2002). From Holloway to Hollywood. In P. Du Gay & M. Pryke (Eds.), *Cultural economy* (pp. 97–114). London: Sage.

McRobbie, A. (2015). *Be creative: Making a living in the new culture industries*. Cambridge: Polity Press.

Miller, T. (2004). A view from a fossil: The new economy, creativity and consumption—Two or three things I don't believe in. *International Journal of Cultural Studies, 7*(1), 55–65.

Miles, A., & Sullivan, A. (2009). *Understanding the relationship between taste and value in culture and sport*. London: DCMS.

Mommaas, H. (2004). Cultural clusters and the post-industrial city: Towards the remapping of urban cultural policy. *Urban Studies, 41*(3), 507–532.

Montgomery, J. (2005). Beware 'the creative class'. Creativity and wealth creation revisited. *Local Economy, 20*(4), 337–343.

Mould, O. (2017). *Urban subversion and the creative city.* London: Routledge.

Mould, O., & Comunian, R. (2015). Hung, drawn and cultural quartered: Rethinking cultural quarter development policy in the UK. *European Planning Studies, 23*(12), 2356–2369.

Nathan, M. (2005). *The wrong stuff: Creative class theory, diversity and city performance.* London: IPPR Centre for Cities.

Nesta. (2006). *Creating growth—How the UK can develop world class creative businesses.* London: Nesta.

Oakley, K. (2004). Not so cool Britannia: The role of the creative industries in economic development. *International Journal of Cultural Studies, 7*(1), 67–77.

Oakley, K. (2009). The disappearing arts: Creativity and innovation after the creative industries. *International Journal of Cultural Policy, 15*(4), 403–413.

Oakley, K., & O'Connor, J. (2015). The cultural industries—An introduction. In K. Oakley & J. O'Connor (Eds.), *The Routledge companion to the cultural industries* (pp. 1–32). London: Routledge.

Oakley, K., Laurison, D., O'Brien, D., & Friedman, S. (2017). Cultural capital: Arts graduates, spatial inequality, and London's impact on cultural labour markets. *American Behavioral Scientist, 61*(12), 1510–1531.

O'Brien, D., & Oakley, K. (2015). *Cultural value and inequality: A critical literature review.* Retrieved from https://ahrc.ukri.org/documents/project-reports-and-reviews/cultural-value-and-inequality-a-critical-literature-review/.

O'Connor, J. (2005). Creative exports: Taking cultural industries to St. Petersburg. *International Journal of Cultural Policy, 11*(1), 45–60.

O'Connor, J. (2007). *The cultural and creative industries: A review of the literature.* London: Arts Council England.

Osborne, T. (2003). Against 'creativity': A philistine rant. *Economy and Society, 32*(4), 507–525.

Parker, S., Tims, C., & Wright, S. (2006). *Inclusion, innovation and democracy: Growing talent for the creative and cultural industries.* Retrieved from https://www.demos.co.uk/files/creative_race_finalweb.pdf.

Peck, J. (2005). Struggling with the creative class. *International Journal of Urban and Regional Research, 29*(4), 740–770.

Pratt, A. C. (1997). Guest editorial. *Environment & Planning A, 29*(11), 1911–1917.

Schlesinger, P. (2007). Creativity: From discourse to doctrine. *Screen, 48*(3), 377–387.

Schlesinger, P. (2009). *The politics of media and cultural policy*. Retrieved from http://www.lse.ac.uk/media-and-communications/assets/documents/research/working-paper-series/EWP17.pdf.

Scott, A. J. (1999). The cultural economy: Geography and the creative field. *Media, Culture and Society, 21*(6), 807–817.

Scott, A. J. (2000). *The cultural economy of cities*. London: Sage.

Scott, A. J. (2006). Entrepreneurship, innovation and industrial development. *Small Business Economics, 26*(1), 1–24.

Scott, A. J. (2014). Beyond the creative city: Cognitive-cultural capitalism and the new urbanism. *Regional Studies, 48*(4), 565–578.

Selwood, S. (2001). *The UK cultural sector—Profile and policy issues*. London: Policy Studies Institute.

Serota, N. (2017, November 17). More funding for the arts could benefit everyone in the country. *Evening Standard*. Retrieved from https://www.standard.co.uk/comment/comment/more-funding-for-the-arts-could-benefit-everyone-in-the-country-a3694116.html.

Shorthouse, R. (Ed.). (2010). *Disconnected: Social mobility and the creative industries*. London: Social Market Foundation.

Smith, C. (1998). *Creative Britain*. London: Faber and Faber.

Stark, P., Gordon, C., & Powell, D. (2013). *Rebalancing our cultural capital: A contribution to the debate on national policy for the arts and culture in England*. Retrieved from http://www.gpsculture.co.uk/downloads/rocc/Rebalancing_FINAL_3mb.pdf.

Stevenson, R. L. (1892). Letter to a young gentleman who proposes to embrace the career of art. In R. L. Stevenson (Ed.), *Across the Plains*. New York: Charles Scribner's Sons.

Stevenson, D., Balling, G., & Kann-Rasmussen, N. (2015). Cultural participation in Europe: Shared problem or shared problematisation. *International Journal of Cultural Policy, 23*(1), 89–106.

Taylor, M. (2016). Nonparticipation or different styles of participation? Alternative interpretations from taking part. *Cultural Trends, 25*(3), 169–181.

Taylor, M., & O'Brien, D. (2017). 'Culture is a Meritocracy': Why creative workers' attitudes may reinforce social inequality. *Sociological Research Online, 22*(4), 27–47.

Technology Strategy Board. (2009). *Creative industries technology strategy 2009–2012*. Swindon: The Technology Strategy Board.

The Work Foundation. (2007). *Staying ahead: The economic performance of the UK's creative industries*. London: The Work Foundation.

Vanolo, A. (2013). Alternative capitalism and the creative economy: The case of Christiania. *International Journal of Urban and Regional Research, 37*(5), 1785–1798.

Vivant, E. (2013). Creatives in the city: Urban contradictions of the creative city. *City, Culture and Society, 4,* 57–63.

Wynne, D. (1992). Cultural quarters. In D. Wynne (Ed.), *The culture industry: The arts in urban regeneration* (pp. 13–23). Aldershot: Avebury.

8

Epilogue: Ever Decreasing Circles?

The intention of this book has been to demonstrate the way in which a discourse regarding the power of creativity has come to prominence and persisted over two decades, broadly from 1998–2018. By 2018, at the time of this book's completion, we can see a certain stagnation, despite the continuing associations with innovation and newness. Just as creativity was seen as being central to *future* wealth in the late 1990s, for instance, analysis of the creative industries commissioned by the Department for Culture, Media and Sport (DCMS) in 2006 also concluded that these industries are 'certain to become even more important in the future' (The Work Foundation 2007, p. 188). By the late 2010s, the 'Independent Review of the Creative Industries' by Sir Peter Bazalgette concluded that in a 'future economy' some fifteen or twenty years hence, 'in every scenario the Creative Industries are of central importance' (2017, p. 4). Whilst the creative industries thus always seem to be particularly important for their future role as time passes, statistics regarding the economic performance of these industries by the end of this period demonstrated very similar overall patterns to those available in 2001 (as concluded in Chapter 5). Similarly, despite the long history of attempts to develop such creative industries to attract a

© The Author(s) 2019
P. Campbell, *Persistent Creativity*, Sociology of the Arts,
https://doi.org/10.1007/978-3-030-03119-0_8

wider 'creative class', build a 'creative city' or enact 'culture-led regeneration', and the production of a wide range of research considering such attempts, Bazalgette's 2017 report suggests that,

> *emerging* evidence from place-shaping research indicates that growth in Creative Industries is enhanced when an area has a strong cultural, heritage and sporting offer, enhancing the attractiveness of locations to live and work and acting as an accelerator for regeneration. (2017, p. 16, emphasis added)

By this stage, it would be fair to say that any such evidence that is likely to become available on these topics had long since emerged, and as Chapter 4 demonstrated, assessment of the challenges in creating any convincing evidence base in this field has also shown a remarkable consistency for many decades, yet in this area too creativity seems to bring a sense of perennial newness. A goal of yet more evidence production therefore remains. At the time of writing, Arts Council England has awarded a £2.3m contract for a scheme to 'measure perceptions of artistic quality' over four years (Hill 2018), a new Scottish culture strategy is being drafted based in part on the need to develop 'new approaches to measuring and articulating the value of culture' (Romer 2018), and DCMS are conducting a new enquiry seeking evidence regarding the 'social impact of participation in culture and sport' which has gathered 224 items of written evidence (DCMS Committee 2018a), and received oral evidence on a number of topics including the impact of the European Capital of Culture and UK City of Culture awards. This evidence continued the linkage of such awards with the goal of 'regeneration', based on assertions such as 'Glasgow and subsequent Capitals of Culture [...] proved that [the title] was an amazing mechanism for regeneration' (DCMS Committee 2018b, p. 24). The positions encountered in Chapter 6 thus persist, although with the 2016 vote for Britain to leave the EU, the UK will have to rely more on its national awards in the future: despite the bidding process for UK cities to host the European Capital of Culture in 2023 already being underway, the award was cancelled in 2017 (BBC 2017). More broadly the impacts of this vote on the creative industries, not to say the country at large, remain at best unclear but are unlikely to be beneficial (Creative Industries Federation 2018).

In his evidence to the DCMS Select Committee referred to above, Chief Executive of Arts Council England Darren Henley also argued for the need for more 'data' for the Arts Council to make their case (DCMS Committee 2018c, p. 31), raising the spectre of the challenges first encountered in Chapter 4, but also referred to ideas from his recently published book in which he attempts to make the case for a particularly important concept: creativity. In 'Creativity: why it matters', he extols the necessity of a broad-ranging conception of creativity which encompasses any new and different approaches arising from fields as diverse as science, business, the arts and fishing, but which is particularly linked to experience of, and practice in, the arts. This wide-ranging account raises the persistent challenges discussed in Chapter 7 such as a lack of specificity and a questionable sense of openness. By this stage, it may be somewhat surprising that the case for creativity still requires such advocacy, but what is less surprising is that Henley's opening chapter focusses on the specifically *economic* case for creativity. This case is based in part on the statistics relating to creative industries—which put 'a smile on our face as a nation' (Henley 2018, p. 40)—encountered in Chapter 5, but unsurprisingly without the range of issues discussed in that chapter being raised.

Given this further entrenchment of the Creativity Agenda discussed over the previous chapters, we thus end with a brief snapshot of prominent political statements on the nature of creativity after twenty years of persistence. In mid-2018, UK Prime Minister Theresa May announced a new fund to 'support creative projects in the Northern Powerhouse' (Prime Minister's Office and May 2018). On the surface, this might seem a useful step towards addressing the patterns of spatial inequality in the creative sector outlined in Chapter 7. In making the case for this fund, May also drew on the figures considered in Chapter 5, and continued the pattern identified in that chapter of mentioning only culturally expressive activities when referring to the economic output of creative industries:

The Prime Minister praised the creative industries which contribute £92 billion to the UK economy, providing work for more than two million people right across the country [...adding] "Our films captivate audiences the world over, our fashion designers surprise and delight, our architects are shaping skylines and cityscapes on every continent. In publishing, in music, in advertising and more, every day our creative industries fly the flag for Britain on the global stage." (2018)

Again, there is no mention by this stage of the work in software that is the largest subsector included within these figures. In the context of the £92bn of Gross Value Added mentioned, and the recent announcement of a £20m 'Cultural Development Fund' fund (suggested in Chapter 7 to be likely to have a relatively modest impact), the expected impact of this new fund of just £3m may well be questioned. Nevertheless, investment of £3m in areas with little established capacity in these industries could well be of some use. What then are the specific intentions of this fund?

Arts projects and enterprises which support their local communities, in areas including Cumbria, Manchester, Lancashire, Leeds, Liverpool, Sheffield and Yorkshire, can apply for £150,000 of government funding. This could include projects using theatre to improve child literacy or art workshops for disabled people or the elderly. (Prime Minister's Office and May 2018)

Worthy projects, no doubt, but unlikely to deal with the issues of inequality and industrial concentration traced in Chapter 7. Once again, the obscuring veil of the Creativity Agenda descends. A high growth sector, producing most of its billions in London, with software as its largest subsector, is aligned here with the deployment of tens of thousands of pounds of funding for art workshops in the north of England. Both of these can be labelled 'creative', but one has little to do with the other. Nevertheless, Arts Minister Michael Ellis tells us:

Britain's creative industries are an economic and cultural powerhouse that is recognised around the world. This new fund is another vote of confidence in the sector that will develop future talent, benefit communities and provide a lasting legacy from the Great Exhibition of the North. (Prime Minister's Office and May 2018)

The Creativity Agenda, prone to celebratory narratives based on minimal evidence and inappropriate alignments, thus seems firmly in place. Indeed, it seems at this point in time that the key elements of the agenda are effectively not open for question, and so such persistence is essentially the only option available. As noted previously, Schlesinger has argued for the hegemonic nature of the discourse—a 'self-sustaining, self-referential framework of ideas [...] that has become largely impervious to critique' (Schlesinger 2017, p. 86). Any discussion in this field thus rests on a set of 'known', unquestioned, truths. In July 2018, for instance, Jeremy Wright began his tenure as Secretary of State for Culture (the third appointee to this role in a twelve-month period) by noting that the work of DCMS can 'unite the nation' (DCMS 2018), and a current 'cultural cities' enquiry supported by the UK's Arts Councils took as its starting point the notion that,

the contribution of culture to cities is evident throughout the UK. Culture makes cities more prosperous: it has helped to catalyse urban renewal in cities and anchor regeneration. It strengthens city economies through tourism, the night-time economy and creative industries – and in attracting talented people to live, work and study. (Core Cities UK 2018)

If such ideas are taken as read, such an 'enquiry' will likely only be able to build on these foundations, rather than question them, and so only produce findings that fit within this existing framework. The enquiry's website leverages the idea of a new economy, the successful Glasgow Model, the successful Liverpool Model, the creative class, the creative industries—the standard Creativity Agenda, all present and correct (Thomas 2018). Yet, as per the discussion in Chapter 7, the context for this discussion is a pattern of reduced funding which raises the need, yet again, to make the case for the arts and culture, and consider 'how culture can be more effectively resourced across the UK' (Core Cities UK 2018). It seems that decades of increasingly focussing on the economic case for culture have paradoxically ended in ever more reduced levels of funding, and ever more evidence production in the need to produce more evidence. This economic case is arguably made ever more problematic by the shift to a focus on 'creativity'—as Garnham notes, a dilemma is raised for cultural policy if we predominantly think about cultural provision in terms of the operation of a given creative industry: 'if it is successful, why does it need public support? If it is unsuccessful, why does it merit public support?' (2005, p. 28). Contradictions such as this lie at the heart of the Creativity Agenda and, as the imposition of austerity measures continue in the UK, will likely become ever more acute.

At the end of this twenty year period, then, we can identify how the Creativity Agenda is at least partly maintained by the deployment of a range of methodological practices to make this economic case, as these help to represent creative practice in certain forms, and play a key role in the process of global policy transfer which characterises the field (Evans 2009; Schlesinger 2009), based on seemingly 'technical' quantification practices (Prince 2014). These techniques thus 'enact' certain forms of creativity (Law and Urry 2004), and keep the Creativity Agenda rolling forward. The discussion in previous chapters, however, does seem to indicate some obstacles looming in its path. An increasing focus on the economic performance of 'digital' and non-cultural forms of creativity may prove problematic for a narrative persistently aligned to the arts and culture, especially considering the deleterious effect these digital systems may have on some forms of creative practice (Olma 2016, p. 85). Nevertheless, for the time being celebrating the creative economy and promoting culture for economic ends seem likely to continue to be prominent positions. This in some senses takes us back to the issue of an absence of 'creativity' in the application of this agenda: once an idea has gained dominance, who has the time or the inclination to resist it? As Hesmondhalgh et al. note:

> Politicians usually don't have the time or resources to be original or ground-breaking or distinctive, and nor do civil servants. Even policy experts and entrepreneurs (think tanks, consultants and so on) form their

views from ideas circulating in academia and elsewhere, and they often revive older concepts. (2015, p. 185)

Without time to reflect, apparently objective numerical evidence can seem to present an incontrovertible case (Beer 2016, p. 50), leading to entrenchment of certain positions. The neat narrative, and 'objective' indicators, that the notions of the creative class or the creative industries present thus continue to circulate despite the challenges they pose, especially in a context in which institutional memory is weak (Oman and Taylor 2018, p. 239).

Looking closer to home in the field of academia, not only does the acceptance of this agenda continue to proliferate (Schlesinger 2017, p. 84), but even where we may expect to find most questioning, there are recent signs of the 'imperviousness to critique' mentioned above. The Arts and Humanities Research Council's Creative Economy Champion Andrew Chitty set out the organisation's position on the suggestions from Sir Peter Bazalgette ('Baz') considered in Chapter 7 thus:

Baz believes that investing in [...] clusters will unlock huge benefits in jobs, productivity and growth. And we agree with Baz [...] We believe the clusters must also foster a new kind of research – research for and with the creative industries not about them; research that can help develop the new creative content, products, services and commercial models with which UK businesses can conquer the world rather than research that analyses how they work. (Chitty 2017)

If the starting point for academic research is also to accept questionable but pervasive positions regarding creativity, and to focus on the development of commercial models with which businesses may 'conquer the world' rather than models to analyse and understand, it is perhaps time to reflect on how useful an overarching concern with economic forms of value over all others may be in the long term.

Although fighting against this prevailing trend, then, it remains important to continue to argue that this agenda requires clarification, and that evidence must be considered more closely. Just as Chapter 3 argued that in the prominence and persistence of the Creativity Agenda we see something akin to the discursive trait of *catachresis*: 'application of a term to a thing which it does not properly denote' (Catachresis, n.d.), rather as time persists we may see creativity veering towards becoming a *panchreston*: 'an explanation or theory which can be made to fit all cases, being used in such a variety of ways as to become meaningless' (Panchreston, n.d.). This trend is worth resisting. In focussing on the challenges that creativity continues to present, we must not lose sight of potential benefits. Until the concept of creativity is utilised in a more precise way, however, such challenges will remain, as will the potential squandering of opportunities and resources in chasing ill-conceived goals (Markusen and Gadwa 2010, p. 379). There is no need for this to persist.

References

Bazalgette, P. (2017). *Independent review of the creative industries.* Retrieved from https://www.gov.uk/government/publications/independent-review-of-the-creative-industries.

BBC. (2017). *Brexit 'bombshell' for UK's European capital of culture 2023 plans.* Retrieved from https://www.bbc.co.uk/news/entertainment-arts-42097692.

Beer, D. (2016). *Metric power.* London: Palgrave Macmillan.

Catachresis. (n.d.). *Oxford English dictionary.* Retrieved from http://www.oed.com.

Chitty, A. (2017). *Creative industries clusters programme leads the way.* Retrieved from https://ahrc.ukri.org/research/readwatchlisten/features/creative-industries-clusters-programme-leads-the-way/.

Core Cities UK. (2018). *About the cultural cities enquiry.* Retrieved from https://www.corecities.com/cultural-cities-enquiry/about.

Creative Industries Federation. (2018). *Brexit White Paper—Impact on creative industries.* Retrieved from https://www.creativeindustriesfederation.com/sites/default/files/2018-07/Brexit%20White%20Paper%20Summary.pdf.

DCMS. (2018, July 11). [Tweet]. Retrieved from https://twitter.com/dcms/status/1016989876036698112?s=12.

DCMS Committee. (2018a). *Social impact of participation in culture and sport inquiry—Publications.* Retrieved from https://www.parliament.uk/business/committees/committees-a-z/commons-select/digital-culture-media-and-sport-committee/inquiries/parliament-2017/socialimpact/publications/.

DCMS Committee. (2018b). *Oral evidence: The social impact of participation in culture and sport, HC 734*. Retrieved from http://data.parliament.uk/writtenevidence/committeeevidence.svc/evidencedocument/digital-culture-media-and-sport-committee/the-social-impact-of-participation-in-culture-and-sport/oral/86738.pdf.

DCMS Committee. (2018c). *Oral evidence: The social impact of participation in culture and sport, HC 734*. Retrieved from http://data.parliament.uk/writtenevidence/committeeevidence.svc/evidencedocument/digital-culture-media-and-sport-committee/the-social-impact-of-participation-in-culture-and-sport/oral/85763.pdf.

Evans, G. (2009). Creative cities, creative spaces and urban policy. *Urban Studies, 46*(5–6), 1003–1040.

Garnham, N. (2005). From culture to creative industries. *International Journal of Cultural Policy, 11*(1), 15–29.

Henley, D. (2018). *Creativity: Why it matters*. London: Elliott and Thompson Ltd.

Hesmondhalgh, D., Oakley, K., Lee, D., & Nisbett, M. (2015). *Culture, economy and politics—The case of New Labour*. Basingstoke: Palgrave Macmillan.

Hill, L. (2018). *Green light for artistic quality measurement scheme*. Retrieved from https://www.artsprofessional.co.uk/news/green-light-artistic-quality-measurement-scheme.

Law, J., & Urry, J. (2004). Enacting the social. *Economy and Society, 33*(3), 390–410.

Markusen, A., & Gadwa, A. (2010). Arts and culture in urban or regional planning: A review and research agenda. *Journal of Planning Education and Research, 29*(3), 379–391.

Olma, S. (2016). *In defence of serendipity: For a radical politics of innovation*. London: Repeater Books.

Oman, S., & Taylor, M. (2018). Subjective well-being in cultural advocacy: A politics of research between the market and the academy. *Journal of Cultural Economy, 11*(3), 225–243.

Panchreston. (n.d.). *Oxford English dictionary*. Retrieved from http://www.oed.com.

Prime Minister's Office, & May, T. (2018). *PM announces £3 million to support creative projects in the Northern Powerhouse*. Retrieved from https://www.gov.uk/government/news/pm-announces-3-million-to-support-creative-projects-in-the-northern-powerhouse/.

Prince, R. (2014). Consultants and the global assemblage of culture and creativity. *Transactions of the Institute of British Geographers, 39*(1), 90–101.

Romer, C. (2018) *Scotland plans to make culture central to policy-making.* Retrieved from https://www.artsprofessional.co.uk/news/scotland-plans-make-culture-central-policy-making.

Schlesinger, P. (2009). Creativity and the experts: New Labour, think tanks, and the policy process. *The International Journal of Press/Politics, 14*(3), 3–20.

Schlesinger, P. (2017). The creative economy: Invention of a global orthodoxy. *Innovation: The European Journal of Social Science Research, 30*(1), 73–90.

Thomas, H. (2018). *We need new ways of funding culture in our cities—A blog from Cllr Huw Thomas.* Retrieved from https://www.corecities.com/cultural-cities-enquiry/news/we-need-new-ways-funding-culture-our-cities-blog-cllr-huw-thomas.

The Work Foundation. (2007). *Staying ahead: The economic performance of the UK's creative industries.* London: The Work Foundation.

Index

© The Editor(s) (if applicable) and The Author(s) 2019
P. Campbell, *Persistent Creativity*, Sociology of the Arts,
https://doi.org/10.1007/978-3-030-03119-0

285

Printed by Printforce, the Netherlands